AF696460

Learning Law Through Experience & By Design

Learning Law Through Experience & By Design

Carwina Weng

CLINICAL PROFESSOR
& DIRECTOR OF THE DISABILITY LAW CLINIC
INDIANA UNIVERSITY MAURER SCHOOL OF LAW

Danielle R. Cover

ASSOCIATE PROFESSOR
& DIRECTOR OF THE LEGAL SERVICES CLINIC
UNIVERSITY OF WYOMING COLLEGE OF LAW

Margaret E. Reuter

ASSOCIATE CLINICAL PROFESSOR
& DIRECTOR OF FIELD PLACEMENT PROGRAMS AT
UNIVERSITY OF MISSOURI-KANSAS CITY SCHOOL OF LAW

Chris Roberts

CLINICAL PROFESSOR
& DIRECTOR OF THE CRIMINAL DEFENSE CLINIC AT
UNIVERSITY OF TEXAS AT AUSTIN SCHOOL OF LAW

CAROLINA ACADEMIC PRESS
Durham, North Carolina

Library of Congress Cataloging-in-Publication Data

Names: Weng, Carwina, author. | Cover, Danielle R., author. | Reuter, Margaret, author. | Roberts, Chris, author.
Title: Learning law through experience and by design / by Carwina Weng, Danielle R. Cover, Margaret Reuter, Chris Roberts.
Description: Durham, North Carolina : Carolina Academic Press, LLC, 2019.
Identifiers: LCCN 2019014250 | ISBN 9781531014797 (alk. paper)
Subjects: LCSH: Law—Study and teaching (Clinical education)—United States.
Classification: LCC KF282 .C68 2019 | DDC 340.071/173—dc23
LC record available at https://lccn.loc.gov/2019014250

e-ISBN 978-1-5310-1480-3

Carolina Academic Press
700 Kent Street
Durham, North Carolina 27701
Telephone (919) 489-7486
Fax (919) 493-5668
www.cap-press.com

Printed in the United States of America

Contents

Learning Law Through Experience & By Design

Chapter 1

Your Experiential Course and the ABA Standards

Welcome to *Experiential Learning Design.*

Two questions—What is the goal of your teaching? and How will you know if you have succeeded? — capture the core principles of *Experiential Learning Design (EL Design). EL Design* starts at the "end" of your course, with what you want your students to know, be able to do, and value at the completion of the course. The *EL Design* process then asks you to consider the observable evidence needed to assess your students' newly acquired capabilities and how well they achieved your goals. That evidence will form the crux of your final evaluation (assessment) for the course. Once you have identified the goal posts and the measuring stick, then you are primed to select learning outcomes and develop the learning activities that will propel your students to achieve your learning goal.

The principles of *EL Design* work very well on the course level. That's the reason for this workbook. But they can also be applied on the program level, whether for a degree or a concentration. At this larger scale, your school might consider: What educational attributes (knowledge, skills, values) are the intended goals of its Juris Doctor (JD) degree program? How can the faculty at large judge whether the school's curriculum fulfills those aspirations and its students graduate with each of those educational attributes? What assessment mechanism can the school and its faculty deploy? The parallel applicability of the design process to courses and programs is even more important now, given current practices in pedagogy and program assessment.

This focus on the end product of teaching (student learning) and authentic measurement of what students in fact have learned (assessment) has long been applied in higher education—both undergraduate and graduate. U.S. Department of Education-authorized accrediting bodies have used these principles as key to the accreditation process. These principles (end goals and assessment) had not been an explicit part of legal education or its accrediting process until 2014.

In 2014, the American Bar Association (ABA), prompted by the Department of Education,[1] enacted major revisions to its law school accreditation standards. These standards require each law school to define the learning outcomes for its JD degree and to

1. American Bar Association, Section of Legal Education and Admissions to the Bar, Report of the Outcome Measures Committee, at 20–53, Randy Hertz (Chairperson), (July 27, 2008). The ABA

evaluate how well the graduating students have achieved those outcomes.[2] The ABA consequently also requires faculty to include learning outcomes in the syllabus of each course taught. Significantly, the new accreditation standards look to the experiential curriculum to deliver core learning outcomes. Faculty who teach experiential courses will be able to use *EL Design* both to improve their own courses and to comply with the new curriculum requirements their schools face.

A. Outcome-Focused Curriculum Standards

The 2014 revisions to the accreditation standards affected many aspects of law school operations, chief among them, the curriculum standards. Five new standards provide a framework as you design your experiential course. Two standards institute the requirements regarding outcomes-based curriculum: Every school must set learning outcomes for graduates of its Juris Doctor degree (Std. 301), which must include a minimum set of outcomes (Std. 302). As you will see, substantively, these standards shine a spotlight on the experiential curriculum. Another two standards impose new requirements on assessment practices within the law school: the faculty must devise a mix of formative and summative assessments of student learning (Std. 314) and must conduct ongoing evaluation of the curriculum's ability to deliver on the learning outcomes of the JD degree program (Std. 315). Finally, one of the new standards expands the graduation requirement for skills learning to a minimum of 6 credits. (Std. 303(a)(3)).[3]

Standard 301 now requires each law school to *establish and publish learning outcomes* designed to deliver a rigorous program of legal education for JD students (program level learning outcomes). Earlier iterations of this standard merely required that the school *provide instruction* in core areas (inputs) and said nothing about the actual results of the teaching and learning process (outputs).[4] This shift requires that the competencies embodied in a school's learning outcomes be taught and assessed by the completion of the JD program. To enable faculty and students to determine where the school's learning outcomes are being taught, the ABA Managing Director's Guidance Memo (June 2015) requires learning outcomes of individual courses to be published in the course syllabi.

Standard 302 *mandates specific learning outcomes* a school must include and invites schools to customize a list of outcomes:

---

amendments trailed every regional accrediting body and every professional accrediting body in moving to an outcome-based orientation. *Id.*

2. In course and curriculum design, the terms "goals" and "learning outcomes" have distinct but closely related meanings. Both are oriented to the results of teaching, *i.e.*, what will (or did) the students learn. See Chapter 4, *The Course Goal: What Do You Want Your Students to Learn?* and Chapter 7, *Course Outcomes and Learning Activities: What Will Happen in Your Classroom?*. The goals are more teacher-anchored; they are defined from the perspective of the beginning of the course. The learning outcomes comprise the component parts of the goals, are written in concrete and measurable terms, and are the focus of the evaluation of each student's performance. They are the representation of the goals at the conclusion of the course. The ABA and some law schools meld the two concepts. That's fine so long as the focus is on the student acquisition of skills, etc. (end product) and not on the teachers' efforts or aspirations (inputs).

3. These standards now fully apply to all law students who entered in the 2016–17 academic year and later. American Bar Association, Section of Legal Education and Admissions to the Bar, *Transition to and Implementation of the New Standards and Rules of Procedure for Approval of Law Schools*, at 2, August 13, 2014.

4. In 2008, Standard 302 provided: "A law school shall require that each student receive substantial instruction in,"

a) substantive law generally regarded as necessary to effective and responsible participation in the legal profession;
b) legal analysis and reasoning, problem-solving, and oral communication,
c) writing in a legal context, included at least one rigorous writing experience in the first year and at least one additional rigorous writing experience after the first year;
d) other professional skills generally regarded as necessary for effective and responsible participation in the legal profession, and
e) history, goals, structure, values, rules, and responsibilities of the legal profession and its members.

a) Knowledge and understanding of substantive and procedural law;
b) Legal analysis and reasoning, legal research, problem-solving, and written and oral communication in the legal context;
c) Exercise of proper professional and ethical responsibilities to clients and the legal system; and
d) Other professional skills needed for competent and ethical participation as a member of the legal profession.

The ABA's Interpretive Guidance invites schools to customize their list of outcomes (Interpretation 302-2). The Guidance further explains that the required outcome—*professional skills*—can be "determined by the law school and may include skills such as interviewing, counseling, negotiation, fact development and analysis, trial practice, document drafting, conflict resolution, organization and management of legal work, collaboration, cultural competency, and self-evaluation." (Interpretation 302-1).

Standard 314 requires law schools to use *both formative and summative assessments* in the curriculum to measure and improve student learning and to provide feedback to students. The standard does not specify which assessment methods to use, noting that schools need flexibility to choose methods that fit their programs. Nor does the standard require that each course include both formative and summative assessments; rather, the program of education must integrate both in a way that demonstrates serious commitment to the process of program assessment.

Standard 315 requires the dean and faculty to conduct *ongoing evaluation* of the law school program of legal education, learning outcomes, and assessment methods. The ongoing evaluation must assess how effectively the school's JD degree requirements succeed in producing graduates that exhibit the competencies embodied in the learning outcomes. To comply, schools must collect evidence of student learning. That evidence may come from the assessments conducted in individual courses, co- and extracurricular programs, and input from various stakeholders such as students, alumni, employers, and judges. Each school is to adopt an assessment plan by the end of academic year 2018–19. Because the standards require the faculty to monitor attainment of each published outcome by the time of graduation, required coursework will carry the lion's share of the burden of instruction and assessment.

Standard 303(a)(3) mandates a new graduation requirement for each student: at least six (6) credits in experiential coursework, exclusively in clinics, field placement, and simulation courses. In Standard 304, the ABA created more structure, rigor, and consistency to the definitions of each of these experiential courses. Each type of experiential course must provide opportunities for student performance, feedback, and self-evaluation. As experiential courses now take up a larger share of the required courses, the experiential curriculum will shoulder a larger share of responsibility for delivering on their law school's learning outcomes.

B. The ABA Mandated Learning Outcomes and the Experiential Curriculum

A review of the ABA's minimum outcomes includes many elements that are principally, if not exclusively, taught in experiential courses. The minimum outcomes include such elements as problem-solving, oral communication, exercising ethical conduct, and professional skills, among others. While some of these outcomes are introduced or used in podium classes, experiential courses are where students most often are taught the ABA core outcomes and practice these skills from the perspective of a legal professional.

Many schools have gone further than the minimum outcomes; they have taken up the ABA's encouragement to customize their list of learning outcomes. This customization often tilts in favor of outcomes central to experiential learning, as can be seen in the database of program outcomes compiled by the Holloran Center at St. Thomas University School of Law.[5] Some of the common outcomes that expand on the list of "other professional skills" include:

- Responding to differences among the individuals with whom they interact
    - Seattle University School of Law: "Graduates will be able to perform their lawyering tasks . . . with the cultural competence necessary for effective, respectful interaction with individuals from diverse backgrounds."
    - Villanova University School of Law: "Graduates will be able to communicate effectively with a variety of audiences in both written and oral form."
    - Washburn School of Law: "Students will demonstrate active listening in communications with others, including legal professionals and laypersons."
- Committing to lifelong learning
    - Indiana University Maurer School of Law: Our students will empathize with and respect those affected by their work, and employ the habit of dynamic learning; exhibit the capacity for reflection, self-evaluation, and learning from experience, and demonstrate a commitment to professionalism in the workplace and lifelong professional development.
    - Ohio State University, Moritz School of Law: Skills for Continued Development (Metacognition, which it defines as "the ability to reflect on one's own thought processes, to improve those processes, and to adapt them to new situations").
- Fact investigation
    - American University Washington College of Law—fact and other information-gathering skills, including client interviewing.

If your school has adopted learning outcomes like these, consider whether any of the courses you teach might deliver such outcomes. If yes, then consider how important that learning outcome is to your course and how you would determine whether a student had attained some level of competency in that skill through your course. While you do not bear sole responsibility at your school for student attainment of learning outcomes based on professional skills, you might choose (or be required) to include them in your design of an experiential learning course. *EL Design* will help you to do so in a way that maintains the integrity and authenticity of your course.

C. Setting Learning Outcomes and Curriculum Mapping

The requirement of ongoing assessment of a law school's program of education meshes neatly with *EL Design*. Program assessment involves establishing learning outcomes; ensuring the curriculum provides learning opportunities that maximize students' abilities to achieve the outcomes; and evaluating whether students actually achieved the learning outcomes at the expected proficiency level when they finish the program. Program learning outcomes typically are phrased something like: At the end of their JD education, our students will have or be able to do ["x" competency]. The competency will be stated with enough specificity that it can be meaningfully taught and measured. Performance indicators (or sub-components of the learning outcome) provide specificity and depth.

---

5. University of St. Thomas School of Law, Holloran Center, Learning Outcomes Database, www.stthomas.edu/holloran center/resourcesforlegaleducators/learningoutcomesdatabase, *(last visited November 12, 2018)*. This database lists and categorizes all law school learning outcomes that were available on law school webpages as of August 2018.

In choosing a learning outcome, the faculty at large is stating that the learning experiences at their school should provide all students with fertile ground to develop "x" competency. That requires the faculty to identify which learning experiences will lead to such a competency. These experiences can be found in required courses; distribution requirements; other graduation requirements (*e.g.*, capstone presentation, pro bono mandates); coordination of content in upper level courses; academic advising; or other widely available co-curricular opportunities. The matching of the learning experience to the learning outcome is a curriculum map.

Developing learning outcomes and curriculum mapping can start at the micro- or macro-level, or a melding of both.[6] In the micro-level approach, the faculty examines each course and its projected learning outcomes as stated by the teacher. This information could be drawn from the syllabi and/or from surveying the faculty member directly. The survey would include enough detail to identify whether the outcome topic was introduced, practiced and developed, or mastered in the course. The survey would also elicit whether the competency was explicitly assessed and, if so, by what method. From that compendium, the faculty would distill the commonalities and strengths of teaching and student learning; judge whether they comprise a worthy set of outcomes (topics and proficiency levels); and officially anoint those strengths as the school's learning outcomes. As an approach, it offers the benefit of drawing from live data of what faculty actually do and does not require convincing any faculty member to change a course or teaching methods.

Alternatively, the faculty might use a macro-level process. They might identify, at least as a tentative matter, what they think are the most important learning outcomes for their school. Only then would they examine each course to determine where and how those goals/outcomes are taught, at what level of proficiency, and whether/how they are assessed. If the outcomes are not currently taught, or taught only in small-enrollment elective courses, or not to a sufficient level of mastery, then the faculty would adjust the curriculum (*e.g.*, introduce new courses, re-orient the topics or methods of existing courses, initiate new graduation requirements, etc.). This method has the benefit of unencumbered thinking about the aspirations and deliverables of their school's legal education. It is not a post hoc rationalization of what exists.

Either method or a blend of the two should connect a set of learning outcomes to the actual courses being taught and the results of student learning. With either method, of course, faculty must ensure that the curriculum covers all mandatory learning outcomes.

An Example of Curriculum Mapping

Here is an example of a learning outcome, woven from similar outcomes and performance indicators from multiple law schools,[7] and the way a school could map the outcome across its curriculum.

---

6. See, *e.g.*, Anthony Niedwiecki, *Law Schools and Learning Outcomes: Developing a Coherent, Cohesive, and Comprehensive Law School Curriculum*, 64 Clev. St. L. Rev. 661 (2016); Debra Moss Curtis and David M. Moss, *Curriculum Mapping: Bringing Evidence-Based Frameworks to Legal Education*, 34 Nova L. Rev. 473 (2010); Miller, Nelson P., *Mapping Lawyer Competencies Onto the Law School Curriculum to Confirm that Graduates are Prepared for Law Practice* (June 30, 2011). Available at SSRN: https://ssrn.com/abstract=2461037 or http://dx.doi.org/10.2139/ssrn.2461037. The literature regarding curriculum mapping and assessment has grown quickly as law schools have prepared to comply with the ABA standards. *See, e.g.*, Judith Welch Wegner, *Law School Assessment in the Context of Accreditation: Critical Questions, What We Know and Don't Know, and What We Should Do Next*, 67 J. Legal Educ. 412 (2018); Susan Hanley Duncan, *They're Back! The New Accreditation Standards Coming to a Law School Near You—A 2018 Update, Guide to Compliance, and Dean's Role in Implementing*, 67 J. Legal Educ. 462 (2018); Andrea Susnir Frank, The Art of Assessment: Making Outcomes Assessment Accessible, Sustainable, and Meaningful (2017); Lori E. Shaw and Victoria L. Van Zandt, Student Learning Outcomes and Law School Assessment: A Practical Guide to Measuring Institutional Effectiveness (2015).

7. See, *e.g.*, University of Massachusetts-Dartmouth School of Law, https://www.umassd.edu/law/about/learning-outcomes/ (outcome 2.2, problem-solving) *(last visited November 12, 2018)*; University of Memphis Cecil Humphreys School

Graduates will be able to provide client-oriented legal services: Graduates will demonstrate achievement of this learning outcome by:

- Engaging with clients to identify goals, interests and values.
- Diagnosing problems as they relate to their clients' goals.
- Engaging in appropriate legal research, factual development, and strategic analysis.
- Evaluating legal and non-legal solutions, in collaboration with the client.
- Articulating practical considerations, such as cost and effects on other people.
- Implementing plans of action to advance the client's goals.
- Managing a complex workload diligently, reliably, and within deadlines.

For each Standard 301 program goal, the law faculty must identify which courses deliver parts or all of the elements of the learning outcome. For a learning outcome focused on *client-oriented legal services*, with seven performance indicators like these, it's easy to see that the experiential curriculum and especially the live practice courses (externships and clinics) will be critical to teaching and assessing student attainment. But which live experiential courses? A clinic with individuals as clients, where the client matter can be started and concluded within a semester might be a prime course to teach all or nearly all elements. But a civil liberties clinic where students experience only a 13-week slice of multi-year litigation might offer opportunity to advance fewer skills, depending on the stage of the litigation during the student's clinic semester. Some field placement host offices, like a legal services landlord-tenant unit, might provide the training platform for students to acquire most of these component skills. Externships with a judge might provide an opportunity to observe lawyers exhibiting such skills, but no opportunity for the students to practice such client engagement skills personally. A simulation course might provide students with a highly developed case file that offers a platform to learn skills critical to several of the skills. A doctrinal class might engage students in focused legal and strategic analysis regarding a particular legal problem.

The faculty would examine these courses, and others, to discern which component skills are covered and at what level of learning (introductory, practicing, or mastery). They also would consider the proportion of graduating students who will have experienced such classes. The result of the mapping might prompt a re-evaluation of the outcome and the performance indicators if they seem more ambitious than can reliably be delivered to the whole student body.

D. Measuring Progress Toward Attainment of JD Learning Outcomes

Once the learning outcomes are set, it's up to the faculty and dean to monitor attainment (or lack thereof). Faculty are required to monitor the school's program of study to measure how well the newly graduated students succeeded in attaining each outcome. (Std. 315). They cannot rest on the fact that the specific competency is "taught." The law school needs some type of assessment instrument that can answer the question: how do we know whether and to what extent our students have attained the specific competencies? Pragmatically (and mercifully), the ABA Standards *do not require* that a school attest that every law graduate meet every institutional learning outcome at a defined competency level. But the standards do require actual measurement of graduate competency. The

of Law, https://www.memphis.edu/law/current-students/learningoutcomes.php (outcome 3, legal problem- solving) *(last visited November 12, 2018);* University of Washington, https://www.law.uw.edu/academics/jd/curriculum/student-learning-outcomes (outcome 3: client orientation) *(last visited November 12, 2018).*

new standard also assumes a cycle of continuous improvement and accountability, by requiring faculty to "make appropriate changes to improve the curriculum." (Std. 315).

As the cycle for accreditation has lengthened to 10 years, the program assessment cycle will probably follow suit. The ABA has assured schools that they need not assess each program outcome every year—that would be extremely difficult—but must assess all of the outcomes and demonstrate appropriate adjustment to the program within an accreditation cycle.

Measurement of student attainment of the learning outcomes is not limited to course performance. The ABA specifically allows both direct and indirect assessment. Interpretation 315-1 notes:

> Examples of methods that may be used to measure the degree to which students have attained competency in the school's student learning outcomes include review of the records the law school maintains to measure individual student achievement; evaluation of student learning portfolios; student evaluation of the sufficiency of their education; student performance in capstone courses or other courses that appropriately assess a variety of skills and knowledge; bar exam passage rates; placement rates; surveys of attorneys, judges, and alumni; and assessment of student performance by judges, attorneys, or law professors from other schools. The methods used to measure the degree of student achievement of learning outcomes are likely to differ from school to school and law schools are not required by this standard to use any particular methods.

How assiduously the ABA accreditation site visit teams will scrutinize law schools is still unknown. Nevertheless, many schools have embraced the switch to outcomes assessment and approached the task to assess the efficacy of their curriculum comprehensively and analytically.

In these new standards, the ABA is now guiding, slowly and incrementally, law schools to incorporate goal-anchored learning into their curriculum. These standards expect the faculty to look critically at all the course offerings at their school and commit to a set of learning outcomes that their graduates will achieve. The ABA standards help teachers conceive how separate courses fit together within the comprehensive curriculum of their law school. At their fullest expression, the new standards will catalyze a collaborative and revealing dialogue among the full faculty about course design and what a worthwhile legal education should deliver.

E. Goal Setting, Learning Outcomes, and Experiential Learning Design

As noted above, *EL Design* parallels the process of program assessment. After all, program assessment occurs to ensure the program can achieve its learning outcomes. That requires many courses in the program are expressly designed to deliver student learning sufficient to meet the program outcomes.

Similarly, *EL Design* requires close examination of a course for what is learned—not only the topics taught but what students are expected to understand and be able to do at the end of the course. Some of your course goals and outcomes will likely need to align with your school's published learning outcomes. You may well have additional specific goals for your EL course. *EL Design* helps you to achieve your individual course outcomes as well as your school's outcomes.

Experiential teachers must also examine how they assess student performance, how well their assessments align with their teaching goals, and whether their teaching actually produces the desired outcomes. This introspection allows teachers to evaluate their teaching priorities. Whether you are internally or externally motivated, you may well recognize the need for realignment and redesign of your courses. That of course, is why we developed this book.

Chapter 2

Using the Experiential Learning Design Process

> Here we go. Got my icebreaker and housekeeping out of the way. My first "client" is a couple, Jan and Bill. Don't think they really understood my explanation of confidentiality. Not sure I do either. Ask the first question on my list. Remember to listen, really listen. Wait—what did they say? I missed that. Shoot, they've moved on to some other part of their troubles. Do I interrupt or let them come to a stop? Good, they've stopped. Make eye contact. Bill seems uncomfortable. What am I supposed to do to make him more at ease? Ask the next question. Oh, no, that information could mess up the case. Unless that was in the exceptions? Maybe I'll leave it alone till I've had a chance to check the law. Where am I on my list?
>
> —*internal monologue from a clinic student during a client interview.*

Experiential learning courses present special challenges in their design and ambitions. First, the realities of practice create a sense of urgency to cover an unwieldy amalgamation of law, skills, and ethics. That urgency is heightened for those experiential courses that place students in the attorney role, responsible for the legal welfare of a client. Second, experiential courses are dynamic and variable, changing semester to semester. Even more challenging, the learning environment can be very different from student to student. These dilemmas—coverage pressures and the variability of student learning experience—prompted the authors to tackle course design for experiential courses.

A. The Coverage Trap

The transition for law students from doctrinal to experiential courses can be daunting. Students new to practice-based courses have little to no exposure to lawyering or the legal subject matter that typically arises in experiential courses. The role of lawyer requires students to combine knowledge of substantive law and its processes and systems, lawyering skills, professional judgment, ethical rules, and foundational professional skills of service to a client. This situation has its benefits—students are asked to perform authentically, as a practicing attorney would, and to learn by doing.

But the breadth of knowledge, skills, and values required to perform as a lawyer, especially in field placements and clinics, also makes learning more challenging. Experiential courses ask students to run before they can walk, and students can be overwhelmed with the cognitive and emotional demands on them: where should they focus their attention—the law, the underlying concepts for the skills, an individual lawyering skill, or finding their voice? What if they aren't comfortable with the individual components before using them with real clients or in real work settings? What happens when they make a mistake?

This complexity and urgency can push teachers into the trap of "coverage," trying to teach all the law, skills, and values that students might need to represent clients in experiential learning courses. Some of the early rubrics in clinics were so extensive they suggested that the four short months of a semester would develop a student from neophyte to master litigator or dealmaker. Such rubrics comprised long lists of lawyering tasks and values including dozens of litigation skills, sociology of poverty and power dynamics, doctrinal law and theory, and more. Teaching such an extensive set of items is both challenging and counterproductive. Instead, teachers should remember that judiciously covering less content can enhance student learning. Judicious coverage allows students to delve into the material more deeply and to practice it more extensively. That in turn can deliver more durable learning—learning that has meaning and utility long after the course is finished. Less is more.

B. A Common Course? Or a Collection of Independent Study Arrangements?

The "less is more" mantra also helps to unify students in the same experiential learning course in a common academic endeavor, not just a common practice experience. Experiential learning courses differ from doctrinal courses in which students are preparing for a common final exam, from a common set of readings and a common lecture. Experiential courses, focused on real clients and legal professionals, in active law offices or chambers are, by nature, fluid. The experience among students and across semesters can vary substantially. Even simulation courses that start with greater commonality of student experience are more dynamic than podium classes.

Faced with such diversity of student experience, some teachers default to teaching each student individually. The shared classroom component in a clinic then takes second seat to supervision meetings, where the focus might lie exclusively on the student's learning through assigned client matters. And some field placement courses omit a classroom component altogether. In these situations, teachers engage in the equivalent of multiple independent study arrangements, despite a common enrollment. As a series of independent studies, an experiential learning course would offer scant opportunity for scaling efficiencies in teaching and might encourage disengagement from the classroom component. The teacher could be quite restricted from using techniques that place students in pairs or small groups to perform simulations or that take advantage of peer-to-peer learning. The risk of providing uneven learning experiences would be ever present.

The diverse experiences also raise challenges for assessment (and grading). If *student learning*, and *opportunity to learn*, differs significantly from one student to the next, what is the fair reference point for grading? Does the teacher grade on effort and diligence, to account for the different complexities and challenges each client matter presented?

The remedy to these problems is to spend the time to find the commonality of student learning. Identify the meaningful core of your course so that every student will be able to partake and learn and so that you will be able to assess student learning consistently and fairly.

C. The "Experiential Learning Design" Solution

Enter *Experiential Learning Design (EL Design)*. *EL Design* is framed by two presumptions. First, educators teach for transfer. As John Dewey has said, student learning should live "fruitfully and creatively in their subsequent experiences." Second, transfer of learning occurs because students grasp *what* their teachers intend them to learn and *why* that learning matters. In the experiential curriculum, the students' ability to learn lawyering skills mechanistically is not sufficient; they must create meaning around those skills.

EL Design provides a methodology to craft a meaningful set of goals that will beckon all students in a course. A teacher can and should create a well-curated set of teaching objectives and resist the impulse to cover as many topics, skills, and values as might be useful. A teacher can and should identify the core learning that flows from the course, useful to each student no matter how different one student's legal work is from another's.

Of course, a teacher will teach topics other than those most closely tied to the teaching goals. But the imperative in *EL Design* is to guide teachers to keep their eyes on the goals they have set. In experiential lawyering courses, "less is more" means a teaching and assessment focus on fewer laws, skills, and values while emphasizing the purposes and underlying concepts of the content.

Consider a negotiation simulation course. During the course, the students might learn different styles of negotiation, what information to share and what to keep close to the vest, how to identify the BATNA (best alternative to a negotiated agreement) and how to comply with ethical guidelines on truthfulness. But, after the course is over, the knowledge and skills might fade, if the students don't use them again regularly. If, however, the instruction is focused on purpose and underlying concepts—say, "successful negotiators find/create value for all parties"—then the students are more likely to **make meaning** of their learning and use it in other contexts.

EL Design uses the phrase, "make meaning" very deliberately. The more that students can interpret their experiences—make meaning—the more likely they will be able to transfer their learning to new lawyering contexts. Few clinical students will practice in the same area of law, with the same clientele, or in the same setting when they graduate. Teaching for meaning will equip students with the ability to transfer their learning and progress farther wherever they land.

Determining what will help the students make meaning from a course is not simple. If "less is more," how does a teacher figure out what is the most critical "less" to cover? To answer this question, consider what students can use when they complete a course. *Design process*, a method used by engineers, architects, and artists, helps with this consideration. Design process dictates that designers start with the finished product and how the intended user would want the product to look, feel, or work. With that vision in mind, an engineer would next break down a project into manageable steps; insert feedback loops from the users; and use that feedback to inform improvements. In education, design process helps teachers shift to the finished product (learning for transfer) and user (the student) and away from content inputs and fun activities.

Educational designers Grant Wiggins and Jay McTighe adapted design process for K-12 education in their acclaimed work Understanding by Design (2d ed. 2005). Their model, nicknamed *backward design*, identifies students as the users of educational courses and posits that students should use course materials and activities to make meaning of the course content at the unit level and to transfer their learning to new contexts.

The *EL Design* model melds engineering design process, the Wiggins and McTighe model, and the course design model developed by the Indiana University Center for Innovative Teaching and Learning. *EL Design* will anchor your course in its subject matter and your reasons for teaching it before you establish a framework for instruction.

This chapter provides an overview of the *EL Design* model. Chapters 3–7 explore the steps of the model in detail. At each step, a mini-lesson and worksheets walk you through the model. Each chapter also provides examples of the authors' thinking as each worked through *EL Design* to construct their own courses.

Please choose your own entry point!

EL Design is sequential in concept. Start with your goals. Articulate what evidence you want to satisfy yourself that your students have achieved those goals (a.k.a. evidence of mastery) and the prompt they need to elicit that evidence. Use those elements to break down your goals into learning outcomes and then identify your units and select specific lawyering tasks and learning activities (*e.g.*, readings, exercises, discussions, reflections).

That said, you need not use this workbook in consecutive order. Your design work should be organic. Perhaps you are focused on planning your assessment and need help designing a rubric. That's where you should start to use this book. Perhaps you set a magnificent course goal, but you are concerned that it's too amorphous or overly ambitious. You might choose to flip among a few chapters or peruse the worksheet examples for guidance.

Dive in where it suits your course design work. Use it at the scale (unit or course) that feels comfortable.

In the end, keep a key principle in mind. Check that your teaching activities, your final assessment, your evaluation criteria, your course goal, and your animating theory align. And know that you will revisit the process, as you reflect, gather feedback, and finally test your ideas as you teach the course. The *EL Design* process is intentionally iterative. The authors each have examined and re-examined the theories of their courses; taken account of the vagaries of their teaching strengths and schedules, student readiness, law school realities, and the like; and circled back to revisit goals, assessments, and alignment.

The graphic below provides a snapshot of the *EL Design* process. It forecasts the specific questions teachers should ask themselves about their teaching intentions. It will help you decide where best to start your design (or re-design) work.

Experiential Learning Design-A Cyclical Process

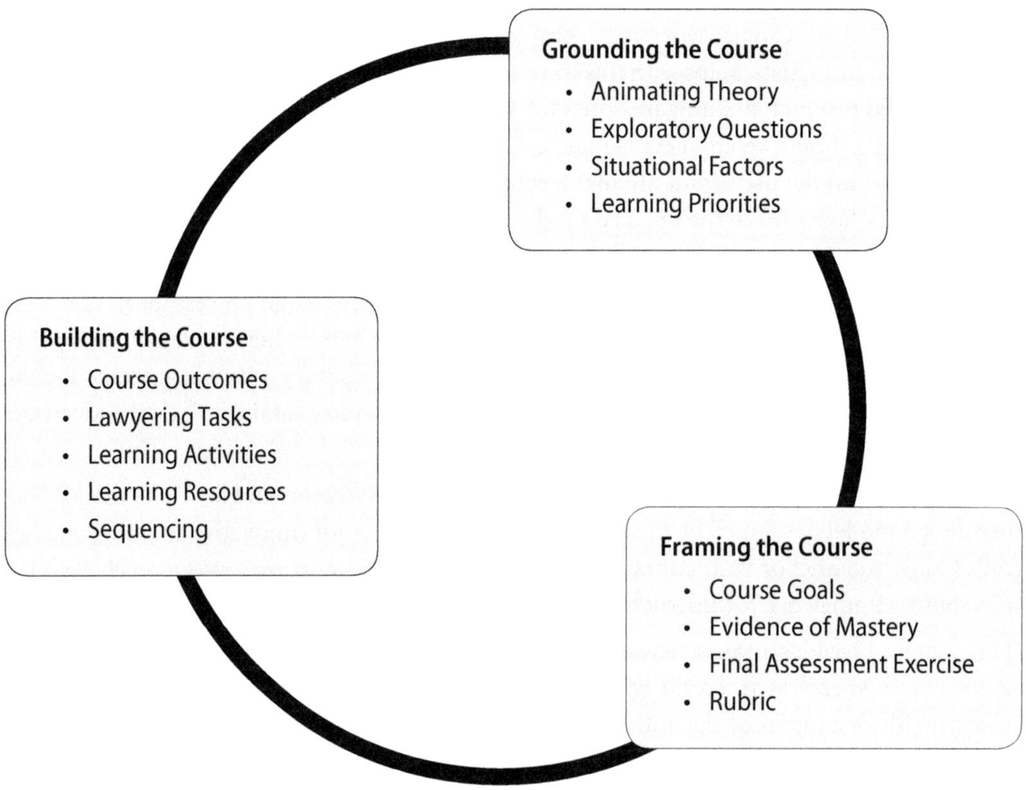

D. Experiential Learning Design in Three Parts

Part 1: Grounding the Course

In Chapter 3—*The Big Picture: What is the Point of Your Course?*—you will take the steps to ground your course. *EL Design* starts with the subject of your course. You are the expert in the subject, and you are teaching it for a reason. Perhaps your focus centers on a particular practice area or lawyering experience, client population, or a set of skills. So, *EL Design* asks a series of questions: Why do *you* think this subject is worth learning? What do you see as the core ideas, principles, and purposes of the subject? Why do they matter? Which ones motivate you to teach? What kind of exploration of the subject do you want your students to engage in? How do you use your expertise in the subject? Your answers to these questions will not necessarily lay out coherent answers. You will have to separate the wheat from the chaff. The result will be your animating theory for the course, and it will help you to focus the content of your course and imbue it with larger meaning.

At the same time, *EL Design* asks the teacher expressly to acknowledge the limitations of the course, whether they stem from the students' or the teacher's circumstances, the school's requirements or culture, or something else. These limitations will affect what can be realistically achieved in the course and how to set priorities for student learning. The limitations will include examination of the diversity of student experiences in your course and require you to identify the common elements pertinent to all of your students. *EL Design* then asks the teacher to determine the vital components of the student learning, in descending order: enduring, important, and "merely" worthwhile. This step helps to define the course goal and prioritize the content of the course.

This part, grounding your course, is usually the hardest in the *EL Design* process. Figuring out what matters most to you in teaching the subject and right-sizing that to something teachable for transfer of learning takes time. But taking the time is worthwhile: exploring these questions first will anchor your course in what is meaningful about the subject and sustainable under the circumstances.

Before turning to examples in legal education, let's walk through a relatable example of how this stage works in an imagined course teaching kids to ride a bike in the suburbs. While the core skills of mounting, pedaling, braking, etc. are vital to student success in the course, *EL Design* asks the teacher to answer the question why it is worth teaching kids to ride a bike. The answer "because everyone should know how to ride a bike" is not enough. Maybe the answer is "because bike riding provides kids independent transportation, no longer beholden to adult willingness and availability to drive. It represents autonomy; with autonomy comes responsibility." Maybe it's about the exhilaration of wind in your face. Maybe the teacher's motivating theory is that biking represents a green lifestyle. These are competing ideas that might animate a bike-riding course. The teacher will consider limitations such as the students' ages, traffic levels, and parental views of children's independence. Let's presume for present purposes that the students' parents and road conditions are such that beginning cyclists will be able to go places quickly and more independently once they know how to ride, whether to soccer practice or to buy bread for dinner. The teacher therefore chooses an animating theory that cycling begets autonomy and autonomy begets responsibility. With that context and teaching vision, the teacher creates the purpose for the course. If the course limitations and opportunities changed, then *EL Design* would ask the teacher to revisit why the course is worth teaching, in order to craft an animating theory that is pragmatic and relevant to the course.

Part 2: Framing the Course

After grounding the subject in its intellectual and logistical context, *EL Design* moves to establishing the framework for the course. The framework is comprised of two major elements—the beginning (teaching intentions) and the end (learning deliverables). These elements of the *EL Design* process are covered in Chapters 4 through 6.

Goal setting: Course goals are forward-looking—what the teacher aspires to teach and expects the students to learn. Course goals transform the teacher's animating theory into a comprehensive, general statement of the students' intended learning. The course goals represent the priorities set for *enduring* student learning as defined in Part 1. What learning should students be able to transfer to new situations after the course ends? Transfer is a performance, in which students use their knowledge, skills, and values creatively and fruitfully in a new context.

Teachers express course goals in terms of the desired student performance and mastery level. The use of specific performance terminology lays out clear expectations for students. Consider the usefulness among these different formulations of the course goal in a Negotiations class. First, "Students will understand the basic principles of negotiations." It's vague; what does "understand" mean in this context? How will the teacher measure "understand"? A second iteration might be "Students will be able to explain the basic principles of negotiations." This iteration is more specific—students will know what kind of understanding is expected, and the teacher can measure the accuracy and depth of their explanations. A third formulation might be "Students will be able to assess and express the motivating interests and values of each party to the negotiation." This iteration also is specific and measurable. Its focus, however, is different from the second iteration's. Here, the teacher expects understanding based on perspective-taking and evaluation. This goal signals to students how they might use their learning, whether or not in a negotiation context.

To help define course goals that are clear and measurable, the *EL Design* process suggests using taxonomies created by learning theorists that describe three domains of learning:

- Knowledge/Cognition: what will the student know or be able to think?
- Skills/Psychomotor: what will the student be able to do?
- Values/Affect: what will the student care about?

The taxonomies stratify learning behaviors into levels from lower to higher cognitive, physical, and affective capability. Using the taxonomy that best encapsulates a course goal, teachers can pinpoint the desired performance and mastery (proficiency) level. The course goals may fall into one or more of the domains and can be crafted as a synthesis of the domains. The three taxonomies help educators phrase their course goal concretely because the levels they describe and the word lists they offer are observable and measurable actions that make the final goal statement clearer. You, however, might find that you situate your learning goals differently from the taxonomies' suggestions. Perhaps you situate a goal across more than one taxonomy or you associate a word with a different mastery level. That variation is normal. What matters more than the taxonomies themselves is clear, observable, and measurable statements of learning to establish the framework of the course.

The knowledge domain provides the framework for goals regarding knowledge content and cognitive skills like legal analysis and interviewing. The knowledge taxonomy differentiates the basic cognitive processing levels needed for lawyering tasks. For example, analysis of a statute is a higher order cognitive process than recalling the elements of a crime. Accurately extracting information relevant to a client's conduct through an interview and analyzing its legal significance represents higher level cognitive thinking as well.

But lawyering skills might also be anchored in the psychomotor domain. The psychomotor taxonomy is intended to capture physical skills like skiing or playing volleyball. But it also can apply to lawyering skills in two ways: to capture physical aspects of lawyering and to capture proficiency in using a combination of cognitive skills for a lawyering task. Thus, an Interviewing course might use the psychomotor domain to establish the goal of using physical elements of interviewing like body language and interpersonal distance effectively. Or it might use psychomotor domain to set a benchmark for how well students should be able to use physical and cognitive skills in interviewing.

Back now to the bike-riding course. Here, the teacher will look mostly to the psychomotor domain for the course goal. That course goal might be "students will be able to ride their bikes safely to school and home." But the teacher can also draw from the affective domain by adding the phrase "while complying with the rules of the road."

Measuring student learning: Having set course goals, *EL Design* moves to crafting the measurement methods for the desired student learning. The vantage point therefore is at the completion of the course. The teacher considers a student who has successfully attained the course goal; deconstructs what that student is able to know, do, and value; and then creates a final assessment to elicit the desired student performance. *EL Design* thus ensures that students are evaluated on their levels of achievement of the course goal, not ancillary learning.

Evidence of student mastery: Most experiential courses will require students to use multiple elements of their newly acquired knowledge, skills, and/or values synchronously and harmoniously. *EL Design* requires the teacher to identify and list the pieces of evidence that will define mastery as it pertains to the course (not veteran lawyer mastery). What would the successful student's performance look like? From that vantage, the teacher can design a final assessment exercise that calls on students to demonstrate their level of learning and can differentiate multiple levels of student accomplishment for building a rubric.

EL Design adapts and uses the concept of the Six Facets of Understanding developed by Wiggins and McTighe in UNDERSTANDING BY DESIGN (2d edition, 2005). The Facets help teachers visualize what they mean when they say they want students to "understand" something. According to Wiggins and McTighe, teachers can describe the evidence of understanding by using one or more of the Facets—Explanation, Interpretation, Application, Perspective Taking, Empathy, and Self-Knowledge. Each of these terms represents a nonhierarchical cognitive behavior that a student uses to make meaning of the course content and to create deep learning. In an experiential lawyering course, each lawyering skill, especially at the advanced levels of the knowledge taxonomy, draws on some of the Six Facets. Thus, a teacher who wants students to learn how lawyers use persuasion successfully might visualize students who are able to explain the law, predict and respond to the perspectives of individual stakeholders, and interpret a problem in a way that acknowledges and speaks to the values and motivations of the decision-maker(s).

Final assessment: With the mastery evidence in hand, the *EL Design* moves to development of the final assessment exercise for the course. The assessment should be authentic—asking students to use their learning as a practitioner would, even if at a lower level of proficiency. The assessment should be forward-looking—asking students to use their learning in a new context that builds on the work they have done in the course. The assessment is summative, to establish student achievement at the end of the course. In experiential courses, typical final assessments might be a live capstone performance, such as a simulated negotiation; or a compilation of work products, such as a portfolio; or perhaps an individual or team presentation. The context and prompt for the final assessment exercise will require students to demonstrate mastery of the course goal.

Evaluative rubric: Although there are many formats for rubrics, *EL Design* uses analytic rubrics as the default. Analytic rubrics have three elements. They identify the key evaluative criteria for examining the student performance. They describe the characteristics of the student work that will be observed. (This is the mastery evidence.) And they differentiate the student performance at multiple levels of proficiency (usually three levels, *e.g.*, developing, competent, exceptional).

When provided to the students at the same time as the final assessment exercise, a rubric communicates expectations and provides the roadmap to meet those expectations. Rubrics thus help students to judge and improve their own work. Rubrics also help teachers to evaluate student work consistently and efficiently. *EL Design* focuses on developing a rubric for the final assessment (summative), as that helps teachers keep in mind the whole course, not individual lawyering tasks or classroom assessments.

Assessments, rubrics, and the feedback loop: The final assessment and the analytic rubric are important to the overall integrity of the course, whether or not a letter grade is given in the course. Unless teachers are willing to assess students, they cannot discern whether their students have learned sufficiently well and whether their teaching is effective. This feedback loop is integral to *EL Design*. Analytic rubrics provide detailed information about what students are learning and where they are getting stuck. Such information helps students and teachers to adjust their learning and teaching respectively. Note that the authors' focus is on assessment for feedback, not grading. Grading may involve other purposes as well, as discussed in Chapter 1, and may also be subject to requirements such as grading curves.

In the bike-riding course, let's assume that the goal is for students to ride a bicycle safely on the streets. The mastery evidence would include performance criteria for the physical acts in cycling—mounting, pedaling, keeping one's balance, stopping, dismounting, and the like. A second set of performance criteria might focus on responsibility—using hand signals, wearing a helmet, courtesy and predictability toward pedestrians (and drivers), etc. From here, the final assessment might contain two parts: a written test requiring mastering rules (rules of the road) and demonstrating judgment (responses to various hypotheticals), and a performance test of actually riding a bike from their home to their school. The rubric would set levels of performance based on how well the student rides, knows safety rules, and can apply the rules with a sense of personal responsibility.

Part 3: Building the Course

After drafting the rubric for the final assessment, *EL Design* turns to filling out the course content and planning the semester. This part of the design process is covered in Chapter 7. It involves working with the nitty gritty of a course—course learning outcomes, lawyering tasks, and learning resources and activities—and how to organize them. The *EL Design* process places these tasks last. The teacher thus can identify the instruction, lawyering tasks, and other practice (topics, exercises, resources) to emphasize so that students can succeed on the final assessment the teacher already has drafted.

Course outcomes: Course outcomes represent the building blocks of learned knowledge, skills, and values necessary to achieve the course goals. Each course outcome corresponds to a particular set of knowledge, skills, or values that the student will integrate when completing the final assessment. Sometimes, when a course goal is written narrowly and specifically, one of the course outcomes may end up being the same as the course goal. That is O.K., as is revising the course goal to be more general.

Course outcomes also may connect to the school's ABA-mandated program outcomes (see Chapter 1, *Your Experiential Course and the ABA Standards*). Some of the ABA minimum learning outcomes are quintessentially the province of the experiential curriculum, and the ABA accordingly now mandates that all students enroll in at least six credits of experiential coursework in order to graduate.

Learning activities and resources: At last, *EL Design* turns to the simulation, fieldwork, and classroom work that will help students to achieve the course goals. Teachers carry out this step last to avoid stringing together learning activities, no matter how interesting, and calling them a course. Rather, in *EL Design*, the course goals serve as the reference point for choosing the kinds of legal matters, field placements, and clients the course involves. With this orientation, lawyering tasks and learning activities become the forum in which course outcomes are introduced, practiced and mastered, not the ends in and of themselves.

Develop teaching plans for each unit of instruction, recognizing that a course outcome might appear across multiple, nonadjacent topics and classes. Organize resources and learning activities across the unit. Think chronologically: What should students do at the beginning of a unit or class to introduce or reinforce content? What activities in class, with clients, or at their field placement will allow practice of their learning? What feedback do they and the teacher need to assess how well students are learning and teachers are teaching? What final unit activity will demonstrate student mastery of the unit's outcomes? Note that designing units of instruction rather than individual lessons makes it easier to see how content in a unit might be distributed throughout the course. This distribution encourages spaced practice, and the use of course outcomes in multiple lawyering tasks and units will encourage learning for transfer.

In the bike-riding course, the outcomes derive from the performance criteria used in the final assessment: Students will be able to mount and dismount a bike. Students will be able to pedal their bike while balanced. Students will be able to comply with the rules of the road. (Notice that the last outcome does not include the word "know"—rather, "knowing" is embedded in "comply with.") Students will be able to explain how their cycling impacts others (fellow travelers, caregivers). The learning activities will focus on the trial and error of mounting the bikes, riding, turning, etc. They will be given demonstrations. The steps of mounting and pedaling will be conducted in a protected lot and mastered before the lessons move to turning, stopping, and signaling. Eventually, the students will take rides on the roadways in light traffic. The instructor will introduce rules of the road, whether in written form and/or orally; quiz the students about them; and give feedback when observing the students bike on the streets. The instructor will begin and end each class with a question about responsibilities to others and have the students discuss who matters and why.

Course Outcomes	Learning Activities	Materials/Resources
Students will be able to mount and dismount a bike.	Read an instruction manual or watch a video. Practice doing so, in increasingly more difficult situations.	Manual Video Bicycle + Helmet + Pads Pick out parking lot, streets, and paths to follow. Props: cones, barriers, etc. to simulate road and traffic conditions.
Students will be able to pedal their bike while balanced.	Same as above.	Same as above.
Students will be able to comply with the rules of the road.	Read rules of road manual. Watch video. Test recall of rules; application to hypotheticals. Test hand signals, use of bell. Simulation in parking lot. Live road practice; different times.	Same as above.
Students will be able to explain how their cycling impacts others (fellow travelers, caregivers).	Discussion of concerns from different perspectives. Role plays of different perspectives. Assessment—written?	Bring in parents, teachers, others?

E. Alignment—From Law School Mission to Course Learning Activities

This overview has used examples from generic courses on negotiations, interviewing, and bike riding. Now it looks at a genuine mini-course on professional identity and career development to illustrate how a course created through *EL Design* fits within the law school's stated mission from its goal to its learning activities.

Carwina Weng created and taught a one-credit, pass/fail course called The Legal Profession: Professional Identity Formation. It is a laboratory or exploration course, connected to the law school's 1L professional responsibility course, which Weng and Meg Reuter have both taught.

Let's start with the **mission** statement of the law school. The mission of the Indiana University Maurer School of Law is to "make a transformative contribution to the lives of our students . . . so they may become accomplished, *ethical leaders and professionals*." (emphasis added).

In service to that mission, one of Maurer's program **goals** pertains to Professionalism: "Our students will . . . take ownership of their own career development ...."

When setting the ABA-mandated **learning outcomes** for the JD degree, Maurer faculty included an outcome to support its Professionalism program goal: Students will be able to "identify personal skills, interests, priorities, and values and incorporate them in developing a career plan."

With these components of the law school goal and program JD learning outcomes in mind, Weng developed her animating theory for her course: Satisfied lawyers know who they are (or want to be) personally and professionally. If Maurer intends to prepare ethical leaders and professionals, her course will help students sync their personal identities with their professional ones.

Weng converted her animating theory to a concrete course goal for *The Legal Profession: Professional Identity Formation*: By the end of the semester, students will be able to shape their professional identity based on their personal skills, interests, priorities, and values. Weng crafted a reflective essay as the final assessment exercise. In the essay, students were instructed to describe their newly developed and refined career aspirations and an action plan of steps to take during law school to further those aspirations.

That final essay included many elements that had been introduced in the course and drew from many activities (readings, self-assessments, programs, field exploration) that the students undertook. Weng teased apart these elements to formulated course outcomes:

By the end of the course, students will be able to:

- Assess their personal values, skills, interests, and experiences.
- Choose the kinds of clients they seek to serve and the kind of lawyer-client relationship they prefer (*e.g.*, directive, cooperative, collaborative, client-centered).
- Evaluate practice settings and areas in light of personal and professional values and skills.
- Describe their currently held career aspirations.
- Develop a short-term plan to pursue those desires.

Weng created a set of learning activities that introduce students to these outcomes and provide multiple fora to allow them to test their ideas of the future careers. They included:

- Self-assessment of personal and workplace values.
- Self-assessment of current skills based on work and academic experience.
- An exercise to identify practice areas, settings, and geographic locations to consider and investigate.

- Exposure to multiple lawyers with diverse practices and career trajectories through attendance at five practitioner workshops on campus.
- Post-workshop written reflection regarding the values, skills, and interests represented by the speaker and how those might be applicable or dissonant to the student.
- Informational interviews with at least five legal professionals that focus again on values, skills, and interests.

Each learning activity aligns with one or more of the course outcomes above and prepares the student to write a reflective essay as the capstone of their career exploration.

Alignment: Law School Mission to Individual Course Outcomes

Next steps

You now have an overview of the *EL Design* process. Each of the subsequent chapters provides detailed guidance for the parts of the process. Each chapter comes with a worksheet or more to help you gather and refine your thoughts. Without context, the theory of course design can be too vague or conceptual to be readily used. That's why each chapter also includes an example or two of how the authors handled that design step in their courses. These courses show the applicability of *EL Design* to many kinds of courses. The book also includes appendixes of a complete set of worksheets for each of the featured courses. The worksheets show how the authors implemented each step of the *EL Design* process. Helpfully the completed worksheets contain the authors' process notes to demonstrate the concerns they considered; efforts they attempted that failed; and what they regarded as happy successes.

With the theory and logic of the *EL Design* process behind you, use the following chapters as a workbook to build or refine your experiential course. Feel free to tear out the worksheet templates at the back of the book, make copies of them, fill them in, cross out what you wrote, crumple up drafts, and repeat until you are satisfied.

Chapter 3

The Big Picture

What Is the Point of Your Course?

The experiential course design process described in this workbook seeks to impart transferable learning. When students transfer their learning to new and different contexts, then they have grasped what teachers intend them to learn and why that learning matters. For this transferable learning to occur in the experiential legal curriculum, the students' ability to learn lawyering skills mechanistically is not sufficient: they also must take in the concepts underlying the skills. To maximize this synthesis of skill and concepts, the *Experiential Learning Design model*, or *EL Design*, emphasizes i) the big picture that you want students to see as the core of your course and ii) alignment of your course goals, assessments, and learning activities with this big picture. This chapter takes you through the steps to identify your big picture. These steps will then prepare you to set your course goal in Chapter 4.

Identifying the big picture is harder than it sounds and is shaped by many contextual factors. In part, you are identifying the intellectual home for your course: what ties the whole course together and your motivation in teaching it. We call this the animating theory. What are the questions you would like students to engage and struggle with? *EL Design* also cautions and guides you to adjust your animating theory to take account of the situational constraints on your course. What are the boundaries and opportunities of your course within your school's curriculum? What are your priorities for what your students will use fruitfully and creatively in their future endeavors? Although these steps are preparatory, you may profitably use this chapter at any point in your course design and may find yourself revising your initial animating theory as a result of later steps in the *EL Design* process. Regardless of when and how often you return to this chapter, spend the time and thought to ground the course in the larger intellectual and teaching environment in which your course sits.

A. The Big Picture: Crafting the Animating Theory for the Course

Most teachers are accustomed to writing course outcomes that look something like this: At the end of the course, my students will be able to interview a client; create the documents necessary to challenge the denial of a government benefit; gather necessary facts, etc. This list is useful to tell the student the discrete skills that a lawyer might use to represent a particular litigation client. But the list doesn't illuminate the larger purpose for the student learning or guide the student to transfer the skills to another context.

To avoid merely listing topics or skills to be covered, *EL Design* draws on the work of educational designers, Grant Wiggins and Jay McTighe, and their seminal work, UNDERSTANDING BY DESIGN (2nd ed. 2005). Wiggins and McTighe recommend that educators ground their courses in a "big idea" along with a set of questions to be pursued. Their "big idea" becomes a focal point for determining course priorities and content. To offer guidance on how to craft one's big idea, Wiggins and McTighe suggest considering questions such as: What is the value of studying your subject? What larger concept, issue, or problem underlies the subject? What lesson can we glean from this subject that our students can use in other contexts (even in areas that, at first glance, seem dissimilar to your subject)? If this course is a story, what is the moral of the story?

EL Design shifted the phrase "big idea" to "animating theory" intentionally. Many experiential educators teach out of a desire to inculcate societal and professional values and traits. Some seek to teach students to recognize and understand the flaws in our system of justice. Some want to help students understand lawyering practices through a particular lens regarding the attorney client relationship. Some strive to instill in their students the habits of life-long self-development. Others strive to develop habits of mindfulness. "Animating theory" better reflects these broader motivational goals.

Your animating theory and related exploratory questions will serve as the focal point for your course. Articulating your theory will help your students to understand the importance of the subject matter. The way you articulate your theory will implicitly or explicitly reveal your motivations and ethos. Thus, you might frame your animating theory as a declarative statement that indicates a specific approach the students should adopt, as these theories do:

- "A client's wishes inform the lawyer's path," from Chris Roberts's criminal defense clinic.
- "Society expects lawyers to have the skills for and to exhibit professional judgment," from Meg Reuter's externship seminar.
- "You are an advocate for children in a system of justice," from another colleague's family law clinic.

Your animating theory might be reduced to a phrase such as "Lawyer as human-centered problem-solver" from Carwina Weng's Disability Law Clinic. Or your animating theory might be in the form of a question that conveys the heart of the subject matter, such as "Who writes the check?" from Danielle Cover's Torts II class.

As you can see, the animating theory is not your course goal. It is not phrased as "what will my students know, be able to do, or value at the end of the term." Rather the animating theory sets the parameters for your course. What is the theoretical environment in which you and your students are going to wrestle with concepts, realities, and lawyering technique? The animating theory functions as the intellectual home for your course.

Regardless of how it's phrased, your animating theory will require students to engage in reflection about its meaning and function. Your students will use the animating theory as a guiding principle, not only as they work their way through your course, but as they move forward into new situations and other areas of practice. When your students are unsure what to do, they can retreat to the unifying principle embodied in the animating theory to help them resolve the dilemma at hand. The animating theory should permeate your experiential course, and it will provide the starting point for your course goals. So, as your first *EL Design* step, it's time to articulate the animating theory of your course.

To conceive and craft the animating theory for your course, consider these prompts.

- What is your chosen subject matter?
- What is the purpose of the skills and values you will teach?
- Why is it valuable that your students learn them?
- What will make your students effective at using the skills or integrating the values?
- How deep do you need the students' learning to be?
- In what ways will they use these skills or values in their future law practice?
- What concept does the expert grasp, perhaps automatically, that the novice does not yet understand or appreciate?

Your animating theory should provide the fuel for transfer of learning, require synthesis of complex material, and offer genuine intellectual and reflective challenge. Wiggins and McTighe have identified some criteria to test your animating theory.

An animating theory:

- Provides a concise statement, principle, theory, or generalization.
- Stands the test of time, and students' thoughts about it might change over time.
- Promotes depth of understanding and helps us make sense of things.
- Is open to disagreement (even if the teacher's views are apparent).
- Applies to students' lives.

Some teachers will have two theories that interlace, but have different conceptual moorings. If this describes you, try to synthesize the two theories into a unified animating theory that applies *throughout* your course or make explicit how the two interlace. This will help you to set attainable course goals in the next step. Indeed, setting two related and attainable course goals may help your students to concretize the animating theory.

B. Exploratory Questions: The Power of Your Animating Theory

When the animating theory is open to exploration, you will cultivate an environment for rich reflective learning. Exploratory questions expose your animating theory to debate and reflection. These questions and the dilemmas that give rise to them are not so much to be answered as they are to be pondered through diverse perspectives, lingering in our students' consciousness. The hope is that the pursuit of answers will deepen the understanding that students have regarding the most important ideas, processes, skills, or values flowing from your course. Together the animating theory and exploratory questions comprise the intellectual home for your course. And they nourish your motivation for teaching the course.

Exploratory questions promote genuine and sustained inquiry. They reveal new understanding and beget more questions for the students. Exploratory questions, at their best, catalyze students to consider alternatives, examine their experience in the course against their prior experience, and stimulate rethinking of their assumptions. Therefore, to give students sincere and supportive room to explore, phrase these questions in an open-ended and non-judgmental manner.

Let's examine one clinician's approach to his animating theory and exploratory questions. Chris Roberts views his Criminal Defense Clinic as working on dual tracks, as he seeks to instill an ethos and an ethic in his clinical students. As a result, he found it easier to work with two separate (though certainly related and often intertwined) animating theories.

■ Criminal Defense Clinic—Animating Theory and Exploratory Questions

Animating Theory 1: The client's wishes inform the lawyer's path.

Exploratory questions:

What does it mean to be client-centered?
How does one take a client-centered approach in the context of counseling clients; conducting negotiations; implementing a litigation strategy; and courtroom advocacy?

Animating Theory 2: The best lawyer is the best-prepared lawyer.

Exploratory questions:

What does "good" preparation entail?
How does one prepare for a seemingly endless list of contingencies?

* See worksheets 1 and 2.

Roberts's exploratory questions channel students into deeper personal inquiry about the meaning of these animating theories. The animating theories are stated as a professional ideal and as a truth. The questions require students to examine their experiences and expectations, and hopefully to ask themselves further questions. The exploratory questions make apparent that there is more than one way to pursue or mold the ideal.

Clinics, externships, and simulation courses are ripe for developing animating theories around a few concepts: the role of lawyer in a system of justice, the benefits and limitations of the rule of law, the dimensions of the attorney-client relationship, or the values of a profession of service. These concepts are too nebulous, as written, to function as a viable animating theory. However, if such concepts have natural tethers to your course, you may find a way to germinate the concept and give it more shape and direction sufficient to be a viable animating theory.

Let's play out some variations. You might imagine a legal educator's first notion of the animating theory for a course could flow from a personal mission, "Lawyers must advocate for social justice." But remember, to be a rich learning platform, the animating theory and exploratory questions should be open to divergent viewpoints; the animating theory is not ineffable dogma; and the exploratory questions should elicit multiple perspectives. You need a platform for genuine inquiry and debate. So, grill yourself: are you open to divergent views about this theory? Perhaps the animating theory can be re-framed as, "Our system of justice is flawed and run by flawed humans." Such a re-characterization certainly opens inquiry about justice and injustice. Importantly, the re-framing cues up exploration about the nature, causes, and impacts of flaws; strategies to correct or overcome the flaws; or how to represent marginalized clientele within such a flawed system. The animating theory might morph further, to "A flawed legal system requires more diligent lawyering." So amended, the animating theory is now both a catalyst to examine the flaws and a call to arms for the students to define diligence. In this formulation, the animating theory lends itself easily to developing attainable course goals that focus on select skills, strategies, and tactics necessary to counter the flaws.

Ruminate about the course you hope to teach and how you hope students will be transformed. As you think about the content of your course, possible course goals, and what drives you personally, start brainstorming your animating theory. Use pencil, not indelible pen. As each of the authors has found, you too may find that this will be an iterative process toggling among animating theory, course goal, and the final assessment.

Animating Theory Checklist

- Is your animating theory open to disagreement?
- Does it stand the test of time?
- Can students' thoughts about it develop or change over time?
- Does it promote in-depth understanding and help make sense of things?
- Does it provide a concise statement, principle, theory, or generalization?

Exploratory Questions Checklist

- Are your exploratory questions open-ended, nonjudgmental, meaningful, and purposeful?
- Do your exploratory questions have emotional appeal?
- Is there more than one valid answer to the questions?
- Do the questions probe for deeper meaning and explore ideas and beliefs?
- Do the questions encourage collaboration?

C. The Realities and Circumstances of Your Course

Shortly, you will turn to crafting course goals. But you have a couple more preparatory steps to consider. It's important to situate your teaching *on the ground* and *over time*. Here you will start, rather explicitly, to vanquish the "coverage" threat, referenced in Chapter 2. Within the confines of a single course, teachers cannot cover everything that goes into their animating theory. Nor can teachers assure that students develop personal responses to every exploratory question. Accordingly, in these next two steps, you will i) list the situational constraints that shape your course, *e.g.*, credits, caseload, mix of field placement host offices; number of students; and ii) set priorities for the learning that you want to be most durable and transferable for your students. Namely, you will identify what can and cannot be covered given your course's circumstances and what elements of the course will be covered in a primary versus secondary or tertiary manner. Strategic course design requires teachers to be clear about what will be covered—and just as clear about what will not be covered.

You are well aware of situational constraints that impact how you will write your course goals. Some circumstances apply to all your students. For instance, the number of credits or hours/week in clinic, grading, enrollment numbers, curriculum requirements, and client stream are circumstances typically common to all your students. Your school's published learning outcomes (ABA required) also may have set teaching and learning expectations for all courses in the experiential curriculum.[1] Be smart about what you can productively and sustainably accomplish within these parameters.

Other realities remind you that, in live practice courses, your students' individual experiences can vary substantially. Coursework focused on real clients—in active law offices or chambers, or in live simulations—is dynamic, has limited predictability, and requires in-the-moment response. As a result, the experience among students will vary, and the variation can be substantial. Some clinics cover many kinds of client matters and law. Most clinics have matters that do not fit snugly within a 13-week semester, and students will work on very different stages of a matter from one another. Field placement courses may include the mix of host offices and practice settings, with diversity in the responsibility and complexity of assignments given, in the manner of supervision, and in office culture. Even simulation courses that start with greater commonality of student experience are more dynamic than podium classes. The teacher strives to insert unpredictability into the live simulations to help

---

1. *See* Chapter 1, *Your Experiential Course and the ABA Standards* for an examination of ABA curriculum standards, requirements regarding institutional learning outcomes, and effect on your course design.

students test their adaptability. Each of these factors—both common and varied—represents limits as well as opportunities for your course.

Your puzzle is to find the learning potential that every student has in common so that you can create course goals that *each and every student reasonably can achieve.* Your students encounter different clients, lawyering and simulation tasks, field placement cultures, and supervision styles. Despite the differences, each student should be able to relate to the animating theory and your chosen learning objectives in their personal experience. Indeed, the variety of student experiences will enrich the exploration of the animating theory and encourage transfer of learning. Moreover, focus on the learning common to all students will decrease resentment that any individual student did not get to do the "exciting" lawyering. It also will make your task in assessing student learning easier, as you can separate the "chaff" of individual encounters from the "wheat" of expected learning. This concept bears repeating. Your course goals should denote the same essential learning for every student. Second, your course goals set a mastery finish line that every student reasonably could achieve. Without working through this puzzle, you run a significant risk that your course could devolve into a collection of independent studies with private tutorials rather than a community of students engaged in a common learning enterprise.

The course design process for Roberts's Criminal Defense Clinic illustrates how to take account of on-the-ground realities to find attainable course goals. A natural focus for a criminal defense clinic might be the development of trial skills with a goal of producing attorneys who are prepared, by the end of the course, to try cases with little or no supervision. After all, trial advocacy is at the heart of being a criminal practitioner. Indeed, many long-time practitioners would argue that being an effective trial attorney is the most essential quality. But then Roberts starts to take account of his course's circumstances. The clinic is a one-semester course for six credits that provides a significant number of hours per week of legal work. The classroom component meets once per week for an hour and fifty minutes. Enrollment is capped at 16 students. [At the point that Roberts developed the worksheets included here, the student supervision was divided among Roberts and two adjunct supervising attorneys, private practitioners who were generally in the clinic workspace only one day a week.] From the time a case begins, it can take two years for a case to get to trial. As a result, the clinic is structured to give students a mix of new cases and cases at various later stages of the process.

Given these factors, how could Roberts develop a course goal to prepare students with "trial-ready" skills? Too few students handle a trial. Additionally, trial itself entails jury selection, delivery of an opening statement, cross-examination, objections based on evidentiary concerns, direct examinations, closing arguments, and critical analysis of jury instructions. Preparation for trial further involves other sets of skills that include legal research, motions drafting, and investigation. Given the limitations of Roberts's clinic and course, getting students to have "trial-ready" skills just isn't realistic. With a lot of one-on-one supervision, he might be able to push the ball forward quite a bit with a student who actually goes to trial during the clinic semester, but developing trial-ready skills simply isn't a viable unifying theory in this setting.

■ Criminal Defense Clinic—Situational Factors

Length (e.g., semester, year), number of credits, number of hours in field, casework, or classroom	6 credits: 1 class per week that lasts 1 hour, 50 minutes + a couple of intensive sessions at the beginning of the semester + 150 hours of casework
Grading scheme	P/F
Student preparedness (typical, high/low)	Consistency of reading is not ideal.
Student motivations	Students tend to prioritize casework, and assignments related to class can suffer from that.
Uniformity, dissimilarity, or variety of student work (in type and complexity)	Casework varies a lot. If a case goes to trial in our county court, it often takes around 2 years to get there. This long life of the case results in different experiences based on stage of case. Like any trial clinic, experience varies based on client objectives, as well.
Teaching Assistance	Roberts supervises the students with 2 private practitioner adjuncts, who come once a week to the clinic. [The clinic has since expanded attorney supervision].
Personal responsibilities that constrain my availability for class or individual student engagement	Roberts supervises anywhere from 6 to 10 students each semester in their casework. Needless to say, if students are approaching trial or some other contested hearing, preparation will take a lot of time and necessarily takes priority over other aspects of the class.

* See worksheet 3.

D. Learning Priorities:

What Do You Want Your Students to Remember Well Past Your Course?

You just considered the circumstances of your course to set realistic goals. You still have one more exercise to undertake before creating your course goals: what do you want students to remember well past your course? Identify the knowledge and understandings, skills, and/or values that flow from your animating theory and exploratory questions. Then categorize them based on their long-term importance to student learning, using the degrees of transferability below: Enduring, Important to know, and Worth being familiar with. Note that the course will cover content in all three categories, but the goals, and therefore the summative (final) assessments, will focus on the *Enduring* knowledge and understandings, skills, and/or values that you want students to transfer.

Roberts's Criminal Defense Clinic again shows an example of setting priorities. Of course, everything he wants to cover cannot be treated as the highest importance. So Roberts had to make some hard choices about content in his course.

■ Criminal Defense Clinic—Learning Priorities

Enduring learning:

Client-centered ethos
Good lawyering is not possible without exhaustive preparation.

Important for students to know:

Strategies for preparation, as related to counseling clients, negotiations, trial, and other advocacy opportunities
Strategies for confronting new processes and procedures, such as court appearances, filings, etc.

Worth being familiar with:

Trial skills
Negotiations strategy
Motions strategy
4th and 5th Amendment jurisprudence

* See worksheet 4.

As you can see, the *Enduring* learning was drawn from Roberts's animating theories. Roberts rephrased the theories to define his highest teaching priorities. To define the student learning in the *Important to know* priority, Roberts considered his experience over previous semesters in supervising students. He had to consider what goes into successful lawyering, and what he *can* convey within a semester. He came to the conclusion that, before novices can develop skills like delivering a closing argument, executing a cross-examination, or negotiating a plea offer, they need to develop techniques of preparation. As a result, Roberts has increasingly focused on ensuring that his course equips students with basic preparation strategies and techniques. For example, students leave the clinic knowing the "chapter method" of cross-examination, how to digest sources of impeachment and label individual questions with references to those sources, and the value of word choice, primacy, narrative, etc. The overarching lesson throughout the semester is that meticulous preparation will maximize an attorney's effective, client-centered representation. Not only is this goal more manageable, but students can transfer the lessons of preparation for discrete lawyering tasks into other contexts more easily, as well.

In his third learning priority, *Worth being familiar,* Roberts placed various skills and doctrinal foundations, *e.g.*, trial and negotiation strategy, and Fourth and Fifth Amendment jurisprudence. That might seem counter-intuitive given the importance to criminal defense practice of these skills and doctrine. However, these are the skills and doctrine that not every student will have the opportunity to use during the clinic and that are more easily forgotten if students do not have ongoing opportunity to use them after the clinic. So these skills and doctrine become tertiary learning priorities.

With these exercises, you have set the ecosystem of your course. You identified its animating theory and exploratory questions, and you recognized its situational and temporal limits. In the next chapter, you will turn to the task of writing your course goals.

E. Takeaways

- Two preparatory exercises help provide the intellectual roots of your course and the realistic aspirations for your students' most durable learning.
- An "animating theory" provides a principle that helps your students understand the importance of the subject matter, however you define that term for your course.
- Exploratory questions relate to your animating theory; they are not so much to be answered as they are to be churned, grappled with, and pondered.
- Recognizing on-the-ground circumstances of your course allows you to identify a common learning enterprise for all your students and to right-size your teaching ambitions.
- Determining the durability of student learning allows you to prioritize your teaching goals.

Chapter 4

The Course Goal

What Do You Want Your Students to Learn?

In Chapter 3, you formulated a theory for your course, accounted for the constraints on the course, and set priorities for the most important learning. Now, you turn to constructing the learning goal(s) for your course. That is the objective of this chapter. Your course goals will be written as comprehensive, general statements that i) align with your animating theory, ii) account for the limits of the learning environment, and iii) support your teaching priorities.

In *Experiential Learning Design* process (*EL Design*), the course goal(s) sets the finish line for your teaching and your students' learning. This is where you identify the type and extent of student learning and then construct the course to meet them. Hence, a fourth criterion for creating a viable course goal: your goals must also be observable and measurable. Without a measuring stick, you have no ability to monitor your students' progress and achievement. Even if you are teaching a pass/fail class, your goals will need to be observable and measurable to assess the extent to which your students reach those goals. Course goals are not hortatory statements. They are meant to be achieved.

Course goals take a form that answers one or more of the following questions.

> What do you want your students to know at the end of the course?
>
> What do you want them to be able to do?
>
> What do you want them to value?

If you are a more holistic thinker, ask instead, "How do I want my students to be different at the end of the course?"

To foster deeper learning, you should limit yourself to one or two course goals. Later in the *EL Design* process, you will devise course outcomes (Chapter 7). Course goals and course outcomes sound very much alike, but they are conceptually and functionally different. The course goal is comprehensive, integrated, and general (*e.g.*, students will develop persuasive, client-centered narratives) and the corollary course outcomes indicate the component parts of the goal (*e.g.*, students will be able to apply relevant law to facts of the case; marshal, weigh, and use both convincing and undermining facts; recognize and adjust to a forum's perspective; and use emotional content.). The course outcomes will help set the learning activities for the course. We don't want to get too far ahead of ourselves. Suffice to say, we are not defining the course goal and the course outcomes simultaneously. We simply note the complementary step in *EL Design* so that you can anticipate how your course goal will operate.

To note the obvious: the course goal is phrased with a subject, verb, and object. "At the end of the course, students will be able to [x], [regarding y]. The subject is set, "students." The verb chosen will indicate the type of learning to be acquired (*e.g.*, memorize, synthesize, compose). The object will represent the task or subject matter of the learning.

To help with this process, carefully review the learning taxonomies provided below. The first taxonomy is the best-known one, the brainchild of educational psychologist Benjamin Bloom. Bloom designed the taxonomy for higher education teaching and so focused it on the cognitive domain of learning. The remaining two taxonomies capture the other domains of learning: psychomotor and affect. Each taxonomy provides an inventory of action verbs that are observable and measurable to help shape your goals. The lists obviously are not exhaustive or exclusive. The taxonomies for three domains of learning—Cognitive, Psychomotor, and Affective—track the form of the seminal questions for setting course goals: What will your students *know*, be able to *do*, or *value* at the end of your course?

1. Cognitive—The cognitive domain focuses on knowledge, comprehension, and critical thinking.
2. Psychomotor—In a legal education context, the psychomotor domain is geared toward mastery of specific lawyering tasks and skills (*e.g.*, client counseling, negotiating with opposing counsel, witness interviewing).
3. Affective—Affective learning relates to awareness and growth in attitudes, emotion, feelings, and/or a value system (*e.g.*, commitment to client-centered lawyering, appreciation for the unevenness of justice).

The taxonomies give teachers a structure for thinking through the depth of a student's learning in a given area.[1] Each chart is organized hierarchically. As you move through the charts (left to right; top to bottom) the categories describe learning at deeper or higher levels of difficulty. Use these charts to choose the point(s) that corresponds to a realistic learning goal, given the subject matter, animating theory, and the situational constraints of your course.

When you scroll through the lists of learning levels and types in each domain, you may find that you are uncertain where your course content best fits. It isn't unusual for one teacher to see a goal as cognitive and another teacher to see it as psychomotor-based, or a third teacher to see it as affective. You may change your view over time as well. These taxonomies do not represent the sharp definitions of the periodic table of elements. Rather they represent a fluidity that is intended to be helpful, not dogmatic. So, use the grids as a brainstorming platform. Maybe you will pencil in learning targets for your course in several cells to test out different ways to characterize the course goal(s) you want to pursue. Don't let the taxonomies mold your learning goal to something that doesn't feel right to you. In the end you should articulate one or two course goals.

Descriptions of each of the domains, their progenitors, and the taxonomy charts follow. The charts for the cognitive and affective domains are marked where Roberts situated the course goals for his

1. Chapter 5, *The Final Assessment*, introduces the concept of six facets or dimensions of "understanding," to help define the evidence teachers need to determine whether a student has shown achievement of the course goal. Each Facet also comes with progressively difficult levels of performance, similar to these taxonomies. You might prefer to use the Facets to help situate the objectives of your course and ultimately your course goals. See Chapter 6, *Rubrics*, Addendum 6-A (*Progressive Levels of Performance*).

Criminal Defense Clinic. The chapter ends with a description of Roberts's thinking as he chose where to situate his course goals.

Nouns versus verbs

You might think it's pedestrian to reduce course design to the process of choosing "verbs." Bloom's original taxonomy used a hierarchy of cognitive concepts phrased as nouns (*i.e.*, knowledge, comprehension, application, analysis, synthesis, and evaluation). In a 2001 update, the abstract nouns were converted to observable action verbs, and instantly it became readily usable for university faculty to create course goals, plan learning activities, and design assessments. Faculty were able, more easily, to identify the mastery goals they had for their courses and to appreciate the component parts necessary to reach those goals. Thus, each chapter of this book contains actionable and concrete learning verbs for you to use in each *EL Design* step.

A. Taxonomy of the Cognitive Process and Knowledge Domain

What Do You Want Your Students to Know?

Benjamin Bloom's life's work was to promote deeper thinking in higher education. His taxonomy encompasses two axes. The horizontal cognitive processing axis depicts a continuum of increasing cognitive complexity (skills that demonstrate understanding). The vertical knowledge axis depicts types of knowledge from concrete to abstract. Bloom's taxonomy was later revised by Lorin Anderson and David Krathwohl.[2] The authors have added some adaptations as well that comport with experiential courses in legal education.

Of the taxonomies included here, the cognitive domain taxonomy is the only grid that is arrayed with intersecting cells of cognitive processing and knowledge. Definitions of the terms and associated learning verbs follow the chart.

2. Adapted from Anderson, L.W., Krathwohl, D.R. et. al. (2001). *A Taxonomy for Learning, Teaching, and Assessing: A Revision of Bloom's Taxonomy of Educational Objectives*. Abridged ed. New York: Longman

■ Cognitive Domain: Cognitive Process and Knowledge Taxonomy

1. Knowledge and Cognitive Processing Domain

		Cognitive processing			
		1. Remember	2. Understand	3. Apply	4. Analyze, Evaluate, or Create
Knowledge	A. Factual	[your course goals]			
	B. Conceptual				
	C. Procedural				Students will compose persuasive narratives for use in advocacy.
	D. Meta-cognitive				

Knowledge types	Definition	Examples
Factual	Basic elements to be acquainted with the discipline and solve problems	Terminology, vocabulary, elements, and details
Conceptual	Interrelationship among basic elements	Categories, principles, theories, models, and structures
Procedural	How to do something *(overlaps with psychomotor domain)*	Subject-specific skills, methods of inquiry and criteria for using, and techniques and procedures
Meta-cognitive	Knowing about knowing	Strategic knowledge, reflections, and self-knowledge

Cognitive processing	Definition	Action Verbs
Remember	Retrieve relevant knowledge from long-term memory	Retain, recall, recognize, memorize, recollect, think of, define, identify, list, name, record, repeat, underline, select
Understand	Construct meaning from instructional messages; can be in oral, written or graphic formats	Interpret, exemplify, classify, summarize, infer, compare, explain, give examples of, describe in own words, differentiate between, discriminate, restate, review, translate, respond, practice, discuss, identify, review, simulate
Apply	Carry out procedures	Execute, implement, apply, demonstrate, dramatize, generalize, illustrate, operate, operationalize, practice, use, utilize, initiate

Analyze	Break material into parts and determine relationships	Differentiate, organize, attribute, analyze, appraise, categorize, compare, conclude, contrast, correlate, deduce, diagram, distinguish, estimate, examine, experiment, infer, predict, question, solve, diagnose
Evaluate	Make judgments based upon criteria or standards	Check, critique, assess, judge, appraise, choose, compare, evaluate, measure, rate, revise, score, select, validate, value
Create	Put elements together into coherent or functional whole, reorganize into new patterns	Generate, plan, produce, invent, arrange, assemble, collect, compose, construct, create, design, develop, formulate, manage, modify, organize, prepare, propose, synthesize

B. Taxonomy of the Psychomotor Domain—Skills

What Do You Want Your Students to Be Able to Do?

The psychomotor domain, in its most literal form, consists of learning related to physical movement, coordination, and motor skills. Bloom did not fully describe the psychomotor (skills) domain because he believed that the academic environment did not contain sufficient expertise to analyze and create a reliable taxonomy. Other contributors were less daunted and built on his work to develop psychomotor taxonomies. Ravindra H. Dave developed a Psychomotor Taxonomy that is probably the most commonly referenced, especially for adult training.[3] Elizabeth Simpson's version addresses sensory perception and preparation and is therefore useful when learning a new behavior that pushes learners out of their comfort zone.[4] The authors have adapted and re-conceptualized their psychomotor domain as a *skills* domain where *physical (e.g.*, shaping questions, using body language and tone) and *mechanistic (e.g.*, learning a protocol for interviewing or negotiations) fluency are intertwined with cognitive and strategic aspects of a lawyering skill. As a rookie does for any physical activity (*e.g.*, playing soccer)—the law student needs repeated practice to integrate cognitive and physical bundles of skill into lawyering. The psychomotor taxonomy thus establishes a hierarchy of increasingly independent and fluid use of lawyering skills.

3. Adapted from Dave, R.H. (1970), "Developing and Writing Behavioral Objectives."

4. Simpson E. J. (1972). *The Classification of Educational Objectives in the Psychomotor Domain*. Washington, DC: Gryphon House.

2. Psychomotor Domain: (can be used by experiential faculty to set goals for lawyering skill development)

	Definition	Action Verbs	Your Course Goals
Perception	Actively using sensory cues to attend to the behavioral skill. *E.g.*, student observes a seasoned attorney perform the behavior.	Choose, describe, detect, differentiate, distinguish, identify, isolate, relate, select, separate	
Imitation	Copying the behavior. The student attempts the behavior, with direction and feedback from an experienced person. The student shows desire and motivation to learn the behavior.	Adhere, begin, attempt, carry out, copy, duplicate, follow, mimic, repeat, replicate, start, try	
Practice	Using the behavior repeatedly. The student performs the behavior multiple times, and her actions become more automatic and smooth. The experienced person need not be present.	Codify, discriminate, display, order, organize, systematize, weigh, discuss, theorize, formulate, balance, examine, adhere to	
Naturalization	Performing two or more skills in combination or sequence, with consistency and ease. The student can combine the behavior with other behaviors independently and with little mental exertion.	Adapt, automatize, combine, complete, demonstrate, internalize, master, perform, show, succeed	
Origination	Creating new behaviors, combinations, or sequences to respond to a new situation. The student creates new methodologies or techniques to improve on or re-imagine how the needs can be met.	Create, design, compose, refine, arrange	

C. Taxonomy of the Affective Domain

What Do You Want Your Students to Value?

Benjamin Bloom, with his collaborator David Krathwohl, created a taxonomy of the affective domain as well. This domain focuses on learning goals characterized by a feeling, emotion, or degree of acceptance or rejection of a value. The affective taxonomy is organized based on the concept of internalization, the process by which a person moves from recognizing that something evokes an affective response, to the point at which that affect has been incorporated into the person's value system and consistently guides the person's behavior.[5]

3. Affective Domain: (can be used to set goals related to professional values, affect, or work approach, *e.g.*, with regard to the attorney client relationship, the rule of law, or other professional value)

	Definition	Action Verbs	Your Course Goals
Receive	Be aware of; attend to something; be willing to tolerate it.	Accept, attend, develop, ask, recognize, listen for, describe, differentiate, receive, identify, tolerate	
Respond	Incorporate a new behavior as a result of the experience.	Complete, comply, cooperate, discuss, examine, obey, assist, respond, follow, volunteer, perform	
Value	Show specific involvement or commitment.	Accept, defend, devote oneself to, pursue, seek, justify, join, debate, value	"Value" is my verb for the goal related to the client's wishes informing the lawyer's path. I'd love to get the students beyond this level, but I see this as the bare minimum.
Organize	Integrate a new value into one's general set of values, giving due ranking among other priorities.	Codify, discriminate, display, order, organize, systematize, weigh, discuss, theorize, formulate, balance, examine, adhere to	
Internalize the value set	Act consistently, conscientiously, and pro-actively with the new value.	Internalize, verify, be rated high in the value, require, resolve	

5. Adapted from Krathwohl, D.R., Bloom, B.S., and Masia, B.B. (1964). *Taxonomy of Educational Objectives, Book II. Affective domain*. New York: David McKay Company, Inc.

As you consider these taxonomy grids and identify the kinds of learning you expect of your students, you may have penciled in multiple ideas. To draft your course goals, synthesize or winnow those ideas down to one or two. You may find it useful to revisit the myriad learning goals you penciled. Some may help you later when identifying the evidence necessary to determine whether students have achieved the course goals (Chapter 5, *The Final Assessment*).

Make sure your course goal aligns with and flows from the animating theory, exploratory questions, and the teaching priorities you set earlier (Chapter 3, *The Big Picture*). The course goals will be more narrowly and concretely drawn. One strategy is to distill from the animating theory a specific exemplar of performance of the animating theory.

D. Course Goals: Drafting in Action

Roberts's translation of animating theories to course goals took two different approaches. For his first animating theory—*The client's wishes inform the lawyer's path*—he used the affective domain. This animating theory is an expression of client-centered lawyering and Roberts expects his students to **value** a client-centered ethos which they will demonstrate through their diligent work in pursuit of the client's priorities. He therefore phrased a first course goal to give the animating theory more form and concreteness.

■ Criminal Defense Clinic—Animating Theory and Course Goal 1

Animating Theory: The client's wishes inform the lawyer's path.

Affective domain: The animating theory is translated to a type of learning that shows the student's appreciation and adoption of a particular value—client-centered practice—as a result of his course.
Course goal: Students will (1) consistently seek to identify the client's priorities for the representation and (2) diligently pursue strategies that promote those priorities within the confines of the student-attorney's professional obligations

* See worksheets 1 and 5.

Roberts's second animating theory—*The best lawyer is the lawyer who is best prepared*—relates grandly to a professional work ethic. To make it tangible, he reduced it to a specific lawyering activity to illustrate the high-preparation ethic. His second course goal is centered, well-grounded persuasive arguments. He chose the cognitive domain to keep the focus on the careful synthesis of *fact, law, and audience orientation,* in a manner that is distinctly practice-oriented.

Animating Theory: The best lawyer is the lawyer who is best prepared.

Cognitive domain: The animating theory is translated to an example of this work ethic. Lawyers require persuasiveness on many levels. Since persuasiveness has many factual, critical assessment, and analytical elements, he used the cognitive domain to ground his second course goal.
Course goal: Students will compose persuasive narratives that apply relevant law to facts of the case; marshal, weigh, and use both convincing and undermining facts; recognize and adjust to a forum's perspective; and use emotional content.

* See worksheets 1 and 5.

In both instances, Roberts chose and framed course goals that fit his learning priorities. He had noted that his most enduring learning priorities were for students to inculcate a client-centered ethos and understand that good advocacy is not possible without exhaustive preparation. Each course goal represents his highest priorities.

Now it's time for you to reduce your animating theory and exploratory questions to a viable course goal.

Course Goal Checklist

- Does the goal align with your course animating theory, exploratory questions, and learning priorities?
- Is it clear?
- Is it amenable to measurement?
- Is it sustainable, *e.g.*, by taking account of the situational factors you identified?

Through these *EL Design* exercises, it becomes apparent how word choice is critical to your conception of your course, its direction, and its objectives. Careful choice of the learning verb and subject matter is vital. If you find yourself having trouble articulating course goal(s) that are aligned, attainable, and measurable, it is possible that your animating theory may be "too big." You may need to re-assess your animating theory and consider whether or not it is so far-reaching that it cannot be translated into useful learning goals for your course. Such a determination would prompt you to reformulate your animating theory and then return to setting course goals. Each of us has spent fruitful time toggling between characterizing our animating theories and articulating our course goals. That iterative process helped each of us to clarify our course and our aspirations more clearly to ourselves and for our students.

E. Takeaways

- Course goals that align with your animating theory and take account of your limits and priorities are attainable.
- No matter how your course is graded, you need course goals that are amenable to measuring observable student learning so that you can assess achievement of the course goals.
- Taxonomies for cognitive, psychomotor, and affective domains of learning help you to situate and describe the kind of learning that we plan for our students to learn.
- Careful attention to word choice (learning verbs and subject matter) will greatly facilitate your thinking about your course, specific learning activities, and readings

Chapter 5

The Final Assessment

How Do You Know That Your Students Learned?

Now that you have your course goal(s) in hand, you are ready to build the course around them. You may have a variety of learning activities in mind for your clinic, field placement, or skills course, which would bring your course goal to life. *Experiential Learning Design (EL Design)*, however, suggests an alternate sequence. Plan and design your final assessment exercise first. If that sounds out-of-order, that is because most teachers do not start here when crafting their courses. Instead, most tend to jump from a primary textbook to coverage identification to development of learning activities, without much consideration of how to evaluate whether students have achieved the course goals.

The basic theory of *EL Design* is backward design or ends-means thinking. Teachers start at the end (the course goal) and work backward in discrete increments. To demonstrate the next steps moving backward from the goal, this chapter examines Danielle Cover's Torts II course[1] and Carwina Weng's Disability Law Clinic.

Cover and Weng have set course goals like these:

- Students will be able to contextualize liability in tort as malleable in terms of fact characterization and legal framework.
- Students will be able to address client problems effectively and humanistically.

With their respective course goals in hand, Cover and Weng had to give them depth. How would they know that their students can contextualize tort claims or apply problem-solving techniques in a human-centered manner? They needed first to determine what they would want to observe about a student's work product or performance to convince them that the student had mastered the goal(s) set for the course. Often teachers can visualize the student who exemplifies mastery level performance. But it takes effort to move from "I know it when I see it," to "I can explain what I expect to see." This is a vital step in experiential course design. Unlike knowledge content-based courses that culminate in a final written exam, experiential courses have diverse types of

1. Cover's doctrinal course provides a more straightforward model for using backward course design, especially the use of the cognitive domain taxonomy discussed in Chapter 4, *The Course Goal,* and Wiggins and McTighe's *Facets of Understanding,* discussed in this chapter. As an attorney must learn doctrine and use cognitive skills to lawyer, the manner in which Cover deconstructs her course demonstrates how doctrine and skills are combined into thoughtful course goals and assessment.

learning objectives, not all of which can be demonstrated in a single final performance, and much of which is outside the view of the teacher.

With their list of mastery evidence in hand, Cover and Weng each crafted a final summative assessment exercise through which their students showcase their learning, hitting each piece of mastery evidence necessary. When the final exercise was set, they moved to create a rubric that helps them judge whether each student excelled, was competent, or showed subpar performance (Chapter 6, *Rubrics*). Even though many experiential courses are graded pass/fail, students will reap great benefit to know how well they performed and why. That assessment helps students set personal goals. It also helps you gauge your teaching. At that juncture, you can profitably turn to creating and sequencing course activities explicitly designed to bring students to the desired mastery level. (Chapter 7, *Course Outcomes and Learning Activities*). You might be surprised to realize how often a teacher's collection of learning activities does not present a clear path toward student achievement of the course goals and includes detours or neglects to lay valuable foundations. This final assessment design stage of *EL Design* is formulated to mitigate those gaps and diversions.

Note on terminology—Assessment

Let's clarify the various uses of the term "*assessment*." Assessment can be *the process* of judging a student's performance, whether written or live. Assessment also refers to *the tool* that provides the content and instructions for how students will show their learning (*e.g.*, the final exam or a portfolio presentation).

This book uses "assessment exercise" or "assessment tool" to denote the assignment or instruction. Assessment tools take many shapes from performance tasks, to reflection prompts, to final exam questions. The terms "assess" and "assessment" denote the teacher's activity of evaluating student demonstration of learning, whether live lawyering performance, oral presentation, or written work.

Formative assessment refers to interim, coaching-style assessment of student work. Summative or final assessment refers to the end-of-semester evaluation of the student's learning in the course. Of course, teachers still may give feedback to a student as part of summative assessment.

This chapter focuses primarily on the final or summative assessment, although it also introduces types of assessments that might be more amenable to formative assessments. Strong teaching and the ABA standards require formative assessments to let students know whether they are on pace to meet your learning goals, or not.[2]

A. Mastery Evidence of Student Performance

You have combed through the three taxonomies to pick which concrete action verbs encapsulate your course goal (Chapter 4, *Course Goal*). Now answer these questions: What specific details in your students' work product or performance will assure you that the students have achieved the course goal you set? What will students "do" to show you that they can apply what you have taught? Given the goals for the class, how deep or multi-dimensional do you want the student's learning to be? Your answers to these questions will comprise your mastery evidence of student performance. Mastery evidence in law school usually will not mean how a highly skilled attorney performs. Rather, it means mastery for your course. Visualize what the strong, solid, engaged, "A" student would do.

2. ABA Accreditation Standard 314. The ABA does not require each course to include both formative and summative assessment. It merely requires the JD curriculum overall to include both.

You might find it helpful to look back to the taxonomies, for other verbs that round out the student learning necessary to meet your course goal. As you start identifying your mastery evidence, continue the practice of using observable, concrete verbs and terms.

Many additional observable, concrete verbs and terms are available through Grant Wiggins and Jay McTighe's work on the Facets of Understanding. UNDERSTANDING BY DESIGN (2nd ed. 2005). Wiggins and McTighe identify six non-hierarchical dimensions of student cognition: Explanation; Interpretation; Application; Perspective-Taking, demonstrating Empathy; and revealing Self-knowledge. Most likely, your mastery evidence will not touch on all six, but you likely will include multiple Facets in your evidence of mastery. For example, you might have a goal that students develop persuasive theories of a case. This goal could encompass the Facets of interpretation, application, perspective-taking, and/or empathy.

Here are the Facets in a nutshell, with some adaptation for law study:

> ***Explanation:*** Students are able to provide thorough and well-supported accounts of topics, events, or actions backed by reasoning, facts, or experience. Students are able to develop a theory of how and why something happened or should happen, supported by evidence, law, and experience.
>
> ***Interpretation:*** Students are able to articulate the importance, meaning, or significance of what they have learned, with context and awareness of multiple interpretations. Students can create meaning from a set of facts and/or law, with attention to ambiguity, uncertainty, opacity, emotional content, and diverse perspectives.
>
> ***Application:*** Students use and adapt the knowledge or skill acquired to new situations and contexts, showing flexibility and adaptability. They can design, develop, test, and refine responses to a new problem or dilemma presented.
>
> ***Perspective-taking:*** Students can take a step back to appreciate broader and alternative views, to critically assess the value or importance of a topic. They can identify, critique, and give credence to multiple valid perspectives including opposing counsel and opposing party, others involved in the matter, judges, etc.
>
> ***Empathy:*** Students demonstrate ability to accept without judgment the feelings of others, perceive others sensitively using prior or indirect experience, and adjust to difference in reactions, thoughts, and feelings of others. Students need not acquiesce in the feelings of others, but must accept the validity of those feelings to the others.
>
> ***Self-knowledge:*** Students understand that their style, preferences, and habits are personal to them and affect their views of events, information, and other people. They can evaluate the extent of and reasons for their skill development.

Appendix 5-A, at the end of this chapter, contains a table that shows each Facet with definitions, examples of their application in legal education, and related characterizations.

As you read the descriptions of the Facets, you likely noticed how some were quite similar to terms used when you crafted your course goals from the cognitive, psychomotor, and affective taxonomies. All of the Facets are represented in the taxonomies, especially in the cognitive and psychomotor domains. Once a student is able to recall the knowledge, skill, or value taught, then the Facets of Understanding provide a methodology to examine the students' integration and facility with those topics. Thus, the Facets are adaptable to any of the stages of the three taxonomies.

Make sure to revisit your teaching and learning priorities set in Worksheet 4. Your mastery evidence should squarely support those priorities.

B. Mastery Evidence in Action

This section now uses two courses to demonstrate how to develop evidence of student mastery: Cover's Torts II course and Weng's Disability Law Clinic. The section starts with an earlier step, how they formulated their animating theories, exploratory questions, dimensions of learning they hoped to teach, and course goals. This foundation will help show how they then conceived their mastery evidence.

Torts II

Cover, like most doctrinal professors, anchored her Torts II course in the cognitive taxonomy, with multiple benchmarks of increasing difficulty. Her inventory of mastery evidence draws on the different benchmarks she identified.

■ Torts II—Intellectual Moorings: Animating Theory to Course Goal

Animating Theory: Who writes the check?

Exploratory questions: Why do we care who is responsible for what conduct and injury? Why do we decide one person is liable and another not liable for the same behaviors? How do we take account of competing evidence?
Cognitive domain (factual knowledge): Remember elements, factors, and theories of liability; Explain reason liability attaches; Apply law to the salient facts of a hypothetical; Compose counter-arguments.
Cognitive domain (conceptual knowledge): Remember "facts" are subject to flexible interpretation; Evaluate and adjust analysis based on additional or alternative facts.
Course goal: Students will be able to contextualize torts (personal injury practice) as a practice focused on how lawyers select and use facts to make their case within the confines of the law.

* See worksheets 1, 2, and 5.

Torts II—Mastery Evidence

Top-performing students will be able to show they can:

Facet of understanding	Associated verbs & Starter phrases	Evidence of student's mastery in your course
Explanation: Students are able to provide thorough and well-supported accounts of topics, events, or actions, backed by reasoning, facts, or experience. Students are able to develop a theory of how and why, supported by evidence, law, and experience.	Demonstrate, derive, describe, design, exhibit, express, instruct, justify, model, predict, prove, show, synthesize, teach Students will be able to: Explain/teach [x], Give examples of [x]; Make connections with [x]; Offer a theory of [x]; Avoid misconceptions, such as [x].	Explain the elements of a cause of action and relevant defenses, possible policy implications. (Mere recall of the elements is insufficient.)
Interpretation: Students are able to interpret and analyze the importance, meaning, or significance of their knowledge/ skill, with context and awareness of multiple interpretations. Students can create meaning from a set of facts and law, with attention to ambiguity, uncertainty, opacity, emotional content, and diverse perspectives.	Create analogies, critique, document, evaluate, illustrate, judge, make sense of, provide metaphors, read between the lines, represent, tell a story of. Students will be able to: Interpret the [x]; Tell a revealing story of [x]; Provide an apt analogy for [x]; Show the importance or meaning of [x]; Translate [x]; Relate [x] to your experience (or the experiences of others).	Interpret facts to show which pieces of information support their client's theory of liability. Interpret law to formulate a theory of liability.
Application-Adaptation: Students use and adapt the knowledge/skill acquired to new situations and contexts, showing flexibility and adaptability. Students can design, develop, test, and refine responses to a new problem or dilemma presented.	Adapt, create, de-bug, design, exhibit, invent, perform, produce, propose, solve, test, use Students will be able to: Apply [x] in a new circumstance; Show or demonstrate [x]; Use in the context of [x]; Design/invent [x]; Overcome a challenge or constraint, such as [x].	Craft a case theory explaining why the other side should "write the check!" and Explain it clearly to others.
Empathy: Students show the ability to embrace the feelings, reasoning, motivations, and perspectives of others with acceptance and non-judgment. Open-minded insight to others.	Assume the role of, believe, be like, be open to, consider, imagine, relate, role-play. Students will be able to: Walk in the shoes of [x]; Experience directly and see [x]; Reach a common understanding with another concerning [x]; Entertain the seemingly odd or alien view that [x]; Anticipate possible concerns of others regarding [x] based on their interests, values, and circumstances.	From the perspective of judge, apply law to straightforward and ambiguous facts and draw a conclusion about liability (Write a dissenting opinion).

* See worksheet 6.

Cover's mastery evidence readily shows how her animating theory and exploratory questions would weave through the students' coursework. Cover wants her students to examine and understand where the cost of injury lies and how liability schemes differentiate responsibility among victim, tortfeasor, and other parties. She wants her students to appreciate and become facile with the malleability of facts. Her mastery evidence draws on those elements of her animating theory, exploration questions, and course goal.

Disability Law Clinic

Weng's Disability Law Clinic handles claims for Social Security and Veterans' Affairs benefits. The client matters have timelines that typically extend multiple years. Her students do not have experiences in sync with one another, such as client intake, investigation and documentation needs, or preparing for or conducting a hearing. Those situational factors compelled her to identify a theory and goal for her clinic that would be relevant to all of her students, without regard to the stage of a client's matter. Weng tapped into the concept of professional identity formation and its focus on how a student becomes a professional, with attention to the values, skills, traits, and interests involved.

With that platform, Weng chose to organize her clinic around the skills of problem-solving and the role of lawyers as problem solvers. Although her students might not encounter common practice experiences, each of her clinic students will encounter difficulties with no obvious solutions, complicated by diverse personalities, interests, agendas, restraints, and schedules, and they would have to figure out solutions to these situations. It also was important to Weng that her students appreciate the value of human-centeredness as part of their professional identities.

■ Disability Law Clinic—Intellectual moorings: Animating Theory to Course Goal

Animating Theory: Lawyer as human-centered and effective problem solver.

Exploratory questions: How do a lawyer's personal values, identity, and traits affect their ability to serve clients? What do clients want from their lawyers? What makes a lawyer an effective problem solver? How does problem-solving interact with other skills and roles of a lawyer?
Cognitive Domain (conceptual, procedural, meta-cognitive knowledge): The problem-solving model used in the course, Brest-Krieger, offers both a procedural and conceptual construct to guide the student-lawyer in representing the client. The steps of the model are applied, but the solution process is quintessentially creative. The model also serves as an introspection device for students to examine how they use problem-solving for their professional development.
Psychomotor domain: Students will be able to practice the problem-solving model independently by using it in multiple contexts with clients and in their own professional development. Some students may progress to the point where they can naturalize and internalize problem-solving methods without reference to the model or professor.
Affective domain: Students will be able to discuss and respond to values of collaborative work and navigation of cultural and personal difference.
Course goal: Students will be able to address real-life lawyering problems and client matters effectively by applying the provided problem-solving model and by following a human-centered approach.

* See worksheets 1, 2, and 5.

Weng drew on more domains of learning than Cover's Torts II course. Weng identified useful learning objectives in the Psychomotor and Affective domains, as well as the Cognitive domain. Within each domain, she pinpointed performances that enable students to demonstrate problem-solving under complex conditions, naturalizing the skills involved, and showing some internalization of the professional values conveyed. Her course goal is a synthesis of these performances. The breadth of domains grounding her course made sense for a multi-faceted, live client clinic.

Weng faced a few challenges that required some creativity to convert her course goal to observable and measurable evidence of mastery. Human-centered problem-solving, *per se*, is not really a visible act; it's more of a process and an experienced result. So how would Weng evaluate a student's final performance that she is unable to observe? Weng chose to adopt and introduce a specific problem-solving model advanced by Paul Brest and Linda Hamilton Krieger.[3] It provides the armature for her classroom component and introduces students to the discipline, theory, and techniques of problem-solving. The model gave Weng a viable way to devise measurable and observable evidence of student mastery. This is a prime example of how course design toggles among course goal, meta-level learning activities (adopting a model), and mastery evidence.

---

3. Paul Brest and Linda Hamilton Krieger, Problem-Solving, Decision Making, and Professional Judgment (2010).

Disability Law Clinic—Mastery Evidence

Top-performing students will be able to show they can:

Facet of understanding	Associated verbs & Starter phrases	Evidence of student's mastery in your course
Interpretation: Students are able to interpret and analyze the importance, meaning, or significance of their knowledge/skill, with context and awareness of multiple interpretations. Students can create meaning from a set of facts and law, with attention to ambiguity, uncertainty, opacity, emotional content, and diverse perspectives.	Create analogies, critique, document, evaluate, illustrate, judge, make sense of, provide metaphors, read between the lines, represent, tell a story of. Students will be able to: Interpret the [x]; Tell a revealing story of [x]; Provide an apt analogy for [x]; Show the importance or meaning of [x]; Translate [x]; Relate [x] to your experience (or the experiences of others).	Use independently the Brest-Krieger model in two contexts: a client-related problem and a personal professional development problem.
Application-Adaptation: Students use and adapt the knowledge/skill acquired to new situations and contexts, showing flexibility and adaptability. Students can design, develop, test, and refine responses to a new problem or dilemma presented.	Adapt, create, de-bug, design, exhibit, invent, perform, produce, propose, solve, test, use Students will be able to: Apply [x] in a new circumstance; Show or demonstrate [x]; Use in the context of [x]; Design/invent [x]; Overcome a challenge or constraint, such as [x].	Make sense of how they used the model in their clinic work.
Perspective: Students can take a step back to appreciate a broader view, critically assess the value or importance of a topic. Students can identify, critique, and give credence to multiple valid perspectives regarding a topic.	Analyze, argue, compare, contrast, criticize, infer Students will be able to: Analyze [x]; See from the viewpoint of [x]; Compare and contrast [x]; Critique [x]; Critically examine assumptions such as [x]; Show how [x]; See the limits of [x].	Use the elements of the model that require specific attention to learning about and adapting to the perspectives of others (clients and others involved in the problem).
Self-Knowledge: Students accept that their style, preferences, and habits are specific to them and affect their views of events, information, and other people. Students can evaluate their professional development with appreciation of what came easily or not and why; can evaluate personal, emotional responses with detachment.	Be aware of, realize, recognize, reflect, self-assess. Students will be able to: Recognize their own prejudice(s) about [x]; Identify the lens through which they view [x]; Explain how they came to understand [x]; Realize that even with all they now know, they still don't really understand [x].	Examine how their prior knowledge, personal preferences and dislikes, impacted how they engaged problem-solving and how they changed through the process.

* See worksheet 6.

Weng's mastery evidence expresses her animating theory and exploratory questions. Weng wants her students to grapple with the meaning of human-centered problem-solving. The Brest-Krieger model allowed Weng to create a learning environment that helps students become deeply aware of their personal orientation and experience with collaboration; consensus-driven problem definition and goal setting; and division of creative work. The model and mastery evidence weave together her animating theory, exploration questions, and course goal.

Given these examples of course goals matched with mastery evidence, it's time for you to draw up a list of evidence you expect to see from students who have succeeded in your course.

Mastery Evidence Checklist

- Does your evidence of student mastery allow you to translate student understanding or ability to an assessment performance or product that you can observe and evaluate?
- Does your mastery evidence flow from your course goals and teaching priorities, and facilitate exploration of the animating theory?

C. Converting Mastery Evidence to a Final Assessment Exercise

You now will craft a final assessment exercise that calls forth each of the pieces of mastery evidence identified and the level of sophistication that best fits the ambitions of your course. Here are three guidelines for creating your final assessment exercise:

- Build on earlier exercises, especially those that were less complicated because they focused on only a small part of a lawyering skill set. The new problem then will require students to integrate their learning authentically, to approximate the work of lawyers;
- Create a less structured problem, requiring synthesis of the repertoire of knowledge, skills, or values gained during the course. The new problem will require students to transfer their learning and is a valuable learning event in and of itself; and
- Take into account the situational factors you face.

To achieve authenticity in the assessment exercise, design a vehicle for students to demonstrate learning in the manner that mimics the skills an expert would deploy. The vehicle thus requires students to do more than memorize and regurgitate information, as happens on a standardized test. For example, in a course on trial advocacy, an inauthentic final assessment would be a multiple-choice test in which students are given examples of questions and asked to choose the type of question each example represents (*e.g.*, narrative; open-ended; closed; leading). An authentic assessment would be a student's drafting of or performance of a direct examination, albeit in simulated format. Authenticity is almost instinctive in an experiential course, as the purpose of these courses is to help students develop integrated, multi-faceted skills in lifelike circumstances. The proficiency at which you want students to demonstrate learning might be lower, of course, than that of a veteran attorney.

You will communicate your expectations as to proficiency through your rubric (Chapter 6, *Rubrics*). Be mindful, however, to revisit the situational factors that create opportunities and limits in your course (Worksheet 3). These factors can shape the kind of assessment exercise you use as well as the depth of feedback you give regarding student performance.

Format decisions: This list of format considerations may help you frame the final assessment exercise.

- Choose a vehicle for the final assessment exercise: writing(s), portfolio, oral presentation or live performance (to you or before another audience), in pairs, teams, or as individuals, etc.
- Consider the number of parts in the final assessment: An ideal assessment exercise compels the students to synthesize and integrate the full constellation of knowledge, skills, and values represented in your course goal. Yet it may simply be impracticable to create such an exercise. So you will have to determine how best to construct a mix of final assessment exercises.
- Consider the length: What is a sufficient length for the students' performance or work product, in order to showcase their mastery? For instance, if you want to assess the students' depth of reflection, can the students meet your expectations (mastery evidence) in 250 words, 1,000, or 5,000 words? If you want to assess the students' ability to conduct a summation for the jury, should the summation last 5 minutes, 15 minutes, 30 minutes, or more?
- Consider involvement of outsiders and their potential contribution: You might want others to be involved as actors simulating clients, witnesses, opposing counsel, and the like. Do you want them to have an evaluative role as well? You might want others involved to judge by established criteria, or to engage the students in a colloquy.
- Address practicalities: Consider the situational factors that impact what is manageable for you to assess. How many students do you have? If others are involved in the final assessment, consider issues of volunteer recruitment, preparation, and scheduling. How much writing can you assess and quickly turn around? Practically speaking, can you give real-time assessments for live performances? How much work are the students responsible for otherwise in your course (*e.g.*, specific client matters)? How much work is fair for students given the number of credits they are earning in your course? Make sure your assessment exercises are appropriately sized for you given your own competing responsibilities.

With a sense of what format might work well for your course, start to craft the subject and the prompts for the final assessment exercise. What are you asking your students to do? Your prompts, length, and parts should be integrated to provide the student work product or performance that will elicit the mastery evidence you need.

D. Final Assessment Exercises in Action

Torts II

In her Torts II course, Cover designed a summative assessment exercise (a final exam) that requires students to write a dissenting opinion to a majority opinion she provides. She will review the students' performances using multiple criteria, including gauging their capacity to explain why the majority might have ruled as they did and to interpret the facts in a manner that supports a dissent and distinguishes (the facet of explanation) the facts and law from the majority interpretation.

■ Torts II—Final Assessment Exercise

Vehicle	Final take home exam.
Quantity (length, parts)	72 hours to complete from pick up.
Practicalities	80–90 students; two weeks to letter-grade. I usually also have 8–10 students in my clinic who are winding down their representation of their clients—many items have client- and time-sensitive aspects.
Subject	Complex public nuisance case on lead paint poisoning (based on actual case from California). Provide edited majority opinion declaring lead paint manufacture a public nuisance.
Prompts	Review factual summary and majority opinion. Write a dissenting opinion arguing that lead paint manufacture is not a public nuisance.
Materials to develop	Distill lengthy majority opinion down to manageable pieces.

* See worksheet 7.

Cover's dissenting opinion exam replicates ordinary lawyering: creating and reforming the presentation and persuasive focus of a set of facts and law. By asking students to do work that resembles what a legal professional, here a judge, might do in practice, Cover's assessment exercise shifts the focus from a simple recitation of the elements of a tort to a written justification of why one party should prevail over the other. The assessment tool (the exam), a course goal (contextualizing facts to legal position), and mastery evidence (the capacity to explain, interpret, take perspective, and apply) all align to allow Cover to measure how well students can do this lawyering.

Disability Law Clinic

The final assessment exercise for Weng's Clinic requires a student to create a portfolio that includes three essays: i) two that each analyze a problem encountered in the Clinic and ii) one that self-assesses the student's personal growth. Only the details of the analytical essays appear below. Weng is especially interested in assessing the students' ability to understand the perspectives of myriad individuals involved in a problem and its solution, as well exhibiting empathy toward those individuals. The Brest-Krieger model explicitly requires those elements. Thus, her essay prompt and rubric criteria do not need to provide specifics on those elements; they are definitional to the model.

■ Disability Law Clinic—Final Assessment Exercise

Part 1, Analysis of Problem-Solving in Two Situations (2 essays)

Vehicle	Capstone portfolio comprised of two separate essays, due at the end of the semester.
Quantity (length, parts)	Each essay is limited to 1250 words.

Practicalities	8 students; three weeks to give a letter grade to the registrar, and I have a personal deadline to give student feedback within 2 weeks as well. Grading portfolios while reviewing client files and continuing any necessary legal work.
Subject (analyses of problems)	Write 2 essays describing, reflecting upon, and critiquing your involvement with 2 challenging problems encountered during the clinic. Choose one problem where your problem-solving worked well and a second where your problem-solving steps did not work as well.
Prompts	—Choose problems that helped you grow. The growth you describe might be more the pure skill of problem-solving or might be contextualized to specific lawyering situations, e.g., client interaction, development of the theory of the case. —Describe the problem and context; explain how you tackled each problem (strategies, solutions, and implementation). —Evaluate your problem-solving (early planning based on readings, hunches, prior experience; patterns in approach; tactics that worked or didn't; solution effectiveness from the perspective of others impacted).
Materials to develop	None in particular, but work with students throughout semester to identify experiences that might be included in the portfolio.

See worksheet 7.

As students select the problems to feature, they are intrinsically exercising self-awareness and self-critique skills. The students' efforts to characterize their legal work to someone who did not have direct participation (Weng) force them to make strategic and tactical choices about the sequencing and narrative coherence. Each of these steps replicates important tasks that lawyers perform regularly. As with Torts II, the chosen mastery evidence and the final assessment exercise become a platform for examination of the animating theory and exploratory questions that provide the intellectual home for the course—*Lawyers as human-centered and effective problem-solvers, who grapple with the realities of how their personal identities impact client relations and problem-solving effectiveness.*

Bearing in mind your course goal and evidence of student mastery, start to imagine a final assessment that will allow the students to showcase their mastery of knowledge, skills, and values you will have taught them.

Final Assessment Checklist

- Does your final assessment exercise allow students to demonstrate their abilities regarding each piece of mastery evidence necessary?
- Does it approximate how a practitioner would exhibit or use the knowledge, skills, or values taught?
- Does it require demonstration of learning in new, less structured problems?
- Does it reflect an awareness of the realities and practical limits for you and for your students?

E. Takeaways

- A concrete list of evidence that indicates a student has mastered the learning you intended will allow you to develop a final assessment exercise that assesses what you intend students to learn.
- You can design a final assessment exercise relevant to all students, whatever their varied experience in your course. Such an exercise will allow valid evaluation of student learning and its corollary, your teaching effectiveness.
- Defining your evidence of mastery of the course goals and designing the final assessment exercise before creating learning activities ensures that your course serves the course goals.

Appendix 5-A

Mapping Evidence of Student Mastery[4]

Facet	Definition	Example	Associated verbs; Starter phrases
Explanation	Students are able to provide thorough accounts of topics, events, or actions well supported by reasoning, facts, or experience. Students are able to develop a theory of how and why, supported by evidence, law, and experience.	Students can extract the finding in a court's decision, including the rule of law and salient facts. Student can support a court's use of precedent in reaching its decision. Student can predict how a law affects a client's desired transaction.	Demonstrate, derive, describe, design, exhibit, express, induce, instruct, justify, model, predict, prove, show, synthesize, teach Students will be able to: Explain/teach [x], Give examples of [x]; Make connections with [x]; Offer a theory of [x]; Avoid misconceptions, such as [x].
Interpretation	Students are able to analyze the importance or meaning of what they have learned, with context and awareness of multiple interpretations. Students can create meaning from a set of facts and law, with attention to ambiguity, uncertainty, opacity, emotional content, and diverse perspectives.	Student can create a client narrative for an affidavit. Student can create a persuasive analogy to use in a closing argument.	Analogies (create), critique, document, evaluate, illustrate, judge, make sense of, metaphors (provide), read between the lines, represent, tell a story about. Students will be able to: Interpret the [x]; Tell a revealing story of [x]; Provide an apt analogy for [x]; Show the importance or meaning of [x]; Translate [x]; Relate [x] to your experience (or the experiences of others).
Application-Adaptation	Students use and adapt the knowledge/skill acquired to new situations and contexts, showing flexibility and adaptability. They can design, develop, test, and refine responses to a new problem or dilemma presented.	Student can apply active listening and question funneling techniques to gather relevant information from the client and to clarify its completeness and accuracy. Student can apply procedural rules to a real litigation matter, to develop a discovery plan.	Adapt, create, de-bug, design, exhibit, invent, perform, produce, propose, solve, test, use Students will be able to: Apply [x] in a new circumstance; Show or demonstrate [x]; Use in the context of [x]; Design/invent [x]; Overcome a challenge or constraint, such as [x].

4. Adapted and expanded from Grant Wiggins & Jay McTighe, Understanding by Design 85–97 (Association for Supervision and Curriculum Development, 2nd edition 2005).

Perspective	Students can take a step back to appreciate a broader view or to critically assess the value or importance of a topic. They can identify, critique, and give credence to multiple valid perspectives regarding a topic. Perspective involves detached distance to achieve greater objectivity.	Students can anticipate how a decision-maker (judge), opposing party, and opposing counsel might perceive a set of facts and their emotional content. Student can write a reflective essay that addresses multiple perspectives regarding a situation experienced in practice, supported by direct observation, information learned from others, factual background, and/or additional research, as appropriate.	Analyze, argue, compare, contrast, criticize, infer Students will be able to: Analyze [x]; See from the viewpoint of [x]; Compare and contrast [x]; Critique [x]; Critically examine assumptions such as [x]; Show how [x]; See the limits of [x].
Empathy	Students demonstrate the ability to inhabit the lives and feelings of others, without themselves having such experiences, to perceive others intimately using their own prior or indirect experience. They engage difference from the perspective of those who are different. Students show ability to embrace the feelings, reasoning, motivations, and perspectives of others with acceptance and non-judgment. Open minded insight to others.	Student convincingly role plays a client in preparation for a custody hearing. Student accepts that a client masks her psychosocial limitations to deflect stigma and shame and works with the client to describe her situation for a disability hearing. Student searches for reasons from client's perspective as to why clients seem not to care about their case.	Assume the role of, believe, be like, be open to, consider, imagine, relate, role-play. Students will be able to: Walk in the shoes of [x]; Experience directly and see [x]; Reach a common understanding with another concerning [x]; Entertain the seemingly odd or alien view that [x].
Self-Knowledge	Students understand that their styles, preferences, and habits are personal to them and impact their views of events, information, and other people. They can evaluate the extent of their professional development with appreciation of what was easy and why and what was most difficult and why.	The student is aware of and practices de-biasing techniques regularly in her work with co-workers, clients, opposing counsel, and court staff. The student reviews a mediation session to assess what went well, what could be improved, and how.	Be aware of, realize, recognize, reflect, self-assess. Students will be able to: Recognize own prejudice(s) about [x]; Identify the lens through which you view [x]; Explain how you came to understand [x]; Realize that even with all you now know, you don't really understand [x].

Chapter 6

Rubrics

How Do You Gauge a Student's Proficiency Level?

This chapter turns to communicating to your students how you will evaluate them on the final assessment exercise. That communication occurs through the rubric. *Experiential Learning Design* (*EL Design*) uses a grading rubric to evaluate (or score) the final assessment exercise, but a grading rubric of course can be used for formative assessment as well. The focus of the rubric is to grade, that is, to tell students how closely their performances represented "mastery." If your experiential course is graded and the assessment exercise is summative, mastery is an "A." If it's a pass/fail course, the measure of progress toward course mastery level is still important for the student, whether or not it is reduced to a transcript grade.

The rubric is also the students' tool to prepare to perform that final assessment exercise, whatever it might look like. Provided ahead of time, the rubric provides the student with a guide for asking questions along the way and engaging in self-directed learning.

A. Rubric Types and Mechanics

A good rubric is both valid and reliable. To be *valid*, the rubric's criteria must align with the course goals, learning activities, class and supervision discussions, and the assessment exercise. The descriptions of proficiency levels also must align with the behaviors required for the performance. Essentially, it is valid when it measures what was actually taught in terms of both subject matter knowledge and learning performances. To be *reliable*, the rubric's evaluative criteria must be sufficiently specific and clear so that teacher and students alike can reach similar results when applying the criteria to the student performance. Indeed, that is one of its useful attributes—to give students a plan of action (what to learn) and predictability (what it takes to warrant a certain grade or proficiency level). Consider the rubric a valuable communication vehicle from you to your students—what should they work toward and how can they judge their own work?

In this chapter, we are principally focused on rubric development process in terms of the final assessment exercise. But, of course, rubrics can be created for any assessment exercise developed throughout the course, including those used for formative assessments. Rubrics come in many forms from the simple to the multifaceted. All identify two things: i) specific evaluation criteria and ii) descriptions of proficiency levels. We describe three types of rubrics—checklist, holistic, and analytic—so that you can see the possibilities. *EL Design* recommends an analytic rubric for the final assessment exercise.

Checklists are akin to a point system, where several aspects of the performance are expected to be evident, with each "graded" in a binary fashion (yes/no). The checklist rubric can be enhanced somewhat by adding scales, such as plus, check, minus. It has the benefit of being quick. It may be particularly useful at the unit level, to gauge whether a student has completed the full set of learning activities assigned, or in a pass/fail course. However, the checklist rubric has limits regarding feedback. While it makes it clear the student must hit each milestone, it gives scant or no indication to a student regarding the quality of the work or performance.

A checklist rubric for a professional exploration unit in a course on the Legal Profession, might include straightforward criteria, such as:

- Did the student submit a reflective essay on his/her career aspirations drawing on interviews with practicing attorneys and career panel presentations?
- Did the student interview 5 or more attorneys?
- Did the student submit a log of all interviews with pertinent details?
- Did the student attend 5 or more legal careers programs?

Students who completed each element receive a Pass grade for the unit. The checklist rubric does not include any evaluation from the teacher as to how well the students gleaned information through their interviews or reflected on their career aspirations.

Holistic rubrics add significantly to descriptions of evaluation criteria compared to checklists. The various grading criteria are intermingled for each proficiency level. For example, to assess a collection of reflective writings for the semester, a holistic rubric might indicate something like:

> "A" level essays show the student used observation and insights drawn from field experience to build lawyering skills or understanding of professionalism. The writing shows the student's capacity to reflect on a situation from the perspectives of multiple individuals, roles, or interests. Writing quality is superior, personal, and paints a vivid picture of the work and student's reactions.

The criteria at the "B" and "C" are similarly consolidated and described with relevant changes in phrasing about the quality of the work expected regarding observation, reflection, and writing quality. The holistic rubric allows the evaluator to provide significant direction to the students about the elements to be scrutinized and evaluated, but the blended grade doesn't help the student to understand which aspects of her work were higher or lower in proficiency. Similarly, it is less useful to the educator to extract the aspects of her teaching that were more or less effective in achieving the objectives of her course.

Analytic rubric. The most structured rubric is the analytic. It takes the form of a grid, with the evaluation criteria along one axis and the levels of proficiency or performance along the opposing axis. An analytic rubric provides descriptions for each evaluative criterion at each level of proficiency.

Analytic rubric format

	Highest proficiency	Mid-level proficiency	Low level proficiency
Criterion 1			
Criterion 2			
Criterion 3			

B. Constructing the Final Assessment Rubric

EL Design process adopts the analytic rubric for the final assessment exercise. The analytic rubric allows teachers to provide more detailed guidance and feedback across the many dimensions of a lawyering task or work product. It therefore is well suited to authentic assessments that require students to synthesize multi-faceted knowledge and skills drawn from the course. It also can provide greater guidance to the student for continued development of the course outcomes after the course ends.

Evaluative criteria (vertical axis): Each criterion draws from the instructions on the assessment exercise and from the mastery evidence you developed. You may have three to six distinct criteria that reflect what is essential to your course goal and the final assessment exercise. Providing weights for each factor indicates its relative importance to achievement of the course goal. Make a quick mental check-in with your course goals (Worksheet 5), mastery evidence (Worksheet 6), and learning priorities (Worksheet 4). Eliminate any criterion that adds little value to those goals. Use nouns to name each criterion.

Proficiency/performance levels (horizontal axis): The descriptions of the performance levels provide the specifics of what students must do or demonstrate, and how that demonstration varies from one level to the next. The descriptions should be observable, measurable, and written in neutral, clear terms with as much precision as practicable. Three proficiency levels (*e.g.*, some variation of exceptional, acceptable, and developing) are enough to allow easy differentiation among the levels and significant guidance to students. Having more than three levels makes it difficult to describe each level distinctly and to apply the rubric reliably. The proficiency descriptions should contain consistent terms and components across each level. Words that describe amounts, frequency, or intensity indicate how the measured behavior varies from the top level. As a practical matter, when drafting descriptions for each performance level, we often find it easiest to start with the highest and lowest levels and then finish with the middle level.

When displaying the performance levels on the rubric grid, placing the highest proficiency level first (followed by the lower levels of proficiency) helps focus student attention on the descriptors of mastery. Other educators prefer to display the proficiency levels from lowest to highest to convey that progress is expected and to convey that students should continue to develop after the course ends.

To set the progressive performance levels, you might find it useful to revisit the work of Grant Wiggins and Jay McTighe, cited in earlier chapters, UNDERSTANDING BY DESIGN (2nd ed. 2005). Recall that their work on facets of understanding was useful to defining the mastery evidence we needed to create a final assessment exercise (Chapter 5). The facets are non-hierarchical among each other. But Wiggins and McTighe also provide descriptions of proficiency (or performance) levels for each facet (*i.e.*, explain, interpret, apply, see in perspective, demonstrate empathy, and reveal self-knowledge). Their progression covers five levels of development and can be useful to you in setting the desired proficiency levels for your assessment. Here we show the proficiency progression for one of the facets, *Explanation*. (Levels for each of the six facets are described at the end of this chapter in Appendix 6-A.)

Explanation *(from highest to lowest level of performance)*

1. ***Sophisticated and comprehensive:*** An unusually thorough, elegant, or inventive account (model, theory, explanation); fully supported, verified, and justified; deep and broad; goes well beyond the information given.
2. ***Systematic:*** An atypical and revealing account, going beyond what is obvious or what was explicitly taught; makes subtle connections; well supported by argument and evidence; novel thinking displayed.
3. ***In-depth:*** An account that reflects some in-depth and personalized ideas; the student is making the work his own, going beyond the given; there is supported theory, but insufficient or inadequate evidence or argument.
4. ***Developed***: An incomplete account but with apt and insightful ideas; extends and deepens some of what was learned; some reading between the lines; account has limited support, argument, data, or sweeping generalizations. There is a theory, but limited testing and evidence.
5. *Naïve:* A superficial account, more descriptive than analytical or creative; a fragmented or sketchy account of facts, ideas, or glib generalizations; a black and white account; less a theory than an unexamined hunch or borrowed idea.

A word to the wise: This might be one of the places where you re-examine your animating theory, exploratory questions, and course goal. Perhaps your evaluative criteria do not align with the early course design work you labored over. Perhaps your first draft of the goal for a trial advocacy course was trial strategy focused. But you realize your students have significant foundational learning to master. Rather than focus on direct and cross examination, you realize that you need to focus their learning on the form of the question. Dare to tear up your course goal and re-orient to one that realistically fits your course, your teaching, and your students.

C. Rubrics in Action

This section illustrates rubric development through two courses, a clinic and an externship seminar. First comes Carwina Weng's Disability Law Clinic, which centers on human-centered problem-solving. Her final assessment appeared in Chapter 5. Second comes Meg Reuter's field placement seminar, which focuses on the nature of professional judgment. Both courses center on forming students' professional identities.

Disability Law Clinic

Weng's clinic focuses on the professional values of human-centered lawyering, and she is especially interested in assessing students' abilities to account for the perspectives of individuals involved in a problem and its solution. These aspects of lawyering and problem-solving are core (definitional) to the Brest-Krieger model. Thus, her essay prompt and rubric criteria do not need to provide specifics on those elements. Simply referring to the Brest-Krieger model makes clear to the student that the interpersonal dimensions of problem-solving should be prominent in their essays.

■ Disability Law Clinic—Rubric

Portfolio Essay on Problem-Solving

Criteria	Excellent: A, A-	Competent: B+, B, B-	Developing: C+ & below
Choice of Problem (10%)	Identifies a problem that was personally challenging and substantively complicated.	Identifies a problem that was not reasonably challenging or complicated.	Identifies a problem for which you did not implement/evaluate a solution or which you did not process sufficiently.
Description of the Problem and your Problem-solving (30%)	Provides vivid, specific details that allow me [teacher/evaluator] to understand the problem, its context, the stakeholders and your thought processes, emotions, and actions in solving the problem using the model we learned.	Provides sufficient detail to allow me [teacher/evaluator] to understand what was going on but missing the details that tell me what you did and why.	Provides perfunctory detail that doesn't allow me [teacher/evaluator] to understand what was going on.
Evaluation (50%)	Assesses the effectiveness of your problem-solving, in terms of both the outcome and collaborative process. Explains your conclusions with support from your description of the problem and your problem-solving efforts, the readings, or other life experiences.	Assesses effectiveness without sufficient support to allow me to understand the assessment.	Assessment is incomplete (only outcome or process but not both) OR lacks support.
Writing Mechanics (10%)	0–3 grammar, spelling, or usage errors. 0 run-ons or fragments. Logical organization with appropriate roadmap, signposts, and transitions. Clear, supported conclusion.	4–8 grammar, spelling, or usage errors. 1–2 run-ons or fragments. Logical organization but missing roadmap, signpost, or transitions. Vague OR unsupported conclusion.	> 8 grammar, spelling, or usage errors. > 2 run-ons or fragments. Confusing organization. Missing conclusion.

* See worksheet 8.

Notice that Weng gave the heaviest weighting to the "Evaluation" criteria (50%), showing that she sees this as the most important. Evaluation represents the keystone of the problem-solving model. In setting her teaching priorities, this was what she hoped would be the most enduring or transferable learning for students.

Weng also added a criterion of writing mechanics to reinforce her expectation of professionalism in all student work products. But she assigned a modest weight to writing mechanics, lower than the others (10%)—not because she does not see writing quality as central to professional attorney work, but because the weight informs students where to devote the most effort, namely to the substantive problem-solving course goal.

Learning from Practice—Professional Judgment Seminar

One of Reuter's course goals is that each student should develop a personal definition of "professional judgment" which, among other things, takes into account the necessity to interpret a set of circumstances through the eyes of others. Through readings, small group exercises, class discussion, and fieldwork-focused reflective writing, her class explores the values and skills inherent in professional judgment. The final assessment exercise for this course is an essay in which the students develop their personal definitions of professional judgment, covering four elements: a coherent definition; references to readings and other class work; examples from the student's fieldwork; and a pragmatic view of how the student will continue to advance toward this ideal definition.

■ Learning from Practice—Professional Judgment Seminar—Rubric

Essay on Personal Definition of Professional Judgment

	Well-developed	Emerging, effective work	Under-developed
Personal definition-clarity	Student thesis or definition of professional judgment has 1–3 elements. The thesis is meaningful, coherent, and concise.	Student thesis is overburdened with an extended list of elements that fails to show significant distillation or consideration.	Student thesis is disjointed and/or simplistic.
Academic anchor	Student's thesis is supported by detailed reference to readings, class discussions, and/or class exercises.	Student's thesis has some support, but the contextual references are thin or have weak connection to the thesis.	Student makes little or no reference to the work undertaken in the seminar.
Integrates field learning	Student's thesis is grounded in multiple examples drawn from his/her field experience, whether demonstrating the exercise of professional judgment or a missed opportunity to exhibit professional judgment.	Student's thesis makes some reference(s) to field experience, but in a superficial manner.	Student suggests that he/she had little to no opportunity to observe professional judgment or perspective-taking in the course of the field placement.
Personal integration and future orientation	Student offers clear and pragmatic ideas how he/she will incorporate one or more elements of professional judgment in future endeavors (work, school, other leadership activities). Student acknowledges barriers to implementing the characteristics of professional judgment, but has thoughtful ideas how to overcome the impediments.	Student suggests some ways in which to adapt behaviors going forward, but the suggestions are simplistic without acknowledgment that new habits take deliberate attention to incorporate effectively.	Student suggests that he/she currently practices and exhibits all elements that comprise his/her definition of professional judgment.

Perspective-taking/ Self-awareness	Student presentation shows self-awareness how his/her experience and preferences can impede professional judgment. Presentation shows ability to anticipate, recognize, and adapt to the viewpoints and cultural values of others.	Presentation makes reference to perspective or self-awareness, but does not show how they are related or have meaningful significance in law practice.	Student glosses over or rejects the notion that professional judgment necessarily requires empathy and the ability to understand circumstances through the eyes of another, without offering a supported counter position.
Writing mechanics	Writing is personal, flows well, and paints a vivid picture. Uses clear and concise sentences, appropriate word choice, effective paragraph structure using topic and transition statements. Negligible errors in grammar, usage, punctuation, or style. Reflects careful proofreading /line editing.	Writing is strong, but shows weaknesses in flow or structure (e.g., rambling, mechanical, cliché). Sentence structure is competent, but needs editing for transition, concision, and/or word choice. Mostly free of grammatical, spelling, punctuation, and other style errors.	Writing is poorly organized. Requires extensive editing for concision, word choice; most paragraphs poorly structured. Multiple distracting errors in grammar, punctuation, style, and/or spelling.

* See worksheet 8.

To assess the depth and breadth of a student's definition of professional judgment, Reuter developed six evaluative criteria. The first criterion is a coherent articulation of the student's definition. The next four criteria tease out the distinct elements that the definition must incorporate—academic (readings, etc.); live/practice connection (fieldwork); professional development agenda; and self-awareness (empathy; cognitive biases). Her final criterion is presentation delivery. She chose not to weight each criterion differently.

Rubric Checklist

- Does your rubric align with the course goals and the prompt for the final assessment exercise?
- Did you keep any criteria not closely related to the course goal (*e.g.*, participation) to a minimum?
- Are the proficiency descriptions written in neutral, clear terms with as much precision as practicable?
- Do the proficiency descriptions use consistent terms and components across each level?

D. Takeaways

- The criteria in a rubric should match the evidence needed for students to demonstrate mastery of the course content.
- An analytic rubric communicates to students your concrete expectations for the assessment exercise. It therefore helps students to focus their learning on the criteria you establish and to self-assess their work product against the performance levels you set.
- A rubric helps teachers to grade consistently across multiple student submissions and performances. The more specific the descriptions of each performance level, the less individualized feedback is needed. The teacher therefore can focus on feedback to those students who need greater guidance.

Appendix 6-A

Facets of Understanding: Progressive Levels of Performance

From Grant Wiggins and Jay McTighe, Understanding by Design *(2nd ed. 2005)*

Explanation

- *Sophisticated and comprehensive:* An unusually thorough, elegant, or inventive account (model, theory, explanation); fully supported, verified, and justified; deep and broad; goes well beyond the information given.
- *Systematic:* An atypical and revealing account, going beyond what is obvious or what was explicitly taught; makes subtle connections; well supported by argument and evidence; novel thinking displayed.
- *In-depth:* An account that reflects some in-depth and personalized ideas; the student is making the work his own, going beyond the given; there is supported theory, but insufficient or inadequate evidence or argument.
- *Developed:* An incomplete account but with apt and insightful ideas; extends and deepens some of what was learned; some reading between the lines; account has limited support, argument, data, or sweeping generalizations. There is a theory, but limited testing and evidence.
- *Naïve:* A superficial account, more descriptive than analytical or creative; a fragmented or sketchy account of facts, ideas, or glib generalizations; a black and white account; less a theory than an unexamined hunch or borrowed idea.

Interpretation

- *Insightful:* A powerful and illuminating interpretation and analysis of the importance, meaning, significance; tells a rich and insightful story; provides a revealing history or context.
- *Revealing:* A thoughtful interpretation or analysis of the importance, meaning, or significance; tells an insightful story; provides a telling history or context; sees subtle differences, levels, and ironies in diverse interpretations.
- *Perspective:* A helpful interpretation or analysis of the importance, meaning, or significance; tells a clear and instructive story; provides useful history or context; sees different levels of interpretation.
- *Interpreted:* A plausible interpretation or analysis of the importance, meaning, or significance; makes sense of a story; provides history and context.
- *Literal:* A simplistic or superficial reading, mechanical translation, a decoding with little or no interpretation; no sense of wider importance or significance; a restatement of what was taught or read.

Application

- *Masterful*: Fluent, flexible, and efficient; able to use knowledge and skill and adjust understandings well in novel, diverse, and difficult contexts.
- *Skilled*: Competent in using knowledge and skills and adapting understanding in a variety or appropriate and demanding contexts.
- *Able*: Able to perform well with knowledge and skill in a few key contexts with limited repertoire, flexibility, or adaptability to diverse contexts.
- *Apprentice*: Relies on a limited repertoire of routines; able to perform well in familiar or

simple contexts, with perhaps some needed coaching; limited use of personal judgment and responsiveness to specifics of feedback/situation.

Novice: Can perform only with coaching or relies on highly scripted, singular "plug-in" (algorithmic and mechanical) skills, procedures, or approaches.

Perspective

- *Insightful*: A penetrating and novel viewpoint, effectively critiques and encompasses other plausible perspectives; take a long and dispassionate, critical view of the issues involved.
- *Thorough:* A revealing and coordinated critical view; makes own view more plausible by considering the plausibility of other perspectives; makes apt criticism, discriminations, and qualifications.
- *Considered*: A reasonably critical and comprehensive look at all the points of view in the context of one's own; makes clear that there is plausibility to other points of view.
- *Aware*: Knows of different points of view and somewhat able to place own view in perspective, but weakness in considering worth of each perspective, especially one's own; uncritical about tacit assumptions.
- *Uncritical*: Unaware of differing points of view; prone to overlook or ignore other perspectives; has difficulty imagining other ways of seeing things; prone to egocentric argument and personal criticisms.

Empathy

- *Mature*: Disposed and able to see and feel what others see and feel; unusually open to and willing to seek out the odd, alien, or different.
- *Sensitive*: disposed to see and feel what other see and feel; open to the unfamiliar and different.
- *Aware*: Knows and feels what others see and feel differently' somewhat able to empathize with others; has difficulty making sense of odd or alien view.
- *Developing*: Has some capacity and self-discipline to "walk in another's shoes" but is still primarily limited to one's own reactions and attitudes; puzzled or put out by different feelings or attitudes.
- *Egocentric:* Has little or no empathy beyond intellectual awareness of others; see things through own ideas and feelings; ignores or is threatened or puzzled by different feelings, attitudes, or views.

Self-Knowledge

- *Wise*: Deeply aware of the boundaries of one's own and other's understanding; able to recognize prejudices and projections; has integrity; able and willing to act on what one understands.
- *Circumspect*: Aware of one's ignorance and that of others; aware of one's prejudices, know the strengths and limits of one's understanding.
- *Thoughtful*: Generally aware of what is and is not understood; aware of how prejudice and projection can occur without awareness and shape one's view.
- *Ineffective*: Generally unaware of one's specific ignorance; generally unaware of how subjective prejudgments color understandings.
- *Innocent*: Completely unaware of bounds of one's understanding and of the role or projection and prejudice in opinions and attempts to understand.

Chapter 7

Course Outcomes and Learning Activities: What Will Happen in Your Classroom?

The previous chapters described ways in which teachers can clarify what they want their courses to achieve and how to ensure they accomplish those ends. Thinking about your own course, you considered: What are the animating theory and exploratory questions that provide the intellectual home for my course? What is the essential learning goal for the course? What kind of student mastery evidence and final assessment will allow me to see if the goals have been realized? The *Experiential Learning Design* (*EL Design*) tasks associated with each question helped you to ground your course and define the goal posts. Your next step is to establish the semester plan. That is the mission of this chapter. You will set your course outcomes (the discrete learning achievements), consider and choose the most useful learning activities, and decide how best to sequence them.

EL Design focuses consistently on the course goal. Each step of *EL Design* requires breaking the goal down to smaller parts for specific purposes. You will repeat the process in this chapter to determine the course outcomes that students will have to achieve to succeed on the final assessment exercise. Your course outcomes therefore will mirror the mastery evidence and the rubric you developed earlier. Defining your course outcomes and publishing them in your syllabus is also required by American Bar Association accreditation standards.

The final question you now ask is: Given my course goal and outcomes, what resources, instructional techniques, and experiences or activities will get the students where I want them to be? The task of selecting, devising, and sequencing learning activities is driven by the course outcomes, final assessment exercise, and course goal. What will help the students move from here (their current state of knowledge and skill) to there (proficient in the things you taught)? As the course designer, you will move back and forth between your goals, mastery evidence, and learning activities to determine whether you are in fact meeting your goals and whether the activity lends itself to meeting your specific criteria for success.

A. Course Outcomes

Course outcomes translate course goals for students to know what they will be able to think and do, after they complete the course. Course outcomes have a few purposes. First, they represent the component parts of the course goal. An easy example: If the course is aimed to teach someone how to ride a bike, the goal drafted broadly might be stated something like this: Students will be able to ride a two-wheeled bike on city streets. The course outcomes would be something like: Students will be able to mount a freestanding bike; to pedal while balancing; to brake safely; to make turns; and to dismount. The outcomes signal to the students the different component tasks they need to master.

Second, the outcomes reveal to the teacher which lawyering tasks and learning activities will help the student master each building block sufficiently to attain the overall course goal. The bike-riding example is simple. It requires a relatively straightforward sequence of skills. In contrast, experiential learning courses generally require a constellation of knowledge, skills, and values, in interpersonally dynamic circumstances. It is far more challenging to disaggregate experiential course goals to their component parts. But, then again, breaking down complex topics into a progression of building blocks is the core of teaching.

Third, the American Bar Association standards for law school accreditation require course outcomes in two forms. The standards require course outcomes to be published in each course syllabus. (Standard 301, Managing Director's Guidance Memo (June 2015)) The ABA standards also require the faculty of each law school to adopt a set of institutional learning outcomes for the whole of the JD program and then to monitor the school's progress toward attaining those outcomes. (Standards 301 and 315). As described in Chapter 1, *Your Experiential Course and the ABA Standards*, when faculty undertake this responsibility to set and evaluate degree-level outcomes, they will draw from individual course outcomes to demonstrate both the teaching offered and the learning attained. All schools must include institutional learning outcomes for skills keyed to lawyering practice. The courses in the experiential curriculum are vitally important here.

Note on terminology—
Course Goals, Course Outcomes, and Learning Outcomes

Educational designers speak in terms of course goals and course outcomes. This book uses the same terminology. The course goals represent the one or two major learning objectives of the course. Course goals are each comprised of multiple course outcomes that represent distinct elements of the student's learning within a course goal. The ABA uses the term "*learning* outcomes." This term is the same basic idea of course outcomes applied to the JD program: the distinct individual competencies students will have acquired once they have completed their degree requirements. (The ABA does not mandate a holistic learning goal for JD programs.)

ABA Standard 302 provides the minimum all schools must include among their stated learning outcomes: substantive and procedural law knowledge, ability to perform legal analysis, research, problem-solve, communicate, exercise professional responsibilities, and other skills needed for competent practice. Their core list has a generic quality. The course goals and outcomes described in this book are more granular and specific to your subject matter and clientele.

Like mastery evidence and rubric evaluative criteria, course outcomes should be specific, observable, and measurable. Course outcomes enable students to gauge for themselves what their starting points are for each course outcome and where to focus their efforts to achieve the course goal.

Course outcomes are phrased similarly to the course goal. They start with a phrase like, "At the conclusion of the course, students will be able to..." To complete that sentence, add:

– ***a verb*** that identifies the observable and measurable task to be performed by the student;

– ***an object of the verb*** that identifies the learning (factual knowledge, process, skill, or value) being demonstrated;

– ***the circumstance*** in which the students will perform; and

– ***criteria*** for acceptable performance.

Here are three iterations of an outcome (in progressive stages of usefulness) for a course that has the goal: "Students will be able to follow a model of client-centered lawyering." An important component of client-centered lawyering is the attorney's ability to discern the client's wishes with enough detail to serve the client's interests fully and respectfully. Hence this course outcome:

Vague: Students will be able to understand their client's situation.

The verb "understand" is amorphous. How will the students demonstrate their understanding? The object—their client's situation—is terribly broad. Specifics about the object would help to focus student learning and plan the learning activities.

Better: Students will be able to identify accurately the priorities among the client's values, interests, and objectives that affect the client's legal problem.

The verb "identify" explains the measurable task students will perform to demonstrate their understanding. "Client's values, interests, and objectives" helpfully specifies what details about the client's situation the students should gather. But the term "accurately" is only really measurable by the client, not the clinical teacher.

Detailed, measurable: Students will be able to confirm with the client priorities among the client's values, interests, and objectives as they apply to the client's legal problem.

This phrasing of the course outcome shows the key features: observable and measurable ("confirm," which encompasses "identify"); expressly focuses on critical aspects of understanding a client (priorities among values, interests, objectives); and illuminates a critical condition (a lawyer's understanding of the client requires re-evaluation to check for misperception, inaccuracy, or changes).

Typically, teachers identify three to six course outcomes for each course goal, to reflect priorities for student learning and to be realistic about what the students can accomplish. As you convert your course goals to multiple course outcomes, check whether you have achieved the right level of specificity and effectiveness for assessment purposes.

B. Course Outcomes in Action

This section explores examples of course outcomes in three different courses: a traditional live client clinic (Carwina Weng's Disability law Clinic), a simulation skills course (Danielle Cover's Interviewing, Counseling, and Negotiation), and a field placement seminar (Meg Reuter's Learning from Practice—Professional Judgment Seminar).

Disability Law Clinic

Weng set a course goal in her clinic focused on human-centered problem-solving. To craft her course outcomes, Weng started with the application of the specific problem-solving model advanced by Paul Brest and Linda Hamilton Krieger.[1] Drawing on her client-centered orientation, Weng identified course outcomes that represent skills students need to use the model collaboratively with their clients. Her law school's institutional learning outcomes include problem-solving, interpersonal skills, advocacy, self-evaluation, and commitment to lifelong professional development. Her course outcomes support her school's program outcomes.

■ Disability Law Clinic — Course Goal // Course Outcomes

Course Goal:

Students will be able to: address real-life lawyering problems and client matters effectively by applying the provided problem-solving model and by following a human-centered approach.

Course Outcomes:

Knowledge, skills and/or values	Students will be able to: Verb (performance)	Object (the learning statement)	Condition and/or Criterion
Know the Brest-Krieger model; value collaboration	Apply	Brest-Krieger model	Humanistically with client.
Skill—asking questions to be able to diagnose the problem, to identify its causes, to brainstorm options that will advance the client's position	Ask	Questions	To elicit factual detail, emotions, interests, values, motivations, and priorities relevant to the problem.
Skill—take perspective	Explain	The perspectives of different stakeholders	In a client or lawyering problem.
Skill—interaction Value—identities of others (cultural competence, empathy)	Interact	With clients, co-counsel, and others	With respect for their cultural and personal identities.
Skill—self evaluation	Evaluate	Their growth	In problem-solving.

* See worksheets 5 and 9.

Interviewing, Counseling, and Negotiation

The animating theory undergirding Danielle Cover's Interviewing, Counseling, and Negotiation course is that effective, problem-solving lawyering requires strong, pliable, adaptive communication skills. She seeks for her students to understand the professional value of collaborative, client-centered lawyering. Without strong communication skills, a lawyer is ill-equipped to discern a client's view of the problem presented or to work collaboratively with the client to advance her interests.

1. Paul Brest and Linda Hamilton Krieger, Problem Solving, Decision Making, and Professional Judgment (2010).

Interviewing, Counseling, and Negotiation — Course Goal // Course Outcomes

Course Goal:

Students will be able to: internalize frameworks for speaking and listening that support a client-centered lawyering approach to their attorney-client relationship with their simulation client.

Course Outcomes:

Knowledge, skills and/or values	Verb (performance)	Object (the learning statement)	Condition and/or Criterion
Ask questions that generate high-quality information	Use	Journalism questions, t-funneling, and active listening	To manage and direct client conversations in furtherance of the simulated case.
Use t-funneling techniques to focus conversation	Be flexible	In generating questions and conducting funnel-like follow up	To explore the factual circumstances, context, and motivations of the communication partner.
Use feedback cues to convey engagement with clients, counsel, partners, etc.	Offer	Body language, verbal critique, and positive responses	In a constructive manner that keeps communication channels open.

* See worksheets 5 and 9.

Learning from Practice—Professional Judgment Seminar

Meg Reuter's Learning from Practice—Professional Judgment Seminar has two goals: i) to help students develop a personal definition of professional judgment, cognizant of the barriers to professional discernment, and ii) to teach students the techniques and value of deliberate and reflective practice. The skills of deliberate and reflective practice can mature into a career-long orientation toward personal development. They depend on the ability to pause and examine what is transpiring—what things need to be seen and understood that are initially obscure to us. Reuter shines a light on professional judgment as a way to focus student attention on the ways in which we are reflexive, jump to conclusions, and have blind spots in how we view and respond to circumstances and events. Her course goals and outcomes support her school's institutional learning outcomes of life-long learning, self-development, and cultural competence.

Learning from Practice Seminar—Course Goals // Course Outcomes

Course Goals:

Students will be able to: develop personal definition of professional judgment that, among other things, takes into account the need to appreciate and interpret a set of circumstances through the eyes of others.
Students will be able to: demonstrate the ability to put deliberate and reflective practice into use to amplify his/her learning from experience.

Course Outcomes:

Knowledge, skills and/or values	Verb (performance)	Object (the learning statement)	Condition and/or Criterion
Deliberate practice.	Devise	A learning plan	Based on self-assessment and professional development needs.
Deliberate practice.	Effectuate	The learning plan	Through fieldwork experience, careful observation, and continuous self-assessment.
Reflective practice.	Articulate	The benefits of reflective practice.	
Reflective practice.	Apply	Reflective practice in multiple contexts	To amplify learning and professional judgment.
Reflective practice.	Deploy	Active and careful observation skills	To facilitate perspective taking and self-assessment.
Perspective taking and its barriers (cognitive biases) Reflective practice.	Describe	Multiple examples how perception and interpretation	Of the circumstances of others is necessary for professional judgment and effective lawyering.
Perspective taking and its barriers (cognitive biases)	Illustrate	How cognitive biases and patterned behaviors can impede	One's ability to see through the eyes of another.
Perspective taking and its barriers (cognitive biases)	Identify and Evaluate	His/her own cognitive biases, patterned behaviors, and gut reactions	In multiple instances.

* See worksheets 5 and 9.

Drafting course outcomes sets the framework for our courses. It is finally time to put together a set of learning activities that will complete the course.

C. Learning Activities: Syncing with Your Course Outcomes

A well-designed learning plan focuses on the learners. Your objective is to create a robust relationship among learning activities, course outcomes, and course goal. Ask yourself, "What will the students need from my planning to make it more likely that everyone will achieve my course goal?" This phase includes several components:

The ABA accreditation standards set some expectations on this score. For a clinic, field placement, or simulation course to satisfy the experiential graduation requirement, it must be "primarily experiential in nature" and i) integrate doctrine, theory, skills, and legal ethics; ii) engage students in performance of professional skills; iii) develop the concepts underlying the professional skills; iv) provide opportunity for student self-evaluation; v) provide faculty and/or supervisor feedback; and vi) include a classroom instructional component or other means of ongoing, contemporaneous, faculty-guided reflection. (Std. 304). You will want to be conscious of this checklist as you start to weave your course plan together.

The course components and planning steps to consider include:

- *Identify the topics represented in the course outcomes*: This becomes your to-do list. You may want to aggregate a few of the topics into "units" or you may choose to present them individually.
- *Project the level of your students' readiness*: This will set your "starting point" and reveal how you should prepare the students for the lessons to follow. Sometimes teachers have to help students "unlearn" things that the students feel quite confident they already know or perform well. For example, students cannot conduct good interviews if they do not know how to ask questions or have a sense of what information is relevant; they cannot work on developing empathy if empathetic communication is a foreign concept. So, the learning plan should make the content accessible, keyed to the students' current level of maturity, self-directedness, knowledge, skill, and value orientation. Teachers must estimate what the students already know about the topic and what information will be new to them. If your school has mapped out its curriculum based on its program outcomes, you may have a better sense of what students should have learned or been exposed to before entering your course. Even without a curriculum map, you expect some students to come in with strong skills or experiences, others with no skills or relevant experiences, some who are self-directed learners, and others who need help to build that orientation. Fortunately, the smaller size of many experiential classes provides the opportunity for teachers to be more aware of (and responsive to) differences in abilities and preparation.
- *Brainstorm possible learning activities:* List these ideas freely, not yet developing them for implementation. Take into account different learning styles of your students. These activities will span the gamut from readings and other media to lectures; from individual student exercises to group activities; to demonstrations, simulations, and live performances. The activities might take place outside the classroom, during supervision meetings, and inside the classroom. As you prioritize the students' learning needs, you will undertake a dynamic analysis of your wish list and course outcomes to determine what is essential and what is less needed. The appendix to this chapter provides an extended selection of possible experiential learning activities that you might use for inspiration.
- *Consider your course priorities:* Examine your topics and learning activities to assure yourself that they fit your priorities and do not devolve to cramming in as many topics and activities as possible. Review the learning priorities you set in Worksheet 4 and check that you allow students to engage the material in multiple environments with diverse conditions and increasing complexity.
- *Generate a sequencing plan:* Choose how to sequence the learning activities within the course and within any specific unit. This step is closely tied with the earlier step of projecting the level of students' current abilities and prior experience. When you sequence an experiential learning course you may need to introduce foundational legal knowledge, values, and skills and then move to building the more nuanced skills and values integration that comprise the goals of your course. *EL Design* asks: How do you want to organize the information to be imparted to the students (topically, thematically, chronologically, etc.)? Do your course goals

require that you start and end with certain lessons or that you start with foundational skills and move to increasingly more complicated topics, etc.? Does it make sense for you to start with theory and then move to application or start with an attempt at application and then discuss theory? The answers to these questions will vary from professor to professor, class to class, and course goal to course goal. In a live-client representation clinic, sequencing priorities might look different from how they look in a simulation course or in a field placement seminar.

- ***Possible sequencing models:*** These sequencing models may help you to design the organization that makes most sense to you and your course outcomes and goals. There is no reason to constrain yourself to a single organizational model. Oftentimes, a combination of models might prove more useful in balancing the different needs of an experiential learning course.
    - *Order of process*: Sequence material along the arc of a process, beginning to end; *e.g.*, litigation sequence (complaint to trial); attorney-client relationship (first meeting through resolution of the matter)
    - *Simple to complex:* Sequence material from simple concepts or skills to more sophisticated ones; *e.g.*, memorizing the elements of intentional torts to analyzing cases for precedent to developing theories of a claim or defense.
    - *Dependent or supportive relationship between units of study:* Sequence together topics or units that are connected; *e.g.*, use where the learning is cumulative; concepts or skills may not be "simple," but represent pre-requisite knowledge or skill necessary (or helpful) for later units.
    - *Cause & Effect:* Introduce a range of problems followed with the types of solutions to be applied.
    - *Spiral or cyclical:* Introduce and revisit concepts multiple times throughout the term.
    - *General to specific or Concrete to abstract*: Introduce general principles and then apply to specific situations; alternatively, start with specific examples of a phenomenon and move toward what they represent on at the conceptual or abstract level.
    - *Thematic or topical:* use when individual units represent independent concepts, *e.g.*, a survey course.
- ***Order your learning activities:*** Winnow your list of learning activities to those that meet your core priorities, and then align with the sequencing or organizing theme you set. Make adjustments for the situational factors and practicalities you face. And now you can graft it to the semester calendar.
- ***Find opportunities for synthesis of substantive law, lawyering skills, and ethical and professional values.*** The ABA standard defines experiential courses in terms of this synthesis. Experiential teachers tend to integrate these learning goals and help students understand the concepts underlying the focal professional skills for the course.
- ***Provide multiple practice opportunities***: To state the obvious for experiential courses, you want to build a learning environment in which students receive adequate information and instruction on core concepts, but also enjoy repeated opportunities to practice, in order to generate understanding and apply the lessons. Practice is critical to mastery. For the live practice courses (clinics and externships), some of the practice opportunities will be outside the classroom, in the fieldwork and client work.
- ***Provide reflection, feedback, and assessment opportunities:*** Feedback and formative assessment must be included, whether student self-critique and reflection, peer assessment, or

teacher evaluation and coaching. ABA Standard 304 specifically requires experiential courses to provide multiple opportunities for performance and self-evaluation.

- *Develop each learning activity:* Get your activities ready to present during the semester (*e.g.*, develop fact patterns and exercises, secure simulated clients, set timing). Revisit the animating theory and exploratory questions for the course (Chapter 3, *The Big Picture*). Use these as the backdrop for how you will conduct the classes, from class to class, or unit to unit.
- *Construct units, as useful:* When developing a unit, include these elements:
    - an introduction, the foundation students need for their learning (*e.g.*, readings, lecture, or preparatory exercise);
    - specific learning activities;
    - opportunity for practice and feedback; and
    - closure to help students see the connections in the experiences you have just moved them through.

  For their self-assessment and/or your teaching self-assessment, you might ask the students to summarize the unit in one or two sentences or encourage them to identify the muddiest point in the unit. These reflections can provide useful insight to the students and also to what you should clarify before beginning the next part of your course.
- *Map your units onto the course calendar:* Predict how much time each unit will require, using all the varied student contact opportunities available to you (*e.g.*, classroom, supervision meetings, and asynchronous communication). After the course ends, you might review the time allotments given to various units for modification in the future.
- *Examine your teaching effectiveness:* Take time over the semester to examine your own teaching. We must sit in the shoes of our students when considering the actual effectiveness of our work, no matter how thoughtfully we planned or how carefully we executed. A number of factors might impede an effective learning plan. There might be flawed assumptions from what we think an activity will do for a student and what happens for the student. As experts in our fields, we can see the inherent value in a series of readings and classroom exercises, but that value can be lost on the novice.

D. Learning Activity Plans in Action

To illustrate the development of learning plans, this section tracks the same three courses as featured in the course outcomes section: a simulation skills course (Danielle Cover's Interviewing, Counseling, and Negotiation), a traditional live-client clinic (Carwina Weng's Disability Law Clinic), and a field placement seminar (Meg Reuter's Learning from Practice—Professional Judgment Seminar). A specific unit from each course models how these authors built their own individual collections of learning activities from foundational lessons to start the unit, to experiential teaching activities, to feedback.

Interviewing, Counseling, and Negotiation

In Cover's simulation course, Interviewing, Counseling, and Negotiation, she spends a significant amount of class time working on what she calls "the shape of questions." This concept is embedded in her course outcomes about knowing different questioning techniques, assessing their utility in different situations, and being able to conduct interviews nimbly while moving among techniques. An overarching goal of the course is that students will be more intentional about how they frame their communications with other lawyers, their clients, the court, court personnel, witnesses, and others. Question formation, then, becomes a critical piece of working with students on communication as a foundation for approaching lawyering tasks. Students must be able to explain the differences in shape and impact of leading, non-leading, broad, and narrow questions.

Cover developed a learning plan for her unit on interviewing that incorporates readings, an in-class teacher-led exercise, student-directed exercises, and a consistent feedback loop that engages students in peer review and critique.

■ Interviewing, Counseling, and Negotiation—Unit Plan

Utility of Diverse Questioning Techniques

Provide foundation about the precepts of client-centered lawyering: what it looks like, why it's the ideal to pursue.
Read a chapter from the assigned text for the course, additional outside reading on leading and non-leading questions.
Perform in-class exercises to focus on evaluating the efficacy of different question shapes. Students answer questions about popular culture. The exercise also allows for useful tangential issues such as gaps between speaker and listener in cultural information. Includes self-assessment loop for students.
Conduct peer-to-peer mini-interviews where the students must use each question shape to gather one piece of information from a colleague. The exercise brings student attention to the challenges of asking effective questions when cultural and experiential frames of reference get in the way. Reinforces the connection to client-centered lawyering.
Throughout, probe students regarding how the quality of a question impacts the quality of information received, and why.
At the end of the Interviewing unit, conduct mini learning reviews to gauge what students have retained and can carry to subsequent exercises. When Cover moves to the Counseling and Negotiation segments of the course, she continues her learning reviews.

* See worksheets 10 and 11.

Cover's sequencing method: basic to more complex, repetition, and informal feedback loops (self-assessment, peer feedback, and teacher coaching). The learning activities—foundational reading, instructor-led examination of question shape, student-led question formation exercises, and feedback directly support the assessment tool of a simulated interview. Students are offered practice and feedback throughout the course about how the shape of a question influences the quality of information an attorney receives and thereby how well the attorney can work with the client toward resolution of the case. Then, as they approach the final simulation, students know exactly what they must show Cover in their performance to demonstrate they have internalized the lessons and can transfer them to new situations.

Disability Law Clinic

Weng used multiple sequencing models for her clinic over the semester. The early part of the course follows order of process, *e.g.*, introducing skills for students to establish a new lawyer-client relationship. Through the remainder of the course she threads in units and learning activities to introduce the more conceptual aspects of the course (problem-solving, collaboration, human-centered orientation). This sequencing plan helps Weng to tap into student eagerness to dig into technical lawyering tasks right at the get-go and then flow into her more abstract course goal of learning how to be a collaborative, client-centered problem-solver.

One of Weng's course outcomes is that students will be able to interact with clients and others with respect for cultural, personal, and professional identities. When she began mapping out this outcome for class, she identified three student needs: i) basic knowledge about people with disabilities, including veterans from different eras; ii) self-awareness about the student's culture and its impact on lawyering; skills of careful active listening and demonstration of empathy; and iii) demonstrating values of respect, non-judgmentalism, and collaboration. With this list of "needs," she started to assemble a set of learning activities to support the students.

Disability Law Clinic—Unit Plan

Oral Communication and Interviewing

Readings including ethnographies of people who are similar to the clinic's clients; materials explaining cultural competence; Sue Bryant and Jean Koh-Peters' Five Habits of Cross-Cultural Lawyering.
Icebreaker to help students and teacher get to know each other. Objective—find things we all have in common (finding connection).
Students develop a personal identity map of five most important identities. Paired with personal reflection regarding how those identities affect their work and view of their clients, and then group sharing and discussion.
Student quick write (early semester): profile what he/she expects about a typical client; identify concerns about working with our clients. Sets baseline for student self-awareness.
Student quick write (late semester): describe the clients he/she worked with and what he/she learned from them. Allows self- and teacher-assessment of progress in empathy and cultural competence.
Improvisational comedy exercises for developing listening and empathy skills.
Model interview (fishbowl): teacher role-plays an interview with actor-client; followed by discussion about active listening and empathy.
Students role-play simulations with actor-clients to practice active listening.
Storytelling exercises aimed to distinguish between empathy and sympathy and the impact on client autonomy. Helps students see clients with disabilities as protagonists, not victims. Also helps with case theory development and persuasion.

* See worksheets 10 and 11.

Learning from Practice—Professional Judgment Seminar

Reuter framed her course as a class in professional judgment. She wants to build toward the goal that students will understand that seeing through the eyes of others is a critical factor in lawyer effectiveness; cognitive biases (including implicit cultural biases) impose barriers to exhibiting professional judgment; and cultural competence (minimizing implicit cultural biases) is a requisite part of professional judgment.

Reuter organized her learning activities first to help students "unlearn" their trust in their instincts and judgments and perception that they are rational actors. Given the emotional freight of cultural bias discussions, she also chose a sequence that starts with a non-embarrassing example of cognitive bias. Her preparatory exercise (and several others) are designed to help students examine their assumptions about their actions and work approaches. She weaves in social science and discussion of professional judgment to cement the purpose of the exercises. She closes with skill building on interrupting bias and a reflective essay.

■ Learning from Practice—Professional Judgment Seminar—Unit Plan

Unit on Cognitive Biases, Cultural Biases, and Interrupting Bias

Exercises to reveal to themselves the cognitive biases and preferences that students would not have said they had. The first exercise (simulated negotiation) has the hidden goal to reveal a cognitive bias (partisan or advocate's bias) that they would have no shame in admitting but is reliably present as soon as they are given a side to advocate. Followed with discussion of cognitive bias as a barrier to professional judgment.
Post-exercise lecture to introduce Daniel Kahneman's System 1 and 2 thinking. System 2 thinking is the byproduct of pausing to be deliberate or intentional about how you interpret and react to circumstances. It describes the science behind debiasing techniques.
Move to biases that are more emotionally freighted, i.e., cultural bias. Read chapter on Navigating Cultural Difference.
Students create grid of personal cultural identities, how the students and others characterize those identities, the upsides and downsides of being a member of those cultural identities.
Take implicit bias test online. Discuss how subtle implicit biases impact behaviors.
Move to specific exercises about cultural difference, existence and impact of implicit bias. Examine in context of client intake (unmasking assumptions, generating multiple hypotheses). Consider micro-aggressions in the workplace; troubleshoot how to interrupt.
Reflective essay on cultural differences observed in their field placements.

* See worksheets 10 and 11.

Course Outcome Checklist

- Do the course outcomes describe what students will know, think, and do to perform the final assessment exercise successfully?
- Do they use verbs that represent observable and measurable behavior?
- Do they address a single distinct learning outcome per statement?
- Do they align with specific course goal(s)?
- Do they map onto your school's published JD learning outcomes?

Learning Plan Checklist

- Do the learning activities introduce the course content; allow repeated use of content and practice of skills; and allow students to demonstrate mastery of the course content?
- Do the learning activities integrate doctrine, skills, and ethics?
- Do the learning activities develop the underlying concepts for the skills being taught?
- Do the learning activities include opportunities for formative and summative assessment?
- Are the learning activities sequenced across the arcs of both the course and the units?

E. Takeaways

- Course outcomes communicate to students the observable and measurable building blocks toward the course goal. They should align with the evidence of course mastery and the rubric for the final assessment exercise.
- Course outcomes across the curriculum allow students to select courses that help them build mastery of their school's program outcomes.
- Learning activities introduce to students the information, skills, and values that underlie each course outcome and allow them to practice their understandings and skills repeatedly and with increasing mastery.
- Sequencing learning activities across a course provides structure for student learning, allowing smoother transitions, scaffolding, and assessment checkpoints.

Appendix 7-A

Samples of Experiential Learning Activities

The brief guide below describes some of the learning activities the authors like to use, with an identification of some of the basic outcomes and Facets of Understanding each can support. The guide is not at all exhaustive, either as to the activities or their uses. Rather, the guide illustrates ways to review learning activities from a design perspective.

As you peruse the guide, you will quickly see the malleability of the learning activities. Using the same activity with different prompts will elicit different types of learning from the students. Certain activities are more amenable to certain types of learning. Or not. For example, a multiple-choice quiz is useful to test recall; it is not an effective platform for students to exercise their ability to interpret or take perspective. You will also notice that the guide includes things like quizzes. Consider assessment exercises, especially formative ones, as learning activities in and of themselves. Make a goal that most, if not all, of your chosen learning activities include some kind of feedback.

Preparatory learning activities: Of course, learning activities include student preparation, such as reading, research assignments, or observing an event. The focus here is on the experiential, classroom types of learning activities.

Facet	Activity	Examples, considerations
Remember—concepts	Quizzes at different points of the semester or teaching unit, for different purposes: • to set a baseline of knowledge at the beginning of a class or unit • to test basic tenets of law and procedure after the class or unit • to ascertain problem areas in student understanding	Multiple-choice quiz on legal or procedural concepts before a class room simulation. Quick, can be self-scored. Useful to provide a key explaining correct/incorrect answers. **Memory matrix**: provide students with a table to organize information and illustrate relationships. Provide the row and column headings and have students fill in the blank cells. Show how you would organize the material. Have discussions in class or in supervision meetings. You might prefill some of the cells in the matrix to prime the students' recall. **Puzzle**: provide students with pieces of a puzzle that they must put together correctly to show in order the steps of a legal procedure.
	Time line	Map out the client's situation on a time line. For it to be an exercise of remembering, you should expect the student to be able to do it on the spot. If it is used as a tool to organize a case file, it would be an example of explanation, interpretation, or application.
Remember—accurate and active listening	Repeater exercise in pairs (improv. technique)	In pairs, students make up a conversation. Each new line of dialogue begins with a repetition of the previous line.
Explain	Quick Write	Before class, to explain the key thesis or point of class preparation materials.

Facet	Activity	Examples, considerations
Explain, *continued*	Concept map	Have students create a diagram to show linkages among concepts (*e.g.*, theory of the case). Help students visualize lawyering and storytelling in more ways than the written word and outlines.
	Flow chart	Have students develop a flow chart to illustrate agency or court process with short description of the purposes of each step and the key factors in decision points.
	Organizational chart	Have students plot the different actors (levels of authority) in their field placement law office, including most important constituencies.
Interpret	Quick Write	At the end of class, to interpret the day's instruction—what was most meaningful? What was the biggest take-away? What do I want to understand better?
	Metaphors	In class, have students develop a metaphor for a lawyering process (*e.g.*, the process of gathering information) or for a client's experience with an agency or legal system. Can be verbal or visual.
	Small group or pairs discussions	**Video:** class views as a group, with small group discussions afterwards to assess particular issues (*e.g.*, communication methods exemplified, cultural differences, barriers, strategy choices, what's missing). **Case study/fact pattern/hypothetical:** students read before class or in class (depending on the length) and discuss. Give different prompts or different case studies to the different groups. Follow with a discussion of the whole class, examining a point from diverse perspectives. Small group or paired discussions are useful to acclimate "quiet" students who take time to gather and speak out their thoughts. Allows more peer-to-peer learning.
	Visuals	Have students draw a picture of themselves as a legal professional or a one-page graphic novel of their development as a legal professional (also includes self-awareness). Have students draw a picture of their field placement organization and the people who interact with it (also includes perspective). Have students make a sculpture that represents their core professional values.
	Legal Storytelling	Determine the kind of archetypal protagonist and story to use for the client's situation.

Facet	Activity	Examples, considerations
Apply	Video Review	Watch a video (movie, tv, YouTube, etc.). Have students apply professional responsibility rules to the situation in the video.
	Simulation or Moot (may involve Analysis as well)	In class, have students use and adapt legal concepts and lawyering techniques in a new problem. The problem might be hypothetical or it might be the enactment of an upcoming lawyering event in which the students must try out legal arguments, examination questions, etc. In class, have students practice question forms for fact-gathering in short interview simulations.
	Supervision meetings	Connect the seminar learning to the work the students are performing for the clients. Have them apply and explain how it relates to their casework.
	Field trip to attend a trial or hearing; interview attorneys; bring practitioners to class	Students are given an observation, fact-gathering, agenda. Depending on the prompt, the students could be asked to interpret or apply some concept presented in class; gauge the perspectives and interests of others (perspective-taking; empathy). Students follow with an essay or report back to class to concretize their synthesis of their observations and learning.
Take perspective	Pro/con List	In class, have students develop pro/con lists to a settlement option from the perspectives of their client, the opposing party, the court, and/or non-party impacted by the outcome.
	Venn diagram	Have students develop a Venn diagram showing the interests of different stakeholders to a problem. The diagram should show areas of overlap and separation.
	Role play simulation	Have students take on specific roles, with instructions as to their role and character, for a lawyering event (*e.g.*, a client board meeting, a motion hearing).
Demonstrate empathy	"Yes, and" improv exercise	In pairs or small groups, one student starts by making a statement. The next student follows up by first saying "Yes, and . . . ." to agree with the first statement and then to add new information. The statements continue until the dialogue reaches a natural conclusion. Students develop empathy by being present with their partners in the exercise, responding to the emotional content; practicing nonjudgmentalism; and accepting of whatever their partners say.

Facet	Activity	Examples, considerations
Demonstrate empathy, *continued*	Emotional Roulette (improv exercise):	In pairs, students start a conversation about anything. Every 1–2 minutes, the teacher calls out a random emotion and the pairs must continue their conversation in the tone of that emotion. Students practice a full-range of emotional expression. The learning value is dependent on the student's ability to show emotion with some subtlety.
	List creation; brainstorming	Have students develop a list of possible legal and non-legal (extra-legal) solutions to client's problem, annotated by their projections of how the client would evaluate the option, and identifying what additional information they would want to learn from the client.
	Video review	Class reviews a video of an interpersonal interaction (*e.g.*, student interview of a client). Class has to identify moments of implicit bias or micro-aggression or assess the emotional state of the participants and, where appropriate, offer suggestions for different responses that are more culturally appropriate or show greater empathy.
Have self-knowledge	Quick write or Reflective essay	Students write a paragraph or a longer essay about what they have learned and why; how they would use the information learned; what traits, biases, or habits affect their learning, etc.
	Portfolio	Students compile a portfolio of their work over the course, with an essay discussing what helped them to progress or what hindered their progress; what made a particular item in their portfolio an exemplar of their best work, etc.

Appendix 7-B

EL Design Annotation of a Sample Course Syllabus
University of Wyoming College of Law
INTERVIEWING, COUNSELING, AND NEGOTIATION
FALL 2018

Instructor: Danielle Cover, Assistant Professor of Law
Phone: 307-766-6560
E-mail: dcover1@uwyo.edu
Office: Annex, Rm. 42a
Office Hours: Please make an appointment.

Credits: 3 credits
Classes: **Tuesday/Thursday from 9:30 a.m. to 10:50 a.m.**
Room: 170

COURSE MATERIALS

REQUIRED

Essential Lawyering Skills: Interviewing, Counseling, Negotiation & Persuasive Fact Analysis (5th ed.), Stefan H. Krieger & Richard K. Neumann, Jr. (WoltersKluwer 2015).

Additional readings and/or exercises will be assigned prior to relevant classes. The additional readings will be made available on TWEN.

ON RESERVE

Psychology for Lawyers: Understanding the Human Factors in Negotiation, Litigation, and Decision-Making, Jennifer K. Robbennolt & Jean R. Sternlight (American Bar Association 2012).

COURSE PREMISE & GOALS

This course is crafted around three big ideas of lawyering. First, lawyering is an inherently collaborative endeavor. Second, effective lawyering relationships are built on solid communication skills. Third and finally, the client is and should be an active participant in every aspect of case development and execution.[2]

My goal is to guide you in developing some of the fundamental skills you will need to be effective attorneys, communicators, and collaborators. Ultimately, I want you to be able to critically examine the integral connections between the relationships you build with your clients, partners, and opposing parties and meaningful interviewing, effective client counseling, and ethical goal-driven negotiation.[3] In addition, this course will also introduce you to some lawyering concepts, skills, and processes that may feel disconnected from the main topics of interviewing, counseling, and negotiation. However, through individual exercises, reflection, and discussion you will explore exactly how interrelated all the skills are. By semester's end you will be able to conduct client-centered interviews, counseling sessions, and negotiations. Together with this, you will understand the dynamic nature of

2. DRC Comment: This is a brief summary of my animating theories for the course (Worksheet 1). I revisit these big ideas in my introductory lecture for the course and reiterate it throughout the semester as we explore different aspects of collaboration and client-centeredness.

3. DRC Comment: Here I plant the seed of the kinds of exploratory questions we will use throughout the semester as we approach each new skill or unit in the course (Worksheet 2).

the lawyering process: that no part exists independent of the others and that each simultaneously builds from and informs the others.[4]

The big picture of the course will focus you toward the following goals:

- You will engage in effective collaborative relationships with each other such that you can effectively assess, plan for, and further the positions of your simulation clients;
- You will internalize frameworks for speaking and listening that will support you in developing and mastering a client-centered approach to lawyering relationships;
- You will increase your self-awareness of and flexibility around your communication strengths and weaknesses within the context of major lawyering tasks; and
- You will recognize the dynamic nature of lawyering relationships across the lawyering spectrum (dispute resolution, transactional, criminal, and administrative) and how communication skills can enhance or detract from creating and maintaining those lawyering relationships.[5]

Scope

We will spend the semester working on three primary lawyering skills: interviewing, counseling, and negotiation. We will approach these skills from the perspective that the client is the primary decision-maker in his or her case and that no decisions should be made without the client's agreement and consent. This may sound fundamental and obvious, and yet you may be surprised at how tempting it is to play the role of all-knowing advisor. In addition to the three primary skills, we will explore the relationship between those skills and other pieces of the lawyering process, including, for example, fact investigation, developing a case theory, and storytelling. We will also explore how ethical rules impact our attorney-client relationships and how they inform a client-centered practice. You will spend the coming weeks learning to approach the lawyering process comprehensively, keeping the client at the center of the representation. We will combine dialogue about the readings you have been assigned with in-class activities that require you to engage in skills practice, problem-solving, and analysis. Throughout the semester you will engage in a consistent feedback loop in which you both receive feedback and provide it to your colleagues and professor.

While the relationship between the skills taught in this course is dynamic, the topics are organized in a roughly linear fashion around the major hubs of interviewing, counseling, and negotiation. There will be discreet formative simulations for each topic as well as a course-long simulation involving a landlord-tenant dispute that will offer you the opportunity to carry a client through from initial meeting to negotiation. For each major topic in the course you will have a final summative assessment related to the course-long simulation that you must prepare and execute with the other members of the law firm in which you are registered.

This class is both self-directed and team-based in its approach. You will be actively responsible for a large part of your learning. There is a significant amount of reading necessary to prepare for class; there are also activities that must be prepared outside of the classroom for discussion during class time. If you are unwilling or unable to engage in this kind of learning atmosphere, this may not be the course for you.

---

4. DRC Comment: The class is structured building from foundational skills to more nuanced skills and is cyclical in its revisiting of earlier concepts, exercises, and discussion points (Worksheet 10).

5. DRC Comment: My goals for the course reflect my animating theory—they build from and support how I perceive my course within the larger scope of developing lawyering skills. I add focus on both self-awareness and the client (Worksheet 5).

In addition to this syllabus and the text, you will have access to a TWEN site that will provide you with additional readings, grading rubrics, and reflection prompts.

TWEN Site:

Interviewing, Counseling, & Negotiation

Attendance

Per law school policy, you are required to attend at least 75% of the class sessions. This requirement will be enforced. This means that out of 27 classes, you can miss 7. If you miss more than 7 classes, you cannot pass, even if you're participating fully and intentionally. To be successful you must be in class and be prepared.

On the dates for which final exercises are assigned, you need appear to class only on the day your team is slated to conduct the simulation.

Grading

Letter grades will be given for this course based on the following breakdown:

Individual Participation:	10%
Final Interviewing Simulation:	25%
Final Client Counseling Simulation:	25%
Final Negotiation Simulation & Written Agreement:	25%
Reflection Memos:	15%

The course will be graded on a +/- scale.

Class participation will be primarily voluntary. I expect that you will be prepared for class and will constructively participate on your own initiative. To be successful in the course-long simulation, you will need to research and engage with Wyoming-specific landlord-tenant laws. We will not cover the substantive law in class—that is outside work your firm will need to complete. If you have questions about the substantive law, please make an appointment to discuss them.

For the purposes of grading and performance, the class will be divided into law firms: three firms will represent a tenant and three firms will represent a landlord.

You will choose the members of your law firm and register the firm under a name of your choosing. Firms must be registered no later than Tuesday, {DATE}. The number of students in the course requires that there be 6 teams of 3 members each. I have provided you a list of class participants at the end of this Syllabus for your convenience in identifying firm members. Once the firms are registered, I will assign each firm a party to represent.

Your law firm assignments, once registered, will remain the same for all the final simulations throughout the semester. All graded simulation exercises as described above will be team or firm-wide grades; that means that everyone in the individual law firm will receive the same grade based on the team's performance during the Final Simulation Exercise. If an individual does not appear for a Final Simulation Exercise, that individual will fail the exercise and the remainder of the team will be graded as a group.

In addition, each individual member of the team will be required to write a reflective memo that will be due **one week** after the simulation is complete.[6] Reflective memos will be scored on an individual basis. The law firms will be given their grades within two weeks of each final simulation along with comments that may help you assess where your firm needs improvement or development. Reflective memos will be returned to each individual student at the same time.

For the final Simulations, you may not discuss your firm's strategy with any other firms other than as we discuss specific, limited topics in class. If your team is assigned to participate on the first day of simulation, you may not discuss the exercise with the teams scheduled for the second day until AFTER both simulations have occurred. Violation of these restrictions will be considered cheating and a violation of the Honor Code.

Individual participation grades will be based on the quality of in-class participation and individual preparedness of reading and activities.

You will be provided grading rubrics for your reflective writing exercises, class participation, and each final simulation. You can find these rubrics on the TWEN site.[7]

During the weeks of {DATE} and {DATE}, I will make specific time available to each student to meet to discuss their standing and progress in the course at mid-semester's point. Participation in mid-semester evaluations is voluntary and will not count toward the final grade. I will make a sign-up sheet available on {DATE}.

There will be no final written examination in this course, however you will be required to conduct your final negotiation simulation on {DATE}during the scheduled written exam period. I will provide the specific firm pairings and order of negotiations no later than {DATE}.

Communication

It is difficult for me to set regular office hours because of the nature of the Legal Services Clinic. If you want to speak to me about the course, your progress, or anything else, you can find me in the Annex. If you ask for time to meet, you will be given time.

Although I try to respond to e-mail questions within 24 hours of receipt, I encourage you to ask course-related questions after class or in person in my office. In addition, over the course of the semester I will ask you to evaluate both your own learning and what you would like to see in the teaching of the course. I will ask for these evaluations in writing and anonymously. I will make time for

---

6. DRC Comment: This section outlines for the students some of the situational factors/considerations of the course—because the course is as large as it is and because of constraints I often face with also directing a clinic, I cannot individually assess each student on the skills—assessments of skills must happen in groups or the time requirements would be overly burdensome (Worksheet 3 and Worksheet 7). As a result, each summative assessment consists of 2 parts—the group exercise and the individual reflection. Because reflection, feedback, and critique are built into the daily structure and conduct of the course, and because I provide the students with a detailed reflective writing rubric, I am comfortable that self-reflection and critique serve the larger course goals and provide for meaningful assessment on an individual level.

7. DRC Comment: I provide detailed rubrics for each summative assessment, class participation, and the reflective writing. The rubrics fall somewhere between a holistic rubric and an analytic rubric. The rubrics evolve every year as I get closer to a more analytic model with specific feedback (Worksheets 5–8).

During each summative assessment, I take extensive notes on the student performances within each category. When all the grading is complete, I provide the students with a copy of those notes so they can review their strengths and weaknesses.

When grading reflective writing memos, I provide written feedback on the memos. Students receive that written feedback as well.

them at the end of specific class periods as designated on the syllabus. Please participate in the evaluations so that I can improve your experience in this classroom.

Class Schedule

The schedule below is tentative. I would rather we get the material covered well than move too quickly. Your reading assignments and other items to prepare for each class meeting are described below.

Occasionally I may have to cancel or reschedule class because of court dates. I will schedule make-up classes as needed.

Date	Topic & Assignments[8]
Tuesday, August 28	**Introduction** Client-Centered Lawyering Read – Krieger & Neumann, *Essential Lawyering Skills*, Chapter 3, pages 21-32 – Wyoming Rule of Professional Conduct 1.2, 1.4
Thursday, August 30	**Lawyers as Problem-Solvers** Read – Krieger & Neumann, *Essential Lawyering Skills*, Chapter 4, pages 33-49
Tuesday, September 4	**Communications** Read – Krieger & Neumann, *Essential Lawyering Skills*, Chapter 5, pages 51-63 – Robbennolt & Sternlight, *Psychology for Lawyers*, Chapter 7, pages 141-170 (available on TWEN) Listen Julian Treasure, 5 Ways to Listen Better: www.ted.com/talks/julian_treasure_5_ways_to_listen_better Prepare Think of a time when you told a story or described a situation and the listener misunderstood what happened. In other words, the listener had a different understanding of what had happened than what you intended to convey. Consider the following: – What were the factual differences in the two understandings of the story or situation? – What factors might have contributed to these different understandings? – What strategies could the speaker and/or the listener have used to communicate more effectively? Be prepared to discuss your story and answers in class.
Thursday, September 6	**Interviewing: Question Formation** Read – Krieger & Neumann, *Essential Lawyering Skills*, Chapter 8, pages 95-121 – Robbennolt & Sternlight, *Psychology for Lawyers*, Chapter 9, pages 187-210 (available on TWEN) Prepare Prepare a list of concerns you have about effective interviewing. Bring your list to class for discussion.

8. DRC Comment: I provide a detailed list of all readings, topics, and assignments here so that the syllabus becomes an integral piece of student engagement in the class. The sequencing of units and topics within the unit is driven somewhat by the assigned text for the course and also by outside resources focused on skill developing such as the text "The Clinic Seminar" by Mlyniec, Aiken, and Epstein (Worksheet 10 and Worksheet 11).

Tuesday, September 11	**Interviewing: Litigation Clients** Read – Krieger & Neumann, *Essential Lawyering Skills*, Chapter 7, pages 83-93. – Eviction Client initial information (available on TWEN) Prepare – Develop an interview plan for the client. Use Krieger & Neumann chapters 7&8 as a guide. – Develop a list of goals you would anticipate trying to meet if you are interviewing a litigation client. Do the same for a transactional client. Bring your lists to class for discussion. – Consider what special problems might arise in the context of interviewing clients. Be prepared to discuss your answers in class.
Thursday, September 13	**Interviewing: Litigation Clients (continued)** No new assignments
Tuesday, September 18	**Interviewing: Group/Transactional Clients** Read – Paul R. Tremblay, Counseling Community Groups, 17 Clinical Law Review 389 (2010) (excerpt available on TWEN) – Community Group client initial information (available on TWEN) – Wyoming Rule of Professional Conduct 1.13 Prepare Develop an interview plan for your community group client that covers the following topics: – Opening and role identification – Eliciting client information about goals – Clarifying client priorities – Closing the meeting Consider the following questions and be prepared to discuss your answers in class: – Think about your initial client meeting from the CLIENT'S perspective. – What information does your client need from you in the context of the meeting? – What value do you think your client wishes you to add to their work? – What concerns or questions do you think your client will have regarding the client's relationship with you? – What questions or concerns is the client likely to share with you? – What is your client less likely to share? – Think about your initial client meeting from YOUR perspective. – What are your top three goals for the meeting? How do you prioritize those goals? – What value do you add for the client in the interaction? – What concerns do you have regarding your client relationship? – What concerns would you share with the client? What would you hold back? Why? – What would your next steps be after this meeting? *Distribution of Final Interviewing Simulation client initial information, background facts, and relevant legal authority.*

Thursday, September 20	**Interviewing: Witnesses** Read – Police misconduct incident information (available on TWEN) – Krieger & Neumann, *Essential Lawyering Skills*, Chapter 9, pages 123-140 Prepare – Identify a witness you would like to interview based on the incident report. Develop an interview plan for that witness. What do you need to cover and how would you approach that coverage? – How is witness interviewing different from client interviewing? – Consider how you might motivate a witness to talk to you about the facts of a case. How do your motivation techniques change if your witness is hostile or friendly? How do your motivation techniques change if your witness is indifferent? Be prepared to discuss your answers in class. *Discussion in preparation for Final Interviewing Simulation*
Tuesday, September 25	**Interviewing Final Simulation: Landlords' Attorneys**
Thursday, September 27	**Interviewing Final Simulation: Tenants' Attorneys**
Tuesday, October 2	**Theory of the Case: Developing a Theory of the Case for Your Eviction Client**[9] Read – Steven Lubet, *Murder in the Streets of Tombstone: A Legendary Theory of the Case*, Litigation 35 (Fall 2000) (excerpt available on TWEN) – Roald Hoffman, *Why Buy That Theory?*, 91 American Scientist 9 (2003) (excerpt available on TWEN) Prepare As a law firm, prepare a theory of the case for your client in the semester-long eviction matter. Your theory of the case should be no longer than 40 words. Ensure your theory reflects critical elements of your client's position, your client's biggest point of contention, and your client's primary goal. Bring your theory of the case to class for discussion. Be prepared to share your theory with the entire class. *Teaching and Learning Evaluations*[10]

9. DRC Comment: These two classes (October 2 and 4) on Case Theory and Fact Investigation do not necessarily fit into the major units of interviewing, counseling, and negotiation. I include them in my teaching priorities because they are foundational pieces in building to larger, long-term lawyer-client relationships. They are important for students to know and be able to approach mastering, but I do not include them in my enduring learning category (Worksheet 4). I perceive case theory development and fact investigation/case planning as tools to offer the students but recognize that there may be other tools they find more effective when they move out of my class and into practice. They are required to engage in the models I offer while in my classroom.

10. DRC Comment: I offer one opportunity during the semester for students to provide anonymous feedback to me on the course—I ask two questions which students answer on flashcards and turn in at the end of the class period. The questions are: i) what is working for you in the course and ii) what would you change in the how the course is presented to make it a more effective learning environment for you. I review the cards, make notes on what is working for students and what is not. To the extent I can implement some change as suggested by the information provided, I do.

Thursday, October 4

Fact Investigation

Read

- Krieger & Neumann, *Essential Lawyering Skills*, Chapter 16, pages 215-229
- Krieger & Neumann, *Essential Lawyering Skills*, Chapter 17, pages 231-235

Prepare

Answer the following questions for yourself. Be prepared to discuss your answers in class.

1) Why are facts so important to lawyering?
2) How can an attorney gather factual information?
3) What categories of factual information should a lawyer look for?
4) Which pieces of factual information should a lawyer prioritize?
5) Where can a lawyer obtain factual information?

Tuesday, October 9

Client Counseling: Introduction

Read

- Robbennolt & Sternlight, *Psychology for Lawyers*, Chapter 10, pages 211-231 (available on TWEN).

Prepare

Think of a time when you were dealing with a difficult problem and you sought advice from someone you considered knowledgeable about the issue. The context is not important—it could be a health issue, a friend/family/relationship issue, or anything else. What is important is that you asked for and received advice from someone who you considered an expert on the topic. Answer the following questions for yourself and be prepared to discuss your answers in class.

1) Putting aside the specific course of action the advice-giver recommended (if any), what was the most helpful thing that person said or did? Why was it helpful?
2) What was the least helpful thing the advice-giver said or did? Why was it unhelpful?
3) Did the advice-giver fully understand the specifics of the difficulty you were facing? If so, how did that understanding affect the quality of their advice? If not, how did the lack of understanding affect the quality of their advice?
4) Did the advice-giver fully understand your personal goals in the situation under discussion? If so, how did that understanding affect the quality of their advice? If not, how did that lack of understanding affect the quality of their advice?
5) Would you seek advice from this person again? Why or why not?

Discussion of Interviewing Final Simulation
Distribution of Mid-Semester Meeting Sign-up Sheet[11]

11. DRC Comment: I provide opportunity for students to voluntarily discuss with me how they are doing in the course. A mid-semester meeting is not required. The conversation does not include an estimate of a final grade the student is likely to earn. Rather, the mid-semester meeting is an opportunity for the students to ask questions about previous grading, express concerns, and make suggestions. Most students participate in the mid-semester meetings.

I provide this opportunity along with the anonymous teaching and learning evaluation to demonstrate to the students how important feedback is to the process of growth. I also use it to demonstrate that I am willing to engage in constructive assessments of the course and make changes when something is not working as well as I would like it to.

Thursday, October 11

Client Counseling: What do you counsel on?

Read

- Robbennolt & Sternlight, *Psychology for Lawyers*, Chapter 10, pages 232-241 (available on TWEN)
- Wyoming Rules of Professional Conduct 1.1, 1.2, 1.4, 1.16, 1.18, & 2.1
- The Case of Karen Doe (available on TWEN)
- Developing a Counseling Plan Handout

Prepare

Develop a counseling plan for Karen Doe. What questions do you feel you need to ask? What information do you need that you do not have in hand? Are there relevant statutory provisions you should consider? Why?

Tuesday, October 16

Client Counseling: Client-Centered Counseling

No assignment

Thursday, October 18

Communication Intelligence

Guest Speaker: Ariana Friedlander, Rosabella Consulting

Tuesday, October 23

Client Counseling: Option Generation

Read

- Krieger & Neumann, *Essential Lawyering Skills*, Chapter 20, pages 255-273
- Counseling Exercise: *The Sgt. Pepper Tapes* (available on TWEN)
- *Hillary Clinton Tries to End Controversy Over Private Email Account*, Los Angeles Times, March 10, 2015 (available on TWEN)
- *Clinton's Team Went from Nonchalant to Nervous Over Email Controversy*, The Washington Post, August 14, 2015 (available on TWEN)

Prepare[12]

For the *Sgt. Pepper* Tapes, consider various options, legal and non-legal, available to Pat Bronski. Be prepared to discuss your answers in class.

For the Hillary Clinton email scandal, consider the following questions: If you were Hillary Clinton's lawyer, how might you have advised her in March 2015? How might your counseling have changed between March 2015 and August 2015? What options do you see for her after August 2015? Be prepared to discuss your answers in class.

Distribution of Final Counseling Simulation
Brief Discussion of Counseling Final Simulation

12. DRC Comment: For this learning activity I provide the students the news articles ahead of time. They are expected to come prepared to discuss how counseling might have looked in the immediate aftermath as the email controversy broke. In the subsequent class this semester, I brought articles to class about the Brett Kavanaugh confirmation hearings. I provided the students in-class time to read the articles, after which we engaged in a similar in-class counseling exercise in that context. I underscored that the conversation is not designed to elicit opinions about guilt or innocence, but rather to highlight how counseling happens every day in a variety of situations and it requires detailed understanding of context and motivation to be effective (Worksheet 10).

Thursday, October 25	**Client Counseling:** Read: – *The Caught Baseball* (available on TWEN) *Distribution of Secret Facts for First Negotiation Exercise*
Tuesday, October 30	**Client Counseling Final Simulation: Tenants' Attorneys**
Thursday, November 1	**Client Counseling Final Simulation: Landlords' Attorneys**
Tuesday, November 6	**Negotiation: Introduction** Read – Krieger & Neumann, *Essential Lawyering Skills*, Chapter 23, pages 301-313 – James R. Holbrook & Benjamin J. Cook, *Advanced Negotiation & Mediation*, Chapter 1, pages 3-36 (available on TWEN) – Wyoming Uniform Rules for District Courts 801 Prepare Review the general facts and your client's secret instructions as distributed on October 25, 2018. 1. Draft a statement of the problem that is the subject of the negotiation. a. How might you want to frame this negotiation? What problem do you see as the subject here? b. Is your opponent likely to share that problem definition? c. Why or why not? d. Is there a way to frame the problem that might be agreeable to both? What would it look like? 2. In drafting the statement, identify the common ground or shared interests among the parties. a. How might these common interests guide the negotiation? b. What might you say to establish an initial focus on common interests?
Thursday, November 8	**Negotiation: Powers, Rights, & Interests** Read – Krieger & Neumann, *Essential Lawyering Skills*, Chapter 24, pages 315-331 Prepare Consider the powers, rights, and interests of both your eviction client and the opposing party. Be prepared to discuss in class the relationships between your client's powers, rights, and interests and those of the other side.
Tuesday, November 13	**Negotiation: BATNA** Read – Krieger & Neumann, *Essential Lawyering Skills*, Chapter 25, pages 333-354 – Danny Ertel, *Getting Past Yes: Negotiating as if Implementation Mattered*, Harvard Business Review 454 (November 1, 2004) (excerpt available on TWEN)

Thursday, November 15	**Negotiation: Styles & Strategies** Read – Krieger & Neumann, *Essential Lawyering Skills*, Chapter 26, pages 355-362 – Robbennolt & Sternlight, *Psychology for Lawyers*, Chapter 11, pages 275-286 *Discussion of Counseling Final Simulation*
Tuesday, November 20	**Negotiation: Writing it Down** Read – The Nand & Jeet Khemka Foundation, *Negotiating Agreements* (available on TWEN) – Michael Gregory Consulting, *Writing the Negotiated Agreement*, March 7, 2016 (available on TWEN) – Program on Negotiation, Harvard Law School, *How to Write a Contract: Three Deal-Drafting Pitfalls*, July 29, 2015 (available on TWEN) – ACTRAV Turin Labour Education Programme, Chapter 7: *Drafting the—Agreement* (e-book excerpt available on TWEN) – Checklist for Drafting Agreement, *Modern Real Estate Practice* (available on TWEN) – *Negotiating and Drafting Agreement Considerations*, Missouri Practice Guide (available on TWEN) *Distribution of Client Positions for {DATE}*
Thursday, November 22	No Class Scheduled, Thanksgiving Break
Tuesday, November 27	**Negotiation: The Lead Paint Case**
Thursday, November 29	**Negotiation: The Lead Paint Case (continued)** *Distribution of Final Simulated Negotiation Fact Patterns* *Brief Discussion of Negotiation Final Simulation*
December 13	**Negotiation Simulation** Teams and time slots to be announced 9:00 – 9:50 AM 10:00 – 10:50 AM 11:00 – 11:50 AM **Written Negotiated Agreements and Reflection Memos are due no later than 5 PM Monday {DATE}**

Chapter 8

Course Exemplars

Throughout this guide, we have used our courses to illustrate how the principles of *EL Design* become operational, providing small slices of our course worksheets. We sample courses designed for clinics, a skills course, an externship companion seminar, and a doctrinal course.

In this section, we bring together the full set of worksheets for each of the courses we have featured in the book. They provide a platform to examine the full set of design steps, from soup to nuts to see what choices were made, how steps overlap, and how the grounding and framing steps give clarity and direction to running the course.

- **Criminal Defense Clinic**, by Chris Roberts
- **Torts II**, by Danielle Cover
- **Interviewing, Counseling, and Negotiation**, by Danielle Cover
- **Disability Law Clinic**, by Carwina Weng
- **Learning from Practice—Professional Judgment Seminar** (externship companion seminar), by Meg Reuter

Course: Criminal Defense Clinic, Chris Roberts

Worksheet 1: Animating Theory

To identify the learning goals for your course, first consider the subject matter generally. Because a subject matter has more content than a course can cover, start by articulating the key reason students should take your course. That reason is your course's Animating Theory. Grant Wiggins and Jay McTighe coined a colloquial term for this, "The Big Idea."[1]

Once you choose your Animating Theory, you will flesh it out with a set of Exploratory Questions (Worksheet 2) that illuminate the challenges you want your students to grapple with. Setting the Animating Theory and Exploratory Questions allows you to build your course from course goal, to mastery evidence, to learning activities. The Animating Theory is not the same as your course goal(s) or learning outcomes; it underlies both. You may have more than one, but restrict yourself to at most two so that student learning is focused. Here, less is more.

The Animating Theory for the Course:

- Refers to core concepts, principles, and theories in a field of study—What unifies the field of study? What makes a skill worthwhile or effective?
- Organizes large bodies of information, skills, or values.
- Is amenable to transfer to new fields of study, new situations, and across disciplines.
- Is abstract and requires investigation to probe its implications.

Considerations for a Skills-focused Course:

- What does the lawyering skill help you do more effectively or efficiently for a client?
- What are the underlying concepts or objectives of the skill?
- When and how do you use the skill (strategy and tactics)?
- Why does the skill work?

Examples: The Animating Theory need not be phrased as a complete sentence. A "motto" works.

- Persuasion: Know your audience.
- Sociology: People in a community depend on each other for the things they need.
- History: History is written by the victors.
- Law: The best lawyer is the best prepared lawyer.

Identify the Animating Theory(ies) for your course.

1: The client's wishes inform the lawyer's path.
2: The best lawyer is the best-prepared lawyer.

Checklist:

- Does my animating theory provide a concise statement, principle, theory, or generalization?
- Does it stand the test of time, allowing students' thoughts about it to develop and evolve over time?

1. See Wiggins, G., & McTighe, J., UNDERSTANDING BY DESIGN (2nd ed. 2005).

- Can it promote in-depth understanding and help make sense of the subject matter?
- Can it promote in-depth understanding and help make sense of the subject matter?

CR Process Notes:

I'm working on dual tracks, looking to instill what I refer to as ethic and ethos. It's certainly possible I could articulate one animating theory that incorporates both pieces, but it's been easier to think about these as two separate (though related) ideas. My thinking is that lawyers who maintain consistent focus on serving clients and diligence about preparation will find ways to figure out what else they need to know, develop skills they need to develop, etc.

Worksheet 2: Develop Exploratory Questions

Questions are used to study the Animating Theory for the course and to ground student learning. These questions are open-ended and probing in nature rather than intended to yield specific answers.

An Exploratory Question:

- Opens the Animating Theory for the course to genuine inquiry.
- Provokes lively discussion, sustained inquiry, and new understanding, as well as more questions.
- Requires students to consider alternatives, weigh evidence, support their ideas, and justify their answers.
- Stimulates vital, on-going rethinking of assumptions, prior understanding, and personal experience.
- Naturally recurs, creating opportunities for transfer to other situations and subjects.

Examples of Exploratory Questions that amplify the value of your Animating Theory:

- Persuasion: What's in it for my audience? What are the ethics of persuasion?
- Government and public policy: What makes a good government? How does cultural identity inform one's views of government and its role in society?
- History/Precedent: What patterns recur throughout history and common law? Is all history biased?

Identify 1–2 Exploration Questions for each Animating Theory.

Animating Theory 1: The client's wishes inform the lawyer's path.

What does it mean to be client-centered?
How does one take a client-centered approach in the context of: Counseling clients Negotiations Implementing a litigation strategy Courtroom advocacy

Animating Theory 2: The best lawyer is the best-prepared lawyer.

What does "good" preparation entail?
How does one prepare for a seemingly endless list of contingencies?

Checklist:

- Are my Exploratory Questions open-ended, nonjudgmental, meaningful, and purposeful?
- Do the questions have emotional appeal?
- Do the questions have more than one coherent answer?
- Do the questions probe for deeper meaning and explore ideas and beliefs?
- Do the questions encourage peer learning and collaboration?

Worksheet 3: Identify Situational Factors That Affect Teaching and Learning

The first two Worksheets lay out the scope of the course on a grand scale. Now situate your ambitions for student learning within the realities of your course, the school's curriculum, your students' semesters, and the scope of all your responsibilities. Some of these situational factors are assets to use wisely and fruitfully. Others are limitations. Affirmatively acknowledging that, in your clinic, field placement, or simulation course, you simply cannot cover all that your students need to know, be able to do, or value will help you to make pedagogical choices to maximize student learning.

Possible situational factors

Length (e.g., semester, year), number of credits, number of hours in field, casework, or classroom	6 credits: 1 class per week that lasts 1 hour, 50 minutes + a couple of intensive sessions at the beginning of the semester + 150 hours of casework
Grading scheme	P/F
Student preparedness (typical, high/low)	Consistency of reading is not where I'd like it to be.
Student motivations	Students tend to prioritize casework, and assignments related to class can suffer from that.
Uniformity, dissimilarity, or variety of student work (in type and complexity)	Casework varies a lot. If a case goes to trial in our county court, it often takes around 2 years to get there. This long life of the case results in different experiences based on stage of case. Like any trial clinic, experience varies based on client objectives, as well.
Personal responsibilities that constrain my availability for class or individual student engagement	I supervise anywhere from 6 to 10 students each semester in their casework. Needless to say, if students are approaching trial or some other contested hearing, preparation will take a lot of time and necessarily takes priority over other aspects of the class.

Checklist:

- Do I capture factors that are opportunities for me to maximize the learning in my course?
- Do I capture the most salient factors that limit the scope of what students can reasonably learn in my course?
- Do I capture the most salient factors that limit my ability to execute a course plan and engage my students?

Worksheet 4: Prioritize Learning for Transfer (durability)

Allow your Animating Theory to percolate. Break it down into specific priorities for your students' learning. Identify the knowledge and understandings, skills, and/or values that are essential to the Animating Theory of your course. Prioritize those elements based on long-term importance to the students' learning. The highest level (enduring learning) should be learning that is transferable to different contexts in their professional lives.

Even though your course may cover content in all three levels of priority, your course goals (Worksheet 5) and final assessments (Worksheet 7) will focus on the knowledge and understandings, skills, and/or values that you intend to be long-lived (enduring) for your students.

Enduring learning:

Client-centered ethos
Good lawyering is not possible without exhaustive preparation.
Strategies for preparation (as related to counseling clients, negotiations, negotiations, trial, and other advocacy opportunities)

Important for students to know:

Strategies for preparation (as related to counseling clients, negotiations, negotiations, trial, and other advocacy opportunities)
Strategies for confronting new processes and procedures (such as court appearances, filings, etc.)

Worth being familiar with:

Trial skills
Negotiations strategy
Motions strategy
4th and 5th Amendment jurisprudence

Checklist:

- Do the elements listed as *Enduring Learning* help students to synthesize individual lessons and readings into a deeper understanding of the Animating Theory?
- Do the *Enduring Learning* elements lay a foundation for further study of this subject matter?
- Do the *Enduring Learning* elements help students to figure out issues in the subject matter that are more difficult to master?

CR Process Notes:

Worth Being Familiar With: It may be surprising to see real lynchpins of criminal defense work at the lowest priority. You just can't produce high-quality trial lawyers in a one-semester course. There are too many different aspects of the work, and the depth of understanding to get anywhere near mastery of any given aspect would be enough to fill an entire course on its own.

Important to Know: We try to teach strategies that help students prepare.

Enduring values: The animating theories.

Worksheet 5: Use Learning Taxonomies to Craft Course Goals[2]

Now that you've identified your learning priorities, you will distill the enduring learning into course goals. Course goals represent the essential i) knowledge and understandings, ii) skills, and/or iii) values that you intend your students to attain by the end of the term. One way to unify the enduring learning into goals is to ask: "How will my students be different by the end of the course?" To answer this question in a way that can be assessed at the end of the course, we have collected taxonomies of learning that capture the complexity and depth of learning you want your students to attain. The taxonomies further assist you to establish observable and measurable course goals (amenable to assessment, Worksheets 6 and 7).

The taxonomies cover the three domains of learning:

1. Cognitive domain: Focuses on knowledge, comprehension, and critical thinking.
2. Psychomotor domain: Encompasses learning geared toward executing specific tasks (*e.g.*, client counseling, negotiating with opposing counsel, witness interviewing).
3. Affective domain: Relates to awareness and growth in values, attitudes, and emotional control (*e.g.*, values embedded in the attorney-client relationship, toward justice, and relating to professional identity formation).

The taxonomy grids on the next three pages organize each domain of learning hierarchically. As you move through the grids (left to right; top to bottom) the categories describe learning at deeper levels of difficulty. Use these grids to choose the deepest point(s) that correspond to a realistic learning goal for your course.

The grids, their terminology, and hierarchy are offered as an aid. Some of your learning priorities might fit within more than one taxonomy, and the Action Verbs that exemplify a category might resonate more than the category of learning does. Choose what works for you. Don't let the taxonomies push your learning goal toward something that doesn't feel right to you. Maybe you will pencil

2. Course Development Institute, Indiana University Center for Innovative Teaching and Learning.

in learning targets for your course in several cells on separate grids; that will allow you to test out different ways to characterize the course goal(s) you want to pursue. In the end you should articulate 1–2 course goals. In drafting these goals, keep your verb singular, not compound, as a verb representing the farthest/deepest taxonomy cell that encapsulates your goal will necessarily include the less complex learning needed to reach that goal.

In the following three pages:

- Review the taxonomy for each domain.
- Reflect on your ambitions for your course. Pencil notes in any of the cells.
- Review your notes and distill them to one to two course goals (last page).

The course goals will form the bedrock for your course. Everything else—the final assessment, rubric, outcomes and learning activities—will be aligned to the course goals.

Sources:

Knowledge and Cognitive Processing Domain

Adapted from Anderson, L.W., Krathwohl, D.R. et. al. (2001). *A Taxonomy for Learning, Teaching, and Assessing: A Revision of Bloom's Taxonomy of Educational Objectives.* Abridged ed. New York: Longman.

Psychomotor Domain

Adapted from Dave, R.H. (1970), "Developing and Writing Behavioral Objectives;" Simpson E. J. (1972). The Classification of Educational Objectives in the Psychomotor Domain. Washington, DC: Gryphon House.

Affective Domain

Adapted from Krathwohl, D.R., Bloom, B.S., and Masia, B.B. (1964). *Taxonomy of Educational Objectives, Book II. Affective domain.* New York: David McKay Company, Inc.

Find taxonomies on following pages

1. Knowledge and Cognitive Processing Domain

		Cognitive processing			
		1. Remember	2. Understand	3. Apply	4. Analyze, Evaluate, or Create
Knowledge	A. Factual				
	B. Conceptual				
	C. Procedural				Students will compose persuasive narratives for use in advocacy.
	D. Meta-cognitive				

Knowledge types	Definition	Examples
Factual	Basic elements to be acquainted with the discipline and solve problems	Terminology, vocabulary, elements, and details
Conceptual	Interrelationship among basic elements	Categories, principles, theories, models, and structures
Procedural	How to do something *(overlaps with psychomotor domain)*	Subject-specific skills, methods of inquiry and criteria for using, and techniques and procedures
Meta-cognitive	Knowing about knowing	Strategic knowledge, reflections, and self-knowledge

Cognitive processing	Definition	Action Verbs
Remember	Retrieve relevant knowledge from long-term memory	Retain, recall, recognize, memorize, recollect, think of, define, identify, list, name, record, repeat, underline, select
Understand	Construct meaning from instructional messages; can be in oral, written or graphic formats	Interpret, exemplify, classify, summarize, infer, compare, explain, give examples of, describe in own words, differentiate between, discriminate, restate, review, translate, respond, practice, discuss, identify, review, simulate
Apply	Carry out procedures	Execute, implement, apply, demonstrate, dramatize, generalize, illustrate, operate, operationalize, practice, use, utilize, initiate

Analyze	Break material into parts and determine relationships	Differentiate, organize, attribute, analyze, appraise, categorize, compare, conclude, contrast, correlate, deduce, diagram, distinguish, estimate, examine, experiment, infer, predict, question, solve, diagnose
Evaluate	Make judgments based upon criteria or standards	Check, critique, assess, judge, appraise, choose, compare, evaluate, measure, rate, revise, score, select, validate, value
Create	Put elements together into coherent or functional whole, reorganize into new patterns	Generate, plan, produce, invent, arrange, assemble, collect, compose, construct, create, design, develop, formulate, manage, modify, organize, prepare, propose, synthesize

2. Psychomotor Domain: (can be used by experiential faculty to set goals for lawyering skill development)

	Definition	Action Verbs	Your Course Goals
Perception	Actively using sensory cues to attend to the behavioral skill. E.g., student observes a seasoned attorney perform the behavior.	Choose, describe, detect, differentiate, distinguish, identify, isolate, relate, select, separate	
Imitation	Copying the behavior. The student attempts the behavior, with direction and feedback from an experienced person. The student shows desire and motivation to learn the behavior.	Adhere, begin, attempt, carry out, copy, duplicate, follow, mimic, repeat, replicate, start, try	
Practice	Using the behavior repeatedly. The student performs the behavior multiple times, and her actions become more automatic and smooth. The experienced person need not be present.	Codify, discriminate, display, order, organize, systematize, weigh, discuss, theorize, formulate, balance, examine, adhere to	

Naturalization	Performing two or more skills in combination or sequence, with consistency and ease. The student can combine the behavior with other behaviors independently and with little mental exertion.	Adapt, automatize, combine, complete, demonstrate, internalize, master, perform, show, succeed	
Origination	Creating new behaviors, combinations, or sequences to respond to a new situation. The student creates new methodologies or techniques to improve on or re-imagine how the needs can be met.	Create, design, compose, refine, arrange	

3. **Affective Domain:** (can be used to set goals related to professional values, affect, or work approach, *e.g.*, with regard to the attorney client relationship, the rule of law, or other professional value)

	Definition	Action Verbs	Your Course Goals
Receive	Be aware of; attend to something; be willing to tolerate it.	Accept, attend, develop, ask, recognize, listen for, describe, differentiate, receive, identify, tolerate	
Respond	Incorporate a new behavior as a result of the experience.	Complete, comply, cooperate, discuss, examine, obey, assist, respond, follow, volunteer, perform	
Value	Show specific involvement or commitment.	Accept, defend, devote oneself to, pursue, seek, justify, join, debate, value	"Value" is my verb for the goal related to the client's wishes informing the lawyer's path. I'd love to get the students beyond this level, but I see this as the bare minimum.
Organize	Integrate a new value into one's general set of values, giving due ranking among other priorities.	Codify, discriminate, display, order, organize, systematize, weigh, discuss, theorize, formulate, balance, examine, adhere to	

Internalize the value set	Act consistently, conscientiously, and pro-actively with the new value.	Internalize, verify, be rated high in the value, require, resolve	

Using the taxonomies on the previous pages, draft your top 1–2 Course Goals:

By the end of the course, my students will:

1. Consistently seek to i) identify the client's priorities for the representation and ii) diligently pursue strategies that promote those priorities within the confines of the student-attorney's professional obligations.
2. Compose persuasive narratives for use in advocacy. A persuasive narrative: - Is developed with an understanding of applicable law. - Identifies and marshals any available facts that are likely to be helpful in convincing the applicable decision-maker. - Recognizes facts that may undermine a given narrative (and key components of potential counter-narratives) and incorporates strategic assessments of how and when to address those components. - Frames issues in recognition of a given forum's concerns. - Makes use of appropriate emotional content.

Checklist

- Do my goals fit within the Animating Theory for the course (Worksheet 1)?
- Do my goals reflect the learning priorities I have set for the course (Worksheet 4)?
- Are my goals clear, observable, and measurable (Worksheets 6 and 8)?
- Do my goals reflect the situational limits of my course and my full responsibilities (Worksheet 3)?

CR Process Notes:

The first goal relates to my first animating theory. Over time, I've moved from a goal based in knowledge or psychomotor skills into thinking of this as an affective goal. I've tried to frame it accordingly—students "consistently seeking" to do these things.

The second goal is an example of one that is simply aligned with—and will promote—my second animating theory related to preparation. Because I don't want my goal to be vague, I'm defining the word "persuasive" here.

Worksheet 6: Identify Observable Evidence of Student Mastery

Visualize the student who excels in the course you are designing. What does the student's performance or work product look like? That is your evidence of student mastery. The student's work is not at the level of a veteran attorney's; it's A-level work as a student in your course. Look at your picture closely, using the following six categories, or facets, of concrete, observable performance to assist your efforts.[3] A "masterful" student performance may well involve synchronous use of multiple facets. After you identify your evidence of mastery, then you will i) create a final assessment exercise to allow your students to exhibit this evidence (Worksheet 7) and ii) create an assessment rubric that defines levels of student performance (Worksheet 8).

Facet of understanding	Associated verbs & Starter phrases	Evidence of student's mastery in your course
Explanation: Students are able to provide thorough and well-supported accounts of topics, events, or actions, backed by reasoning, facts, or experience. Students are able to develop a theory of how and why, supported by evidence, law, and experience.	Demonstrate, derive, describe, design, exhibit, express, instruct, justify, model, predict, prove, show, synthesize, teach Students will be able to: Explain/ teach [x], Give examples of [x]; Make connections with [x]; Offer a theory of [x]; Avoid misconceptions, such as [x].	
Interpretation: Students are able to interpret and analyze the importance, meaning, or significance of their knowledge/ skill, with context and awareness of multiple interpretations. Students can create meaning from a set of facts and law, with attention to ambiguity, uncertainty, opacity, emotional content, and diverse perspectives.	Create analogies, critique, document, evaluate, illustrate, judge, make sense of, provide metaphors, read between the lines, represent, tell a story of. Students will be able to: Interpret the [x]; Tell a revealing story of [x]; Provide an apt analogy for [x]; Show the importance or meaning of [x]; Translate [x]; Relate [x] to your experience (or the experiences of others).	

3. Adapted and expanded from Wiggins, G., & McTighe, J., Understanding by Design (2nd ed. 2005) (describing six facets of understanding).

Application-Adaptation: Students use and adapt the knowledge/skill acquired to new situations and contexts, showing flexibility and adaptability. Students can design, develop, test, and refine responses to a new problem or dilemma presented.	Adapt, create, de-bug, design, exhibit, invent, perform, produce, propose, solve, test, use Students will be able to: Apply [x] in a new circumstance; Show or demonstrate [x]; Use in the context of [x]; Design/invent [x]; Overcome a challenge or constraint, such as [x].	Students will understand how statutes and case law apply to the factual circumstances of their cases. Students will be able to propose potential resolutions that take account of client priorities and, to the extent possible, address concerns of the prosecutor. Students will be able to construct persuasive narratives in the context of negotiation, trial work, motions writing, advocacy to judges, et al. Students will be able to use written preparation and mooting to prepare for negotiations, trial work, advocacy to judges, et al.
Perspective: Students can take a step back to appreciate a broader view, critically assess the value or importance of a topic. Students can identify, critique, and give credence to multiple valid perspectives regarding a topic.	Analyze, argue, compare, contrast, criticize, infer Students will be able to: Analyze [x]; See from the viewpoint of [x]; Compare and contrast [x]; Critique [x]; Critically examine assumptions such as [x]; Show how [x]; See the limits of [x].	Students will be able to identify and examine priorities of clients, prosecutors, and judges, in the context of potential case outcomes.
Empathy: Students show the ability to embrace the feelings, reasoning, motivations, and perspectives of others with acceptance and non-judgment. Open-minded insight to others.	Assume the role of, believe, be like, be open to, consider, imagine, relate, role-play. Students will be able to: Walk in the shoes of [x]; Experience directly and see [x]; Reach a common understanding with another concerning [x]; Entertain the seemingly odd or alien view that [x]; Anticipate possible concerns of others regarding [x] based on their interests, values, and circumstances.	Students will be able to consider why clients may not consistently prioritize meetings or other tasks related to their cases.

Self-Knowledge: Students accept that their style, preferences, and habits are specific to them and affect their views of events, information, and other people. Students can evaluate their professional development with appreciation of what came easily or not and why; can evaluate personal, emotional responses with detachment.	Be aware of, realize, recognize, reflect, self-assess. Students will be able to: Recognize their own prejudice(s) about [x]; Identify the lens through which they view [x]; Explain how they came to understand [x]; Realize that even with all they now know, they still don't really understand [x].	

Checklist

- Does my mastery evidence flow from my course goals and teaching priorities?
- Does my mastery evidence facilitate exploration of the Animating Theory for the course?
- Is my evidence of student mastery observable and measureable in an assessment exercise?

Worksheet 7: Create a Final Assessment Exercise

Create a final assessment exercise that will allow you to observe and evaluate each piece of mastery evidence listed. Before crafting the assessment exercise, revisit the enduring learning priorities you established (Worksheet 4) and your course goals (Worksheet 5). Use the measurable language in the goals and the mastery evidence (Worksheet 6) to create the content framework for your final assessment exercise. Note: you may use more than one assessment exercise to determine the final grade for your course.

- Choose the vehicle: a piece(s) of writing, a portfolio, an oral presentation or live performance (to professor or before another audience), etc.
- Quantity—Length: Consider how short or long the students' performance or work product should be to showcase their mastery. For instance, if you want to assess the students' level of reflection, can the students meet your expectations in 250 words, 1,000, or 5,000 words? If you want to assess the students' ability to conduct a summation for the jury, should the summation last 5 minutes, 15 minutes, 30 minutes, or more?
- Quantity—Parts: Determine the number of parts or exercises. While it might be ideal to create an assessment exercise that synthesizes the full constellation of knowledge, skills, and values represented in the course goal, often it might be impracticable to create a single assessment exercise that allows the students to produce evidence of full mastery. How would you segment the parts of the assessment?
- Practicalities: Consider the situational factors that impact what is manageable for you to assess.
- Design the subject and the prompts: This is the meat of the assessment. What are you asking your students to do? Make certain that your prompts, length, and parts will summon the work product or performance that elicits your desired mastery evidence.

Vehicle	Portfolio
Subject and prompts	Students will submit a portfolio that includes the following: 1) A mitigation packet and script for negotiation to be used in a plea-bargaining conversation with a prosecutor. These materials should include the final draft as well as any prior drafts. You will need to "show your work" in your final draft. For example, how did you decide what facts to include? What to omit? The sequence of areas for discussion? Identify any word choice that you see as particularly important and why. What do you expect to be the prosecutor's concerns and/or reactions, and how do you plan to respond to those concerns/reactions? How did you reach your conclusion as to what a reasonable request would be under the facts and circumstances of this case? 2) A sample of other written work produced in connection with your representation of a client Examples of work that would fulfill this requirement include: - A motion (note that a motion that is completely boilerplate will NOT fulfill the requirement) - Preparation for a witness statement or witness interview - Preparation for a motions hearing (i.e., questions or argument) Once you have determined what sort of sample you will submit, you should contact me to set up short conversation about what sorts of annotations may be necessary in the context of your sample. 3) Reflective essay: Please use narrative to discuss examples where you implemented a client-centered approach and where you wish you had been more client-centered in your advocacy. Instances of client-centeredness: Choose 3 of the 4 following areas: - Counseling a client; - Negotiation on behalf of a client; - Implementing an over-arching litigation strategy; and - Courtroom advocacy Questions that may be answered include (but are not limited to): (1) How did the client's wishes inform your path in this setting? (2) How did you go about identifying the client's priorities? (3) What strategy did you pursue to promote those priorities? (4) What benefit(s) (tangible and/or intangible) did the client derive from your actions? Instances for enhanced client-centeredness: Discuss an example of a situation where you wish you had been more client-centered in your advocacy. Questions that should be answered include (but are not limited to): (1) Why do you believe that you could have been more client-centered? (2) What do you think caused you to fall short? (3) How did your client react to the situation? (4) How did you address the shortfall with your client? (5) How did your shortfall affect how you moved forward with your representation? (6) If you could go back, what would you do differently? ***Later-developed alternative to reflective essay component of the portfolio*** Litigation Strategy: In consultation with your supervisor, select one of your cases, and provide a description of your case strategy. This description should be in narrative form, detailed, and annotated (describing the reasons for your choices).

Subject and prompts, (cont.)	Questions that may be answered include (but are not limited to): (1) What are the client's short- and long-term goals for the representation? (2) How have the client's wishes informed your path? (3) How have you gone about identifying the client's priorities? (4) What have you done thus far to advance the client's goals? (5) What tensions, if any, have you identified between the client's short- and long-term goals, and how have you gone about resolving dilemmas caused by those tensions? (6) If initial efforts are unsuccessful, what would you suggest doing next? (For example, if client wants a certain resolution, and you cannot obtain that resolution with your initial effort, what are the next steps?)

CR Process Notes:

As part of a continuing emphasis on preparation, I ask supervisees to submit a written document that details what they will say to the prosecutor in narrative form. We refer to that document as a "script." This practice promotes my course goal regarding narrative (and the various areas identified in that course goal).

By asking them to describe how they determined their request of the prosecutor, I'm in part fishing to make sure that they've discussed the potential resolution and know that they are pitching something that client is on board with.

The "other written work" assignment contains flexibility because of the varied casework of the students.

The reflective essays were my original ideas for additional assignments, but I have since abandoned them. I thought it might nonetheless be useful to see them. I've since decided that the litigation strategy has more utility for the clinic then the reflection that it has replaced. I also think it better assesses what I want the students to learn than the reflection would.

Worksheet 8: Prepare an Analytic Rubric

Whether your course is graded or not, you should assess each student's learning: 1) to inform the students of what they have in fact mastered or not; and 2) to inform you of your teaching effectiveness. An analytic rubric serves both purposes by imparting detailed feedback to each student and by enabling you to analyze where students are having trouble. If you give the rubric to students with the assessment exercise, the rubric also communicates your expectations so that they can self-assess their work before submitting it.

An analytic rubric is easily written as a grid:

- Vertical axis: Identify the assessment (evaluative) criteria to track the course goal and mastery evidence. You may include additional criteria not specifically tied to the course goals (e.g., writing mechanics, class participation), but do not let their grading value dilute the assessment of the course goal. Identify up to 6 criteria.
    - Describe the different elements of performance for each assessment criterion. You may include more than one element of performance in each criterion.
- Horizontal axis: Set and label the different proficiency levels. Levels can be labeled as grades, numeric ranges, or descriptors like exceptional, competent, and developing.
    - Each proficiency level for an assessment criterion should address each performance element in the assessment criterion.

Course Goal (from Worksheet 5): Students will consistently seek to (1) identify the client's priorities for the representation and (2) diligently pursue strategies that promote those priorities within the confines of the student-attorney's professional obligations.

Evaluative criterion; weighting	Highest proficiency	Mid-level proficiency	Low level proficiency
Description of background (15%)	Clear, concise, comprehensive narrative that: (1) Details relative strengths and concerns regarding the facts of the case; (2) Details relative strengths and concerns regarding the client's circumstances; (3) Addresses basic questions; and (4) Provides additional details necessary for context.	Provides adequate description of situation but lacking sufficient level of detail to provide full context.	Falls short in one or more of the following ways: (1) Fails to provide anything beyond a cursory description of situation; (2) Fails to provide more than cursory answers to basic questions; (3) Fails to use narrative form.

Quality of Strategy (40%)	(1) Steps of plan are tethered to client goals; (2) Details selection of steps in a way that describes how student selected each step, describes other options considered, and shows reasoned, logical analysis of issues presented; (3) Details efforts to be made on both fronts (trial and mitigation); (4) Describes tensions between short- and long-term goals and how the plan resolves dilemmas related to those tensions; (5) Consistently recognizes points where contingency planning is needed and details how to proceed in instances where circumstances dictate something other than the preferred course of action.	Details selection of steps in a way that describes how student selected each step, describes other options considered, shows reasoned, logical analysis of issues presented, addresses efforts to be made on both fronts (trial and mitigation); and exhibits no more than 1 of the following problems: (1) Steps appear to be aligned with goals, but the student fails to articulate how s/he anticipates how 1-2 steps advance the goal; (2) Describes tensions between short- and long-term goals but fails to detail how the plan resolves dilemmas related to those tensions; (3) Fails to recognize 1-2 points where contingency planning is needed or fails to present a viable option of how to proceed in instances where circumstances dictate something other than the preferred course of action.	Presents multiple problems (as described above) or falls short in one or more of the following ways: (1) Steps of plan are not tethered to client goals; (2) Gives cursory description of selection of steps such that strategy is not articulated clearly enough to be assessed; (3) Series of steps appears ill-suited to attain goal; (4) Fails to consider efforts to be made on one front (trial or mitigation); (5) Fails to recognize and/or balance tensions between pursuits of different goals; (6) Fails to engage in contingency planning in more than 2 instances.
Quality of Thought Process (40%)	(1) Discusses identification of client goals and priorities; (2) Identifies decision points for client and describes how client decisions informed next steps; (3) Details student-attorney's thought process in a way that describes options considered and shows appropriate depth of thinking about issues presented.	Discusses client goals and priorities, but the student exhibits one of the following problems: (1) Fails to recognize one decision point for client; (2) Next steps appear to follow logically from client decisions, but fails to detail how client decisions informed next steps; (3) Details student-attorney's thought process in a way that describes options considered but fails to exhibit depth of thought in 1-2 areas related to development of strategy.	Presents multiple problems (as described above) or falls short in one or more of the following ways: (1) Fails to recognize multiple decision points; (2) Next steps in strategy do not appear to follow from client choices; (3) Fails to describe student-attorney's thought process or fails to do so in a way that exhibits anything more than cursory thought; (4) Fails to discuss identification of client goals and priorities.

Writing Mechanics (5%)	0-2 total errors in spelling and grammar. No run-on sentences or fragments. Clear structure with transitions as appropriate. Avoids platitudes and vagaries, instead making use of fact-rich description.	3-6 total errors in spelling and grammar. 1-2 run-on sentences or fragments. Structure is clear but less than optimal in ways that should have been apparent to the writer. 1-2 missed transitions and/or platitudes.	One or more of the following problems: >6 total errors in spelling and grammar; >2 run-on sentences or fragments; structure is unclear, confusing; >2 missing transitions; > 2 instances of platitudes and/or vagaries that lack fact-based support.

Checklist:

- Does my rubric track my mastery evidence and the prompt for the final assessment exercise?
- Does my rubric align with the course goals?
- If I include criteria not related to the course goal, do they comprise a minimal part of the assessment?
- Are the evaluative criteria specific and clear?
- Are the proficiency descriptions written in neutral, clear terms using consistent terms and components across each level?

Worksheet 9: Draft Course Outcomes

In this Worksheet, you will convert your course goals into multiple learning outcomes and check whether you have achieved the right level of specificity and effectiveness for assessment purposes. Develop a maximum of 6 outcomes per course goal.

- Align each outcome to one or more specific course goal(s).
- Each outcome should be written as a single statement; do not join multiple outcomes within one statement.
- Use verbs that represent observable and measurable performance (live, written, other type of performance). For each outcome, choose the single verb that represents the deepest level of performance that you want for that outcome; avoid compound verbs.
- Because the ABA now requires at least 6 experiential credits for graduation, you might want to align any clinic, field placement, or simulation course to at least some outcomes that relate directly to both your course goals and your school's program outcomes.

Course Goal (from Worksheet 5): Consistently seek to (1) identify the client's priorities for the representation and (2) diligently pursue strategies that promote those priorities within the confines of the student-attorney's professional obligations.

Students should be able to . . .

Knowledge, skills and/or values	Verb (performance)	Object (the learning statement)	Condition and/or Criterion
	Identify	The client's goals for the representation	Accurately
	Develop	Litigation and/or negotiation strategies	That promote the goals
	Assess	How actions taken to advance one goal of the representation may adversely affect pursuit of another goal	
	Prioritize	Among competing goals (and actions taken to pursue those goals)	With guidance from the client
	Evaluate	Components of litigation and/or negotiation strategy	To determine preferred course of action given prioritized goals
	Assess	Proposed actions in light of ethical rules	To ensure compliance

Course Goal (from Worksheet 5): By the end of the course, students will compose persuasive narratives for use in advocacy.

Students should be able to . . .

Knowledge, skills and/or values	Verb (performance)	Object (the learning statement)	Condition and/or Criterion
	Apply	Relevant law to facts of case	To advance a narrative of innocence or mitigation (as applicable).
	Marshal	Facts	In a manner likely to be helpful in convincing the applicable decision-maker.
	Recognize	Facts that may undermine a given narrative	With an eye towards crafting a narrative that embraces, addresses, or mitigates those facts.
	Frame	Issues	In recognition of a given forum's concerns.

Checklist:

- Do the course outcomes describe what students should know, do, and/or value in order to complete the final assessment successfully?
- Are the course outcomes described with verbs that represent observable, measurable behaviors?
- Are the course outcomes expressed individually, not jointly?
- Do the course outcomes align with a course goal?
- Do the course outcomes align with the ABA-required program outcomes, in whole or in part? (optional)

Worksheet 10: Organize Topics and Learning Activities across the Entire Course

Once you have identified the course outcomes, start identifying the learning activities and lawyering tasks that will enable students to develop the knowledge, skills, or values necessary to achieve each outcome. These activities will then help you choose the materials for the course and to plan individual units and lessons. You will want to organize the units into a sequence that promotes effective learning through smooth and clear transitions from unit to unit.

Situational factors

Before laying out the specific learning activities, re-examine the situational factors that will enable or constrain the types of learning activities you can incorporate, when or how they should be sequenced, and the like. Some of your situational factors may include the pre-requisite knowledge, skills, or values expected of students before taking your course or the availability of a boot camp week or clinic orientation.

Models for organizing and sequencing course content

Consider generally your course's organization. The models below will help you to sequence the course topics, outcomes, and learning activities and to decide what foundation needs to be laid and when. You may combine multiple organizational models.

- *Order of importance*: Because students have highest enthusiasm for a course at the beginning, embed the most important (or difficult) concepts earliest.
- *Order of process*: Sequence material along the arc of a process, beginning to end, *e.g.*, litigation sequence (complaint to trial); attorney-client relationship (first meeting through resolution of the matter; first meeting to transition to the next student-lawyer).
- *Simple to complex*: Because students can build confidence in mastering simple topics and skills, start with these before tackling higher level, more complex tasks.
- *Dependent or supportive relationship between units of study*: If the learning is cumulative, start with the concepts or skills that represent pre-requisite knowledge or skill necessary (or helpful) for later units.
- *Cause & Effect:* Introduce a range of problems and then follow with types of solutions to be applied (*e.g.*, claims and remedies).
- *Spiral or cyclical*: Introduce and revisit concepts or skills multiple times throughout the term, adding complexity with each repetition.
- *General to specific vs. Concrete to abstract*: Introduce general principles & then apply to specific situations. Alternatively, start with specific examples of a phenomenon and move toward what they represent at the conceptual or abstract level.
- *Thematic or topical:* Use when individual units represent independent concepts. Plan transitions carefully. (*e.g.*, a survey course.)

ABA experiential course design standards

Standard 304 provides the elements that any course intended to be counted toward the experiential graduation requirement must have. For each mode of skills teaching (simulation, clinic, externship) Standard 304 includes additional requirements.

Std. 304 (a): Experiential courses [include] simulation courses, law clinics, and field placements that must be primarily experiential in nature and must:

1) Integrate doctrine, theory, skills, and legal ethics, and engage students in performance of one or more of the professional skills identified in Standard 302;
2) Develop the concepts underlying the professional skills being taught;
3) Provide multiple opportunities for performance;
4) Provide opportunities for student performance, self-evaluation, and feedback from a faculty member, or, for a field placement, a site supervisor;
5) A classroom instructional component; or, for a field placement, a classroom instructional component, regularly scheduled tutorials, or other means of ongoing, contemporaneous, faculty-guided reflection; and
6) Provide direct supervision of the student's performance by the faculty member; or, for a field placement, provide direct supervision of the student's performance by a faculty member or a site supervisor.

Topic	Course outcomes in measurable terms	Learning activities / Lawyering tasks	Materials to aid student performance
	What will students be able to think, do, or value to complete the final assessment successfully? Use info developed in Worksheet 9. Organize in a coherent sequence. **By the end of the semester, students will be able to:**	What exercises, performances, discussions, or other learning activity will help students to prepare for and succeed in the final assessment? Identify whether an activity is designed as an introduction (I), practice opportunity (P), or mastery vehicle (M).	What readings, media, information, lecture, and other aids will my students need to perform the lawyering and learning activities successfully? Will it be used before, during, or after the class?
	Apply relevant law to facts of case to advance a narrative of innocence or mitigation (as applicable).	Review of fact pattern and elements of offense to discuss potential defense theories. (Introduced)	Reading on defense theory. Lecture/Class Discussion on Narrative, Theory, and Theme
		Mock negotiation (Introduced/ Practiced)	Review of sample problem and basic rubric for thinking about negotiation.
		Write and deliver opening statement based on a current clinic case. (Practiced)	Reading on opening statements. Lecture/Class Discussion on Opening Statements

Checklist:

- Do the course materials, learning activities, and lawyering tasks provide sufficient foundation for student progress toward course mastery?
- Does the order of materials, learning activities, and lawyering tasks allow my students to apply their learning repeatedly, to make progress toward mastery of the course outcomes?
- Do the learning exercises and lawyering activities include ones where I expect course mastery for each Enduring Learning element (Worksheet 4)?

- Do the course materials, learning activities, and lawyering tasks allow my students to consider the Animating Theory and Exploratory Questions for the course on multiple occasions throughout the semester (Worksheets 1 and 2)?
- Do the learning activities and lawyering tasks cover each criterion in ABA Standards 304 (as applied to all experiential courses and to the provisions specific to my type of course)??

CR Process Notes:

We have generally followed order of process, but I want to take a step back and determine whether something closer to "simple to complex" may be more useful (or could be successfully integrated into our order of process, as the closer to trial we get, the more complex things tend to get).

The effort to apply relevant law will recur over many aspects of our work and appears over multiple units, and some examples have been given in the chart above.

Worksheet 11: Plan Units of Student Learning Activities

For each unit (a single topic/learning activity or chunk of topics or activities), create a plan for work that your students will do before, during, and after class. Make sure that you identify how you will "know" that the students learned what you planned. That might be your own reflection and assessment at the end of the class, supervision, or unit, or it might be some other evidence of student learning (whether direct from the student, or indirect from another source).

Course Unit: Narrative

Relevant Course Outcomes (from Worksheet 9):

Apply relevant law to facts of case to advance a narrative of innocence or mitigation (as applicable).

How will students prepare for the unit/class?	What will students do in class to prepare them to reach the outcomes?	How will I know they learned what I wanted them to learn?
Reading: *The Defense "Theory of the Case": A Flexible Blueprint for Trial Preparation*, an excerpt from a chapter from Trial Manual for Defense Attorneys in Juvenile Delinquency Cases by Hertz, Guggenheim, & Amsterdam. Reading: *Your First Misdemeanor* (case simulation) Reading: Opening Statements: A Roadmap to Victory, from the Gideon's Promise Training Manual (co-authored by Todd Edelman).	Review of fact pattern and elements of offense to discuss potential defense theories (Introduced/Practiced) Mock negotiation (Introduced/Practiced) Write and deliver opening statement based on a current clinic case. (Practiced)	Assess using rubric related to legal narrative. Assess using rubrics related to legal narrative and negotiation. Assess using rubrics related to legal narrative and opening statements.

Checklist:

- Do the unit activities align with one or more of my course's learning outcomes?
- Do the unit activities have a clear purpose to help students learn?
- Is the unit structured to build on existing learning, give clear direction, and give opportunity to practice what students are expected to do?
- Do the unit activities give students time to develop their own thoughts and positions, and to hear others' ideas, perspectives, or positions?
- Do I hold my students accountable for doing the activity, including by giving them feedback?
- Do I provide opportunity for students to reflect on the activities and connect them to their prior learning?

CR Process Notes:

I've been sort of basic in framing the "Course Unit" for the purposes of this worksheet. As with Worksheet 10 and application of the law to fact patterns, I've selected a topic that is developed in multiple sessions. Narrative is at the heart of our subject matter and is one of the overarching course goals, and the notes above are from three different classes, each of which involves the application of narrative techniques in a different context.

Course: Torts II, Danielle Cover

Worksheet 1: Animating Theory

To identify the learning goals for your course, first consider the subject matter generally. Because a subject matter has more content than a course can cover, start by articulating the key reason students should take your course. That reason is your course's Animating Theory. Grant Wiggins and Jay McTighe coined a colloquial term for this, "The Big Idea."[4]

Once you choose your Animating Theory, you will flesh it out with a set of Exploratory Questions (Worksheet 2) that illuminate the challenges you want your students to grapple with. Setting the Animating Theory and Exploratory Questions allows you to build your course from course goal, to mastery evidence, to learning activities. The Animating Theory is not the same as your course goal(s) or learning outcomes; it underlies both. You may have more than one, but restrict yourself to at most two so that student learning is focused. Here, less is more.

The Animating Theory for the Course:

- Refers to core concepts, principles, and theories in a field of study—What unifies the field of study? What makes a skill worthwhile or effective?
- Organizes large bodies of information, skills, or values.
- Is amenable to transfer to new fields of study, new situations, and across disciplines.
- Is abstract and requires investigation to probe its implications.

Considerations for a Skills-focused Course:

- What does the lawyering skill help you do more effectively or efficiently for a client?
- What are the underlying concepts or objectives of the skill?
- When and how do you use the skill (strategy and tactics)?
- Why does the skill work?

Examples: The Animating Theory need not be phrased as a complete sentence. A "motto" works.

- Persuasion: Know your audience.
- Sociology: People in a community depend on each other for the things they need.
- History: History is written by the victors.
- Law: The best lawyer is the best prepared lawyer.

Identify the Animating Theory(ies) for your course.

Who writes the check?
Effective lawyering entails being able to identify competing perspectives and arguments given a factual framework and applicable law.

Checklist:

- Does my animating theory provide a concise statement, principle, theory, or generalization?

4. See Wiggins, G., & McTighe, J., UNDERSTANDING BY DESIGN (2nd ed. 2005).

- Does it stand the test of time, allowing students' thoughts about it to develop and evolve over time?
- Can it promote in-depth understanding and help make sense of the subject matter?
- Can it promote in-depth understanding and help make sense of the subject matter?

DRC Process Notes:

In the first semester of torts students focus on intentional torts and negligence. I start the torts II curriculum with more complicated theories of liability including multiple tortfeasors and vicarious liability. The course also includes strict liability, negligence, and some products liability. "Who writes the check?" is the easiest distillation of this variety of complex liability frameworks. (As a side note, as I develop a Judicial Remedies course, I have been using the animating theory "How big is the {metaphorical} check?" to engage the students in analyzing how you identify and define appropriate remedial approaches to hypothetical problems.)

The second animating theory reflects a more practice-oriented approach to teaching a doctrinal course—I expect the students to engage in analyzing provided hypothetical facts from multiple perspectives in much the same way opposing counsel would.

Worksheet 2: Develop Exploratory Questions

Questions are used to study the Animating Theory for the course and to ground student learning. These questions are open-ended and probing in nature rather than intended to yield specific answers.

An Exploratory Question:

- Opens the Animating Theory for the course to genuine inquiry.
- Provokes lively discussion, sustained inquiry, and new understanding, as well as more questions.
- Requires students to consider alternatives, weigh evidence, support their ideas, and justify their answers.
- Stimulates vital, on-going rethinking of assumptions, prior understanding, and personal experience.
- Naturally recurs, creating opportunities for transfer to other situations and subjects.

Examples of Exploratory Questions that amplify the value of your Animating Theory:

- Persuasion: What's in it for my audience? What are the ethics of persuasion?
- Government and public policy: What makes a good government? How does cultural identity inform one's views of government and its role in society?
- History/Precedent: What patterns recur throughout history and common law? Is all history biased?

Identify 1–2 Exploration Questions for each Animating Theory.

Animating Theory 1: Who writes the check?

Why do we care who should be financially responsible for tortious interactions?
How does the human aspect of analyzing tortious conduct influence how we value injury and liability?
Why do we decide one tortfeasor is liable and one is not for engaging in identical tortious conduct?

Animating Theory 2: Effective lawyering entails being able to identify competing perspectives and arguments given a factual framework and applicable law.

Why might it be important to view case analysis as perspective-based and not just application of facts to elements or factors?
Why might it be important to analyze cases from competing perspectives?
How does the human aspect of lawyering impact advocacy?

Checklist:

- Are my Exploratory Questions open-ended, nonjudgmental, meaningful, and purposeful?
- Do the questions have emotional appeal?
- Do the questions have more than one coherent answer?
- Do the questions probe for deeper meaning and explore ideas and beliefs?
- Do the questions encourage peer learning and collaboration?

DRC Process Notes:

Torts II covers complex tort theory including multiple tortfeasors and vicarious liability. The question of who is responsible to pay for the injury is critical to the course. I hope to use these exploratory questions as a foundation for building case theory without introducing that term. Throughout the course, I work the students toward case theory development, but learned early on that many students were freaked out when I suggested we would be working on more than just complex theories of tort liability.

Worksheet 3: Identify Situational Factors That Affect Teaching and Learning

The first two Worksheets lay out the scope of the course on a grand scale. Now situate your ambitions for student learning within the realities of your course, the school's curriculum, your students' semesters, and the scope of all your responsibilities. Some of these situational factors are assets to use wisely and fruitfully. Others are limitations. Affirmatively acknowledging that, in your clinic, field placement, or simulation course, you simply cannot cover all that your students need to know, be able to do, or value will help you to make pedagogical choices to maximize student learning.

Possible situational factors

Length (e.g., semester, year), number of credits, number of hours in field, casework, or classroom	2 credit/2-hour course taught in 2 1-hour segments per week
Grading scheme	+/- scaled grading with curve
Student preparedness (typical, high/low)	Students have taken Torts I with a different professor in their first semester as well as Property I. As a result, they are familiar with intentional torts, negligence, and some nuisance law. Most students have not had exposure to theories of multiple tortfeasor liability, vicarious liability, and products liability.
Student motivations	The course is a required second semester/first year course.
Uniformity, dissimilarity, or variety of student work (in type and complexity)	Entirely uniform
Personal responsibilities that constrain my availability for class or individual student engagement	I also direct a litigation clinic, scheduling for which sometimes impacts availability to teach during scheduled times and office hours. Students have complained in the past about rescheduling class times.
Continuity with previous faculty	Inherited the text from the first semester professor—feel the need to keep the book because of student comfort with it and keeping textbook costs low.
Changing law and student capacity	Level of nuance and complication in the new, potentially less straightforward liability theories may be hard for some students to process.
Class size	80-90 students per class (the entire first year class); Small sections not available as an option because of faculty size, class size, and clinic responsibilities.

Checklist:

- Do I capture factors that are opportunities for me to maximize the learning in my course?
- Do I capture the most salient factors that limit the scope of what students can reasonably learn in my course?
- Do I capture the most salient factors that limit my ability to execute a course plan and engage my students?

Worksheet 4: Prioritize Learning for Transfer (durability)

Allow your Animating Theory to percolate. Break it down into specific priorities for your students' learning. Identify the knowledge and understandings, skills, and/or values that are essential to the Animating Theory of your course. Prioritize those elements based on long-term importance to the students' learning. The highest level (enduring learning) should be learning that is transferable to different contexts in their professional lives.

Even though your course may cover content in all three levels of priority, your course goals (Worksheet 5) and final assessments (Worksheet 7) will focus on the knowledge and understandings, skills, and/or values that you intend to be long-lived (enduring) for your students.

Enduring learning:

Ability to apply facts to elements/factors from both plaintiff's and defendant's perspectives. *(What will students do?)*
Skill—perspective taking and problem solving
Value—human centeredness, collaboration

Important for students to know:

Lawyering and advocacy are different skills than memorization and recitation *(What will they value?)*
Ability to recall elements/factors of complicated liability schemes/issue spot. *(What will they know?)*
Liability is not predetermined. *(What will they value?)*

Worth being familiar with:

Foundational principles of assessing damages. *(What will they know?)*
Tort law has common principles but the practice is jurisdiction specific. *(What will they value?)*

Checklist:

- Do the elements listed as *Enduring Learning* help students to synthesize individual lessons and readings into a deeper understanding of the Animating Theory?
- Do the *Enduring Learning* elements lay a foundation for further study of this subject matter?
- Do the *Enduring Learning* elements help students to figure out issues in the subject matter that are more difficult to master?

DRC Process Notes:

While this may run contrary to traditional perspectives on doctrinal teaching, I view the course as an early step toward developing practice-oriented skills. The students will need to know elements and factors of specific torts for the bar exam, but upon graduation will be faced with a different schema for approaching the problem-solving that defines lawyering, no matter the practice context.

Based on my comment above, I stress ability to issue spot and discuss elements and factors of specific torts, but it is not my focus in terms of transferrable skills. Issue spotting is also a critical lawyering skill, however, I place it in "Important to Know" because it is a skill they are practicing in other doctrinal courses.

Worksheet 5: Use Learning Taxonomies to Craft Course Goals[5]

Now that you've identified your learning priorities, you will distill the enduring learning into course goals. Course goals represent the essential i) knowledge and understandings, ii) skills, and/or iii) values that you intend your students to attain by the end of the term. One way to unify the enduring learning into goals is to ask: "How will my students be different by the end of the course?" To answer this question in a way that can be assessed at the end of the course, we have collected taxonomies of learning that capture the complexity and depth of learning you want your students to attain. The taxonomies further assist you to establish observable and measurable course goals (amenable to assessment, Worksheets 6 and 7).

The taxonomies cover the three domains of learning:

1. Cognitive domain: Focuses on knowledge, comprehension, and critical thinking.
2. Psychomotor domain: Encompasses learning geared toward executing specific tasks (*e.g.*, client counseling, negotiating with opposing counsel, witness interviewing).
3. Affective domain: Relates to awareness and growth in values, attitudes, and emotional control (*e.g.*, values embedded in the attorney-client relationship, toward justice, and relating to professional identity formation).

The taxonomy grids on the next three pages organize each domain of learning hierarchically. As you move through the grids (left to right; top to bottom) the categories describe learning at deeper levels of difficulty. Use these grids to choose the deepest point(s) that correspond to a realistic learning goal for your course.

5. Course Development Institute, Indiana University Center for Innovative Teaching and Learning.

The grids, their terminology, and hierarchy are offered as an aid. Some of your learning priorities might fit within more than one taxonomy, and the Action Verbs that exemplify a category might resonate more than the category of learning does. Choose what works for you. Don't let the taxonomies push your learning goal toward something that doesn't feel right to you. Maybe you will pencil in learning targets for your course in several cells on separate grids; that will allow you to test out different ways to characterize the course goal(s) you want to pursue. In the end you should articulate 1–2 course goals. In drafting these goals, keep your verb singular, not compound, as a verb representing the farthest/deepest taxonomy cell that encapsulates your goal will necessarily include the less complex learning needed to reach that goal.

In the following three pages:

- Review the taxonomy for each domain.
- Reflect on your ambitions for your course. Pencil notes in any of the cells.
- Review your notes and distill them to one to two course goals (last page).

The course goals will form the bedrock for your course. Everything else—the final assessment, rubric, outcomes and learning activities—will be aligned to the course goals.

Sources:

Knowledge and Cognitive Processing Domain

Adapted from Anderson, L.W., Krathwohl, D.R. et. al. (2001). *A Taxonomy for Learning, Teaching, and Assessing: A Revision of Bloom's Taxonomy of Educational Objectives.* Abridged ed. New York: Longman.

Psychomotor Domain

Adapted from Dave, R.H. (1970), "Developing and Writing Behavioral Objectives;" Simpson E. J. (1972). The Classification of Educational Objectives in the Psychomotor Domain. Washington, DC: Gryphon House.

Affective Domain

Adapted from Krathwohl, D.R., Bloom, B.S., and Masia, B.B. (1964). *Taxonomy of Educational Objectives, Book II. Affective domain.* New York: David McKay Company, Inc.

Find taxonomies on following pages

1. Knowledge and Cognitive Processing Domain

Knowledge		Cognitive processing: 1. Remember	2. Understand	3. Apply	4. Analyze, Evaluate, or Create
Knowledge	A. Factual	Recall elements/ factors of complex torts and liability theories	Describe in their own words why someone is liable	Pull hypothetical facts from a problem and analyze relative to elements/factors/ theories	Contrast discordant facts relative to elements/factors/ theories; Identify what facts matter to plaintiffs and defendants; compose arguments based on an assigned perspective
	B. Conceptual	Remember that facts are often flexible/arguable relative to the tort theory	Factor-based analysis of facts can change based on whether you are representing the plaintiff or the defendant	Adjust analysis when provided additional or different facts	
	C. Procedural				
	D. Meta-cognitive				

Knowledge types	Definition	Examples
Factual	Basic elements to be acquainted with the discipline and solve problems	Terminology, vocabulary, elements, and details
Conceptual	Interrelationship among basic elements	Categories, principles, theories, models, and structures
Procedural	How to do something *(overlaps with psychomotor domain)*	Subject-specific skills, methods of inquiry and criteria for using, and techniques and procedures
Meta-cognitive	Knowing about knowing	Strategic knowledge, reflections, and self-knowledge

Cognitive processing	Definition	Action Verbs
Remember	Retrieve relevant knowledge from long-term memory	Retain, recall, recognize, memorize, recollect, think of, define, identify, list, name, record, repeat, underline, select
Understand	Construct meaning from instructional messages; can be in oral, written or graphic formats	Interpret, exemplify, classify, summarize, infer, compare, explain, give examples of, describe in own words, differentiate between, discriminate, restate, review, translate, respond, practice, discuss, identify, review, simulate
Apply	Carry out procedures	Execute, implement, apply, demonstrate, dramatize, generalize, illustrate, operate, operationalize, practice, use, utilize, initiate
Analyze	Break material into parts and determine relationships	Differentiate, organize, attribute, analyze, appraise, categorize, compare, conclude, contrast, correlate, deduce, diagram, distinguish, estimate, examine, experiment, infer, predict, question, solve, diagnose
Evaluate	Make judgments based upon criteria or standards	Check, critique, assess, judge, appraise, choose, compare, evaluate, measure, rate, revise, score, select, validate, value
Create	Put elements together into coherent or functional whole, reorganize into new patterns	Generate, plan, produce, invent, arrange, assemble, collect, compose, construct, create, design, develop, formulate, manage, modify, organize, prepare, propose, synthesize

2. Psychomotor Domain: (can be used by experiential faculty to set goals for lawyering skill development)

	Definition	Action Verbs	Your Course Goals
Perception	Actively using sensory cues to attend to the behavioral skill. E.g., student observes a seasoned attorney perform the behavior.	Choose, describe, detect, differentiate, distinguish, identify, isolate, relate, select, separate	Even when not assigned to a specific position in the conflict, be able to distinguish facts that support one position or another (relative to the elements/factors); particularly relevant in the factor-based analyses (which factors does one highlight or downplay)
Imitation	Copying the behavior. The student attempts the behavior, with direction and feedback from an experienced person. The student shows desire and motivation to learn the behavior.	Adhere, begin, attempt, carry out, copy, duplicate, follow, mimic, repeat, replicate, start, try	Attempt to articulate a position as assigned

Practice	Using the behavior repeatedly. The student performs the behavior multiple times, and her actions become more automatic and smooth. The experienced person need not be present.	Codify, discriminate, display, order, organize, systematize, weigh, discuss, theorize, formulate, balance, examine, adhere to	Discuss why and how a fact supports or undermines a position; engage with colleagues about differences of opinion in weighing importance of provided facts.
Naturalization	Performing two or more skills in combination or sequence, with consistency and ease. The student can combine the behavior with other behaviors independently and with little mental exertion.	Adapt, automatize, combine, complete, demonstrate, internalize, master, perform, show, succeed	Student reflexively/automatically approaches hypotheticals from a "there may not be one right answer" perspective
Origination	Creating new behaviors, combinations, or sequences to respond to a new situation. The student creates new methodologies or techniques to improve on or re-imagine how the needs can be met.	Create, design, compose, refine, arrange	Student is able to compose a position based on a perspective and articulate with clarity how and why their assigned position is superior to the opposing position

3. **Affective Domain:** (can be used to set goals related to professional values, affect, or work approach, *e.g.*, with regard to the attorney client relationship, the rule of law, or other professional value)

	Definition	Action Verbs	Your Course Goals
Receive	Be aware of; attend to something; be willing to tolerate it.	Accept, attend, develop, ask, recognize, listen for, describe, differentiate, receive, identify, tolerate	Student learns to be comfortable with taking a position and advocating for it not necessarily looking for one right answer.
Respond	Incorporate a new behavior as a result of the experience.	Complete, comply, cooperate, discuss, examine, obey, assist, respond, follow, volunteer, perform	
Value	Show specific involvement or commitment.	Accept, defend, devote oneself to, pursue, seek, justify, join, debate, value	Student can accept that fact-based lawyering work often requires looking at discordant realities and recognize that multiple realities can exist within one factual scenario.

Organize	Integrate a new value into one's general set of values, giving due ranking among other priorities.	Codify, discriminate, display, order, organize, systematize, weigh, discuss, theorize, formulate, balance, examine, adhere to	
Internalize the value set	Act consistently, conscientiously, and pro-actively with the new value.	Internalize, verify, be rated high in the value, require, resolve	

Using the taxonomies on the previous pages, draft your top 1–2 Course Goals:

By the end of the course, my students will:

1. Students will be able to contextualize torts (personal injury practice) as a practice focused on how lawyers select and use facts to make their case within the confines of the law.
2. Student is able to compose a position based on a perspective and articulate with clarity how and why their assigned position is superior to the opposing position.

Checklist

- Do my goals fit within the Animating Theory for the course (Worksheet 1)?
- Do my goals reflect the learning priorities I have set for the course (Worksheet 4)?
- Are my goals clear, observable, and measurable (Worksheets 6 and 8)?
- Do my goals reflect the situational limits of my course and my full responsibilities (Worksheet 3)?

DRC Process Notes:

It is my opinion that the skill of factual assessment has both cognitive and psychomotor components and can fall squarely in either domain. Particularly in the "imitation" and "practice" categories, the "I do, we do, you do" methodology works well to support students in taking risks in class.

Worksheet 6: Identify Observable Evidence of Student Mastery

Visualize the student who excels in the course you are designing. What does the student's performance or work product look like? That is your evidence of student mastery. The student's work is not at the level of a veteran attorney's; it's A-level work as a student in your course. Look at your picture closely, using the following six categories, or facets, of concrete, observable performance to assist your efforts.[6] A "masterful" student performance may well involve synchronous use of multiple facets. After you identify your evidence of mastery, then you will i) create a final assessment exercise to allow your students to exhibit this evidence (Worksheet 7) and ii) create an assessment rubric that defines levels of student performance (Worksheet 8).

Facet of understanding	Associated verbs & Starter phrases	Evidence of student's mastery in your course
Explanation: Students are able to provide thorough and well-supported accounts of topics, events, or actions, backed by reasoning, facts, or experience. Students are able to develop a theory of how and why, supported by evidence, law, and experience.	Demonstrate, derive, describe, design, exhibit, express, instruct, justify, model, predict, prove, show, synthesize, teach Students will be able to: Explain/teach [x], Give examples of [x]; Make connections with [x]; Offer a theory of [x]; Avoid misconceptions, such as [x].	Issue spot consistently (recall of elements/factors/triggers for the tort) in hypotheticals; connect hypothetical facts to elements/factors
Interpretation: Students are able to interpret and analyze the importance, meaning, or significance of their knowledge/skill, with context and awareness of multiple interpretations. Students can create meaning from a set of facts and law, with attention to ambiguity, uncertainty, opacity, emotional content, and diverse perspectives.	Create analogies, critique, document, evaluate, illustrate, judge, make sense of, provide metaphors, read between the lines, represent, tell a story of. Students will be able to: Interpret the [x]; Tell a revealing story of [x]; Provide an apt analogy for [x]; Show the importance or meaning of [x]; Translate [x]; Relate [x] to your experience (or the experiences of others).	Identify basic reasoning behind rulings in case book cases; attach significance to facts chosen by majority to support opinion
Application-Adaptation: Students use and adapt the knowledge/skill acquired to new situations and contexts, showing flexibility and adaptability. Students can design, develop, test, and refine responses to a new problem or dilemma presented.	Adapt, create, de-bug, design, exhibit, invent, perform, produce, propose, solve, test, use Students will be able to: Apply [x] in a new circumstance; Show or demonstrate [x]; Use in the context of [x]; Design/invent [x]; Overcome a challenge or constraint, such as [x].	Hypothesize/brainstorm facts and/or arguments that would have supported a ruling contrary to the majority opinion

6. Adapted and expanded from Wiggins, G., & McTighe, J., UNDERSTANDING BY DESIGN (2nd ed. 2005) (describing six facets of understanding).

Perspective: Students can take a step back to appreciate a broader view, critically assess the value or importance of a topic. Students can identify, critique, and give credence to multiple valid perspectives regarding a topic.	Analyze, argue, compare, contrast, criticize, infer Students will be able to: Analyze [x]; See from the viewpoint of [x]; Compare and contrast [x]; Critique [x]; Critically examine assumptions such as [x]; Show how [x]; See the limits of [x].	Alternate perspectives from Plaintiff side to Defendant side; highlight facts that support each in complex hypothetical scenarios (either discordant facts or same facts with a different focus)
Empathy: Students show the ability to embrace the feelings, reasoning, motivations, and perspectives of others with acceptance and non-judgment. Open-minded insight to others.	Assume the role of, believe, be like, be open to, consider, imagine, relate, role-play. Students will be able to: Walk in the shoes of [x]; Experience directly and see [x]; Reach a common understanding with another concerning [x]; Entertain the seemingly odd or alien view that [x]; Anticipate possible concerns of others regarding [x] based on their interests, values, and circumstances.	
Self-Knowledge: Students accept that their style, preferences, and habits are specific to them and affect their views of events, information, and other people. Students can evaluate their professional development with appreciation of what came easily or not and why; can evaluate personal, emotional responses with detachment.	Be aware of, realize, recognize, reflect, self-assess. Students will be able to: Recognize their own prejudice(s) about [x]; Identify the lens through which they view [x]; Explain how they came to understand [x]; Realize that even with all they now know, they still don't really understand [x].	Recognize how assignment to the Plaintiff side or Defendant side of a scenario impacts reading and interpretation of facts; reflect on potential biases in interpreting facts

Checklist

- Does my mastery evidence flow from my course goals and teaching priorities?
- Does my mastery evidence facilitate exploration of the Animating Theory for the course?
- Is my evidence of student mastery observable and measureable in an assessment exercise?

Worksheet 7: Create a Final Assessment Exercise

Create a final assessment exercise that will allow you to observe and evaluate each piece of mastery evidence listed. Before crafting the assessment exercise, revisit the enduring learning priorities you established (Worksheet 4) and your course goals (Worksheet 5). Use the measurable language in the goals and the mastery evidence (Worksheet 6) to create the content framework for your final assessment exercise. Note: you may use more than one assessment exercise to determine the final grade for your course.

- Choose the vehicle: a piece(s) of writing, a portfolio, an oral presentation or live performance (to professor or before another audience), etc.
- Quantity—Length: Consider how short or long the students' performance or work product should be to showcase their mastery. For instance, if you want to assess the students' level of reflection, can the students meet your expectations in 250 words, 1,000, or 5,000 words? If you want to assess the students' ability to conduct a summation for the jury, should the summation last 5 minutes, 15 minutes, 30 minutes, or more?
- Quantity—Parts: Determine the number of parts or exercises. While it might be ideal to create an assessment exercise that synthesizes the full constellation of knowledge, skills, and values represented in the course goal, often it might be impracticable to create a single assessment exercise that allows the students to produce evidence of full mastery. How would you segment the parts of the assessment?
- Practicalities: Consider the situational factors that impact what is manageable for you to assess.
- Design the subject and the prompts: This is the meat of the assessment. What are you asking your students to do? Make certain that your prompts, length, and parts will summon the work product or performance that elicits your desired mastery evidence.

Vehicle	Final take home exam
Quantity (length, parts)	72 hours to complete from pick up, one question
Timing/sequence	During exam period.
Practicalities	Exam software considerations Honor Code considerations Open book Distill majority opinion to digestible/manageable length Facts must include both sides not just findings
Subject and prompts	Complex public nuisance case on lead paint poisoning (based on actual case from California) Provide edited majority opinion declaring lead paint manufacture a public nuisance Prompt: review factual summary/majority opinion and write a dissenting opinion arguing that lead paint manufacture is not a public nuisance

DRC Process Notes:

I borrowed the idea for my final assessment from a law teaching guide when I first began teaching torts in 2015; I don't remember which one. I did not, at that time, use the backward design process for creating classes, it just seemed like an interesting and challenging way to assess. As I began to work through the model that eventually became EL, I went back several times to this assessment tool, not wanting to give it up, to ensure that what I wanted out of the course and how I was assessing it were aligned.

Worksheet 8: Prepare an Analytic Rubric

Whether your course is graded or not, you should assess each student's learning: 1) to inform the students of what they have in fact mastered or not; and 2) to inform you of your teaching effectiveness. An analytic rubric serves both purposes by imparting detailed feedback to each student and by enabling you to analyze where students are having trouble. If you give the rubric to students with the assessment exercise, the rubric also communicates your expectations so that they can self-assess their work before submitting it.

An analytic rubric is easily written as a grid:

- Vertical axis: Identify the assessment (evaluative) criteria to track the course goal and mastery evidence. You may include additional criteria not specifically tied to the course goals (e.g., writing mechanics, class participation), but do not let their grading value dilute the assessment of the course goal. Identify up to 6 criteria.
  - Describe the different elements of performance for each assessment criterion. You may include more than one element of performance in each criterion.
- Horizontal axis: Set and label the different proficiency levels. Levels can be labeled as grades, numeric ranges, or descriptors like exceptional, competent, and developing.
  - Each proficiency level for an assessment criterion should address each performance element in the assessment criterion.

Course Goal (from Worksheet 5): Student is able to compose a position based on a perspective and articulate with clarity how and why their assigned position is superior to the opposing position.

Evaluative criterion; weighting	Highest proficiency	Mid-level proficiency	Low level proficiency
Recognize applicable law and standards (10%)	Identifies the applicable tort standards (the broad primary category of nuisance is provided) to use in analyzing the problem; Identifies all secondary tort issues/standards that might also apply.	Identifies the applicable tort standards (the broad primary category of nuisance is provided) to use in analyzing the problem; Identifies all but 1 or 2 of the secondary issues.	Identifies the applicable tort standards (the broad primary category of nuisance is provided) to use in analyzing the problem; Identifies most of the secondary issues that might apply, misses 3 or more.
Identify basic premises of majority opinion (10%)	Clearly articulates with restatement support the basis and reasoning of the majority opinion.	Articulates with some vagueness with restatement support the basis and reasoning of the majority opinion.	Cannot articulate with clarity the basis for the majority opinion; does not use restatement support in explanation.
Spot facts discordant with majority opinion or same facts that could have a different interpretation/focus (10%)	Identifies all discordant and flexible facts.	Identifies all but 1 or 2 discordant or flexible facts.	Identifies most of the discordant or flexible facts but misses 3 or more.
Craft and support and alternate argument/interpretation of the law using the applicable law and standards (70%)	Fully applies specific discordant or flexible facts to the applicable law/standards in clear manner; Complete explanation of how and why specific discordant or flexible facts support a different outcome; addresses secondary issues/possible theories that support a different outcome.	Applies discordant or flexible facts to the applicable law/standards in clear manner; explains how and why the discordant or flexible facts support a different outcome; misses no more than 2 areas where the facts may support differing outcomes; is less specific about which facts influence outcome and why, makes reasonable inferences; addresses secondary issues/possible theories that support a different outcome.	Applies discordant or flexible facts to the applicable law/standards; explains how and why the discordant or flexible facts support a different outcome; misses 3 or more areas where they facts may support differing outcomes; vague references to facts without specificity, makes reasonable inferences; fails to address secondary issues/possible theories that support a different outcome.

Checklist:

- Does my rubric track my mastery evidence and the prompt for the final assessment exercise?
- Does my rubric align with the course goals?
- If I include criteria not related to the course goal, do they comprise a minimal part of the assessment?
- Are the evaluative criteria specific and clear?
- Are the proficiency descriptions written in neutral, clear terms using consistent terms and components across each level?

Worksheet 9: Draft Course Outcomes

In this Worksheet, you will convert your course goals into multiple learning outcomes and check whether you have achieved the right level of specificity and effectiveness for assessment purposes. Develop a maximum of 6 outcomes per course goal.

- Align each outcome to one or more specific course goal(s).
- Each outcome should be written as a single statement; do not join multiple outcomes within one statement.
- Use verbs that represent observable and measurable performance (live, written, other type of performance). For each outcome, choose the single verb that represents the deepest level of performance that you want for that outcome; avoid compound verbs.
- Because the ABA now requires at least 6 experiential credits for graduation, you might want to align any clinic, field placement, or simulation course to at least some outcomes that relate directly to both your course goals and your school's program outcomes.

Course Goal (from Worksheet 5): Students will be able to contextualize torts (personal injury practice) as a practice focused on how lawyers select and use facts to make their case within the confines of the law.

Students should be able to . . .

Knowledge, skills and/or values	Verb (performance)	Object (the learning statement)	Condition and/or Criterion
Identify what tort theory or theories apply in a given factual scenario.	Recall	The elements, factors, and theories of liability schema	Implicated in hypothetical scenarios.
Identify facts that support a position (Plaintiff or Defendant)	Brainstorm	Facts that might support or controvert a particular position	Without detailed hypotheticals, using only restatement sections, statutory sections, or hornbook sections as reference.
Explain the influence of representing one side on how you argue facts provided	Identify	Biases implicated by being asked to represent one side or the other	After having prepared to argue for both sides.

Course Goal (from Worksheet 5): Student is able to compose a position based on a perspective and articulate with clarity how and why their assigned position is superior to the opposing position.

Students should be able to . . .

Knowledge, skills and/or values	Verb (performance)	Object (the learning statement)	Condition and/or Criterion
Identify what tort theory or theories apply in a given factual scenario.	Recall	The elements, factors, and theories of liability schema	Implicated in hypothetical scenarios.
Identify facts that support a position (Plaintiff or Defendant)	Spot	Facts that support or controvert a particular position	From both sides of the problem.
Explain the influence of representing one side on how you argue facts provided	Argue	Facts that support an assigned position	Using the restatement sections and case precedent as described in the text.

Checklist:

- Do the course outcomes describe what students should know, do, and/or value in order to complete the final assessment successfully?
- Are the course outcomes described with verbs that represent observable, measurable behaviors?
- Are the course outcomes expressed individually, not jointly?
- Do the course outcomes align with a course goal?
- Do the course outcomes align with the ABA-required program outcomes, in whole or in part? (optional)

Worksheet 10: Organize Topics and Learning Activities across the Entire Course

Once you have identified the course outcomes, start identifying the learning activities and lawyering tasks that will enable students to develop the knowledge, skills, or values necessary to achieve each outcome. These activities will then help you choose the materials for the course and to plan individual units and lessons. You will want to organize the units into a sequence that promotes effective learning through smooth and clear transitions from unit to unit.

Situational factors

Before laying out the specific learning activities, re-examine the situational factors that will enable or constrain the types of learning activities you can incorporate, when or how they should be sequenced, and the like. Some of your situational factors may include the pre-requisite knowledge, skills, or values expected of students before taking your course or the availability of a boot camp week or clinic orientation.

Models for organizing and sequencing course content

Consider generally your course's organization. The models below will help you to sequence the course topics, outcomes, and learning activities and to decide what foundation needs to be laid and when. You may combine multiple organizational models.

- *Order of importance*: Because students have highest enthusiasm for a course at the beginning, embed the most important (or difficult) concepts earliest.
- *Order of process*: Sequence material along the arc of a process, beginning to end, *e.g.*, litigation sequence (complaint to trial); attorney-client relationship (first meeting through resolution of the matter; first meeting to transition to the next student-lawyer).
- *Simple to complex*: Because students can build confidence in mastering simple topics and skills, start with these before tackling higher level, more complex tasks.
- *Dependent or supportive relationship between units of study*: If the learning is cumulative, start with the concepts or skills that represent pre-requisite knowledge or skill necessary (or helpful) for later units.
- *Cause & Effect:* Introduce a range of problems and then follow with types of solutions to be applied (*e.g.*, claims and remedies).
- *Spiral or cyclical*: Introduce and revisit concepts or skills multiple times throughout the term, adding complexity with each repetition.
- *General to specific vs. Concrete to abstract*: Introduce general principles & then apply to specific situations. Alternatively, start with specific examples of a phenomenon and move toward what they represent at the conceptual or abstract level.
- *Thematic or topical:* Use when individual units represent independent concepts. Plan transitions carefully. (*e.g.*, a survey course.)

ABA experiential course design standards

Standard 304 provides the elements that any course intended to be counted toward the experiential graduation requirement must have. For each mode of skills teaching (simulation, clinic, externship) Standard 304 includes additional requirements.

Std. 304 (a): Experiential courses [include] simulation courses, law clinics, and field placements that must be primarily experiential in nature and must:

1) Integrate doctrine, theory, skills, and legal ethics, and engage students in performance of one or more of the professional skills identified in Standard 302;
2) Develop the concepts underlying the professional skills being taught;
3) Provide multiple opportunities for performance;
4) Provide opportunities for student performance, self-evaluation, and feedback from a faculty member, or, for a field placement, a site supervisor;
5) A classroom instructional component; or, for a field placement, a classroom instructional component, regularly scheduled tutorials, or other means of ongoing, contemporaneous, faculty-guided reflection; and
6) Provide direct supervision of the student's performance by the faculty member; or, for a field placement, provide direct supervision of the student's performance by a faculty member or a site supervisor.

Topic	Course outcomes in measurable terms	Learning activities / Lawyering tasks	Materials to aid student performance
	What will students be able to think, do, or value to complete the final assessment successfully? Use info developed in Worksheet 9. Organize in a coherent sequence. **By the end of the semester, students will be able to:**	What exercises, performances, discussions, or other learning activity will help students to prepare for and succeed in the final assessment? Identify whether an activity is designed as an introduction (I), practice opportunity (P), or mastery vehicle (M).	What readings, media, information, lecture, and other aids will my students need to perform the lawyering and learning activities successfully? Will it be used before, during, or after the class?
Strict Liability	Identify the elements of strict liability in a variety of contexts and how to apply the theory in a given factual scenario. Identify facts that support a position (Plaintiff or Defendant). Explain what facts, why, and how would support a particular client in having the other side "write the check."	Review of fact pattern and elements of offense to discuss potential defense theories. (Introduced)	Reading on defense theory. Lecture/Class Discussion on Narrative, Theory, and Theme.

Topic	Course outcomes in measurable terms	Learning activities / Lawyering tasks	Materials to aid student performance
Multiple Tortfeasors	Identify the elements of various theories of multiple tortfeasor liability and which apply in a given factual scenario. Identify facts that support a position (Plaintiff or Defendant). Explain what facts, why, and how would support a particular client in having the other side "write the check."	Lecture/discussion (introduction) Hypothetical review (practice) Bar question review (practice)	Text Restatement Sections relevant to topic Lecture Class discussion Hypotheticals Brainstorming Bar questions
Public & Private Nuisance	Identify the basic factors used in determining nuisance claims and how apply to apply them in a given factual scenario. Identify facts that support a position (Plaintiff or Defendant). Explain what facts, why, and how would support a particular client in having the other side "write the check."	Lecture/discussion (introduction) Hypothetical review (practice) Bar question review (practice)	Text Restatement Sections relevant to topic Lecture Class discussion Hypotheticals Brainstorming Bar questions
Wrongful Death	Identify what statutory sections are relevant in a given wrongful death scenario. Identify facts that support a position (Plaintiff or Defendant). Explain what facts, why, and how would support a particular client in having the other side "write the check."	Lecture/discussion (introduction) Hypothetical review (practice) Bar question review (practice)	Text Wyoming statutes relevant to topic Restatement sections relevant to the topic Lecture Class discussion Hypotheticals Brainstorming Bar questions

Topic	Course outcomes in measurable terms	Learning activities / Lawyering tasks	Materials to aid student performance
Vicarious Liability	Identify the various theories of vicarious responsibility, particularly employer liability, apply in a given factual scenario. Identify facts that support a position (Plaintiff or Defendant). Explain what facts, why, and how would support a particular client in having the other side "write the check."	Lecture/discussion (introduction) Hypothetical review (practice) Bar question review (practice)	Text Restatement Sections relevant to topic Lecture Class discussion Hypotheticals Brainstorming Bar questions
Products Liability	Identify what products liability theory or theories apply in a given factual scenario. Identify facts that support a position (Plaintiff or Defendant). Explain what facts, why, and how would support a particular client in having the other side "write the check."	Lecture/discussion (introduction) Hypothetical review (practice) Bar question review (practice)	Text Restatement Sections relevant to topic Lecture Class discussion Hypotheticals Brainstorming Bar questions
Damages	Identify what damages theory or theories apply in a given factual scenario. Identify facts that support a position for calculation methodology and size of damages (Plaintiff or Defendant). Explain what facts, why, and how would support a particular client in having the other side "write the check.	Lecture/discussion (introduction) Hypothetical review (practice) Bar question review (practice) Oral advocacy with question and answer opportunities by other students in class (Mastery)	Hypotheticals Remedies hornbook sections relevant to topic Lecture Class discussion Brainstorming Oral advocacy Bar questions

Checklist:

- Do the course materials, learning activities, and lawyering tasks provide sufficient foundation for student progress toward course mastery?
- Does the order of materials, learning activities, and lawyering tasks allow my students to apply their learning repeatedly, to make progress toward mastery of the course outcomes?
- Do the learning exercises and lawyering activities include ones where I expect course mastery for each Enduring Learning element (Worksheet 4)?
- Do the course materials, learning activities, and lawyering tasks allow my students to consider the Animating Theory and Exploratory Questions for the course on multiple occasions throughout the semester (Worksheets 1 and 2)?
- Do the learning activities and lawyering tasks cover each criterion in ABA Standards 304 (as applied to all experiential courses and to the provisions specific to my type of course)??

DRC Process Notes:

I tend not to use Socratic methodology, even in the large classroom. I prefer to engage the students in a more active learning environment based on class discussion and hypothetical review. I provide them with the restatement sections for each tort/theory so that as they read cases they can look at the restatement for clarification and so they have a more solid understanding of why the court may have decided as they did. My use of the text is really as a reference point for application of the restatement rather than as a roadmap for learning elements/factors.

It has always been my hope in planning content for the course that we get to Damages at the end of the semester. That has not always been possible as often the other substantive topics take longer to move through than I have anticipated. This presents challenges for me as I map topics onto the semester calendar and continually requires me to think about the coverage/content dilemma.

Worksheet 11: Plan Units of Student Learning Activities

For each unit (a single topic/learning activity or chunk of topics or activities), create a plan for work that your students will do before, during, and after class. Make sure that you identify how you will "know" that the students learned what you planned. That might be your own reflection and assessment at the end of the class, supervision, or unit, or it might be some other evidence of student learning (whether direct from the student, or indirect from another source).

Course Unit: Damages

Relevant Course Outcomes (from Worksheet 9):
Explain what and how specific facts would support a particular client in having the other side "write the check."

How will students prepare for the unit/class?	What will students do in class to prepare them to reach the outcomes?	How will I know they learned what I wanted them to learn?
Read sections of "The Law of Remedies" hornbook Work hypothetical damages problems from both plaintiff and defendant sides Develop oral arguments for both sides' positions on a damage claim, citing to the hornbook and whatever other research/case precedent we discuss in class Review and attempt to answer essay and multiple-choice bar questions from past bar exams relating to damages	Review hypothetical problems Discuss as a class the relevant sections in the Remedies hornbook sections Work on identifying what type(s) of damages may apply in a given situation Brainstorm facts and arguments for the Plaintiffs and Defendants described in the hypothetical scenarios In class mini-oral arguments advocating for a client's damages position Review multiple choice and essay bar questions; connect review to readings and earlier hypotheticals	Discuss, with both prompts and reference to the hornbook, the relevant theory of damages calculation Explain effect of different theories of damages calculation from defendant or plaintiff perspective Analysis of hypotheticals is flexible—same student answering for plaintiff is then asked to answer for defendant Facts generated during brainstorming are relevant to applicable standards, elements, or factors in damage calculation Facts generated during brainstorming can change potential outcomes or considerations depending on whether they are analyzed from defendant or plaintiff perspective Arguments for or against specific damages calculations in a given case are comprehensive, clear, and persuasive Student can articulate how viewing a problem from an assigned perspective influences how they choose which facts to argue and how they argue them

Checklist:

- Do the unit activities align with one or more of my course's learning outcomes?
- Do the unit activities have a clear purpose to help students learn?
- Is the unit structured to build on existing learning, give clear direction, and give opportunity to practice what students are expected to do?
- Do the unit activities give students time to develop their own thoughts and positions, and to hear others' ideas, perspectives, or positions?
- Do I hold my students accountable for doing the activity, including by giving them feedback?
- Do I provide opportunity for students to reflect on the activities and connect them to their prior learning?

DRC Process Notes:

For this unit I step away from the case text book entirely. Damages as a remedy is generally more complex a concept than students realize. I provide them with relevant sections of "The Law of Remedies" by Dobbs instead of the restatement sections. In this unit we work not only on analyzing problems from different perspectives but also on oral advocacy. I approach these problems as though liability has already been established and that all the students are responsible for is expanding or limiting the damages as much as reasonably possible.

Course: Interviewing, Counseling, and Negotiation, Danielle Cover

Worksheet 1: Animating Theory

To identify the learning goals for your course, first consider the subject matter generally. Because a subject matter has more content than a course can cover, start by articulating the key reason students should take your course. That reason is your course's Animating Theory. Grant Wiggins and Jay McTighe coined a colloquial term for this, "The Big Idea."[7]

Once you choose your Animating Theory, you will flesh it out with a set of Exploratory Questions (Worksheet 2) that illuminate the challenges you want your students to grapple with. Setting the Animating Theory and Exploratory Questions allows you to build your course from course goal, to mastery evidence, to learning activities. The Animating Theory is not the same as your course goal(s) or learning outcomes; it underlies both. You may have more than one, but restrict yourself to at most two so that student learning is focused. Here, less is more.

The Animating Theory for the Course:

- Refers to core concepts, principles, and theories in a field of study—What unifies the field of study? What makes a skill worthwhile or effective?
- Organizes large bodies of information, skills, or values.
- Is amenable to transfer to new fields of study, new situations, and across disciplines.
- Is abstract and requires investigation to probe its implications.

Considerations for a Skills-focused Course:

- What does the lawyering skill help you do more effectively or efficiently for a client?
- What are the underlying concepts or objectives of the skill?
- When and how do you use the skill (strategy and tactics)?
- Why does the skill work?

Examples: The Animating Theory need not be phrased as a complete sentence. A "motto" works.

- Persuasion: Know your audience.
- Sociology: People in a community depend on each other for the things they need.
- History: History is written by the victors.
- Law: The best lawyer is the best prepared lawyer.

Identify the Animating Theory(ies) for your course.

Good communication skills enhance effective lawyering and improve lawyer-client relationships.
Effective lawyering includes the ability to navigate multiple collaborative environments and relationships.

Checklist:

- Does my animating theory provide a concise statement, principle, theory, or generalization?
- Does it stand the test of time, allowing students' thoughts about it to develop and evolve over time?

7. See Wiggins, G., & McTighe, J., Understanding by Design (2nd ed. 2005).

- Can it promote in-depth understanding and help make sense of the subject matter?
- Can it promote in-depth understanding and help make sense of the subject matter?

DRC Process Notes:

The student body at my law school is on the smaller side, with the average class size falling in the range of 75-80 people. Many of the students, upon graduation will stay in the Mountain West region, and many will work for the government or in small or solo firms. A significant proportion of the students will find themselves doing transactional work in the extraction industry. In Wyoming, of the 1800 or so barred attorneys, fewer than 200 identify themselves primarily as civil litigators.

As a set of general principles, I want the course to challenge students not only in the development of effective ways to ask questions, give advice, and negotiate outcomes acceptable to their client, but also to recognize the underlying human aspects and characteristics that influence those larger skills. This necessarily means exposing them to their own humanity as well as exploring the humanity of their clients. I do this with both subtle and direct means, e.g., asking them to engage in client-centered analysis of the simulation problems and exploring with them how their own personalities impact how they work in group settings. Given the small region in which many of the students eventually practice, understanding their own tendencies with regard to communication is critical to professional identity development.

Worksheet 2: Develop Exploratory Questions

Questions are used to study the Animating Theory for the course and to ground student learning. These questions are open-ended and probing in nature rather than intended to yield specific answers.

An Exploratory Question:

- Opens the Animating Theory for the course to genuine inquiry.
- Provokes lively discussion, sustained inquiry, and new understanding, as well as more questions.
- Requires students to consider alternatives, weigh evidence, support their ideas, and justify their answers.
- Stimulates vital, on-going rethinking of assumptions, prior understanding, and personal experience.
- Naturally recurs, creating opportunities for transfer to other situations and subjects.

Examples of Exploratory Questions that amplify the value of your Animating Theory:

- Persuasion: What's in it for my audience? What are the ethics of persuasion?
- Government and public policy: What makes a good government? How does cultural identity inform one's views of government and its role in society?
- History/Precedent: What patterns recur throughout history and common law? Is all history biased?

Identify 1–2 Exploration Questions for each Animating Theory.

Animating Theory 1: Good communication skills enhance effective lawyering and improve lawyer client relationships.

What makes someone a good communicator?
In the lawyering context, what communications skills should we develop?
How should we define 'good communication' and what factors influence our individual definitions?

Animating Theory 2: Effective lawyering includes the ability to navigate multiple collaborative environments and relationships.

What does collaboration mean and how does it manifest in lawyering relationships?
Why is it important to foster collaborative skills across lawyering relationships and environments?
How do our individual human characteristics influence our capacity to collaborate effectively?

Checklist:

- Are my Exploratory Questions open-ended, nonjudgmental, meaningful, and purposeful?
- Do the questions have emotional appeal?
- Do the questions have more than one coherent answer?
- Do the questions probe for deeper meaning and explore ideas and beliefs?
- Do the questions encourage peer learning and collaboration?

DRC Process Notes:

Communication is a fundamental foundational piece of the lawyering profession; attorneys communicate in writing, in words, with their body language, and with the choices they make throughout representation relationships. Collaboration is also a foundational piece to lawyering as no one lawyers alone—if there's not a client to work for, there's no job to be done. Collaboration skills impact all lawyering work as the relationships an attorney builds with colleagues, the court, and the surrounding community influence everything, particularly in small regional communities. It is my experience and impression that students haven't taken much time, if any, to consider what it means to be an effective communicator or a collaborator. And, even if they have considered those issues in competition teams or in their brief writing, they have not often approached the issues from the client perspective. Thus, the exploratory questions I have articulated as part of my animating theories create a pathway for thinking about communication and collaboration as 2 building blocks for their future practice.

Worksheet 3: Identify Situational Factors That Affect Teaching and Learning

The first two Worksheets lay out the scope of the course on a grand scale. Now situate your ambitions for student learning within the realities of your course, the school's curriculum, your students' semesters, and the scope of all your responsibilities. Some of these situational factors are assets to use wisely and fruitfully. Others are limitations. Affirmatively acknowledging that, in your clinic, field placement, or simulation course, you simply cannot cover all that your students need to know, be able to do, or value will help you to make pedagogical choices to maximize student learning.

Possible situational factors

Length (e.g., semester, year), number of credits, number of hours in field, casework, or classroom	Semester, 3 credits (Fall semester only)
Grading scheme	+/- graded scale Assessment happens in teams and individually; team assessment requires significant class time to complete.
Student preparedness (typical, high/low)	Most students believe they are highly prepared in all areas of the class except in negotiation—many have expressed the belief that interviewing and counseling skills are secondary to understanding effective negotiation techniques; few students previously exposed to client-centered lawyering perspective or process
Student motivations	Primary motivation = learning negotiation skills; Students perceive themselves to be accomplished communicators Most students do not recognize that lawyering is inherently collaborative across environments (client, other lawyers, opposing parties, court personnel, witnesses, etc.)
Uniformity, dissimilarity, or variety of student work (in type and complexity)	½ class represent a plaintiff in a semester-long simulation ½ class represent defendant in a semester-long simulation All students work on formative assessment exercises—uniformity high
Personal responsibilities that constrain my availability for class or individual student engagement	Clinic litigation scheduling often impacts capacity for class to be held at consistent times Parenting responsibilities preclude most evening work or meetings Significant proportion of older/returning students with children—impacts availability for out of class group work
Enrollment	Growing enrollment in the course has required team performance—class now performs in groups of 3 to ensure everyone has a chance to engage without too much burden on assessment

Scheduling	Must reserve time in all units for practice/formative assessment, feedback loops—limits number/timing of exercises Must build in opportunities for individual assessment as well as group assessment—summative assessments occur in groups of 3 (team); entire team graded together; post-summative assessment each student turns in a reflective writing that is graded individually—lots of assessment time and feedback opportunities also time-intensive commitment
Arranging actors	Scheduling concerns with using students as the actors for the semester-long simulation

Checklist:

- Do I capture factors that are opportunities for me to maximize the learning in my course?
- Do I capture the most salient factors that limit the scope of what students can reasonably learn in my course?
- Do I capture the most salient factors that limit my ability to execute a course plan and engage my students?

DRC Process Notes:

Because of the situational factors such as student over-estimation of their communication skills, as well as their often-expressed dislike of group work, I have felt compelled to approach the class from the perspective that as much feedback as they can receive in the 14 weeks of the class the better. The more often I and the other students in the class can "unpack" and "debrief" the student experiences in the formative assessments, the more I can create pathways by which the students can see their actual strengths and weaknesses.

Worksheet 4: Prioritize Learning for Transfer (durability)

Allow your Animating Theory to percolate. Break it down into specific priorities for your students' learning. Identify the knowledge and understandings, skills, and/or values that are essential to the Animating Theory of your course. Prioritize those elements based on long-term importance to the students' learning. The highest level (enduring learning) should be learning that is transferable to different contexts in their professional lives.

Even though your course may cover content in all three levels of priority, your course goals (Worksheet 5) and final assessments (Worksheet 7) will focus on the knowledge and understandings, skills, and/or values that you intend to be long-lived (enduring) for your students.

Enduring learning:

Communication (written, oral and listening) has patterns that can enhance or detract from the quality of information a lawyer has at their disposal for representing a client
Basic client-centered lawyering theory and transfer of client-centered theory/ approaches to creating and maintaining lawyering relationships in different areas of substantive law and in different contexts, benefits and drawbacks of same
How to engage in meaningful reflection about the lawyering choices students make in each formative or summative assessment exercise

Important for students to know:

How to leverage communication similarities and differences to make the most effective use of collaborative relationships
Impact of individual human characteristics on presentation and reception of information; Neuroscientific explanations of brain function and ability to process information/problem-solve; related: the impact of stress and fear on problem-solving and decision-making
Ethical implications of client/OP communications

Worth being familiar with:

Impact of case preparation/case theory on effective communication
Fact investigation/discovery methods
Case planning

Checklist:

- Do the elements listed as *Enduring Learning* help students to synthesize individual lessons and readings into a deeper understanding of the Animating Theory?
- Do the *Enduring Learning* elements lay a foundation for further study of this subject matter?
- Do the *Enduring Learning* elements help students to figure out issues in the subject matter that are more difficult to master?

DRC Process Notes:

Over time my enduring learning, important learning, and familiarity categories have changed as I have played with the course parameters. I see as a primary purpose of the course the responsibility to introduce students to and engage them in how to use the communication skills needed for interviewing, counseling, and negotiation to influence the quality of the information they elicit and reveal. As a result, while we practice things such as journalism questions and t-funneling, etc., I push them to reflect critically on where their choices had definable and measurable impact on their ability to lawyer a case. We use those reflection conversations (and my feedback on their reflection memos) to think about how to change or improve future communication patterns.

Worksheet 5: Use Learning Taxonomies to Craft Course Goals[8]

Now that you've identified your learning priorities, you will distill the enduring learning into course goals. Course goals represent the essential i) knowledge and understandings, ii) skills, and/or iii) values that you intend your students to attain by the end of the term. One way to unify the enduring learning into goals is to ask: "How will my students be different by the end of the course?" To answer this question in a way that can be assessed at the end of the course, we have collected taxonomies of learning that capture the complexity and depth of learning you want your students to attain. The taxonomies further assist you to establish observable and measurable course goals (amenable to assessment, Worksheets 6 and 7).

The taxonomies cover the three domains of learning:

1. Cognitive domain: Focuses on knowledge, comprehension, and critical thinking.
2. Psychomotor domain: Encompasses learning geared toward executing specific tasks (*e.g.*, client counseling, negotiating with opposing counsel, witness interviewing).
3. Affective domain: Relates to awareness and growth in values, attitudes, and emotional control (*e.g.*, values embedded in the attorney-client relationship, toward justice, and relating to professional identity formation).

The taxonomy grids on the next three pages organize each domain of learning hierarchically. As you move through the grids (left to right; top to bottom) the categories describe learning at deeper levels of difficulty. Use these grids to choose the deepest point(s) that correspond to a realistic learning goal for your course.

The grids, their terminology, and hierarchy are offered as an aid. Some of your learning priorities might fit within more than one taxonomy, and the Action Verbs that exemplify a category might

8. Course Development Institute, Indiana University Center for Innovative Teaching and Learning.

resonate more than the category of learning does. Choose what works for you. Don't let the taxonomies push your learning goal toward something that doesn't feel right to you. Maybe you will pencil in learning targets for your course in several cells on separate grids; that will allow you to test out different ways to characterize the course goal(s) you want to pursue. In the end you should articulate 1–2 course goals. In drafting these goals, keep your verb singular, not compound, as a verb representing the farthest/deepest taxonomy cell that encapsulates your goal will necessarily include the less complex learning needed to reach that goal.

In the following three pages:

- Review the taxonomy for each domain.
- Reflect on your ambitions for your course. Pencil notes in any of the cells.
- Review your notes and distill them to one to two course goals (last page).

The course goals will form the bedrock for your course. Everything else—the final assessment, rubric, outcomes and learning activities—will be aligned to the course goals.

Sources:

Knowledge and Cognitive Processing Domain

Adapted from Anderson, L.W., Krathwohl, D.R. et. al. (2001). *A Taxonomy for Learning, Teaching, and Assessing: A Revision of Bloom's Taxonomy of Educational Objectives.* Abridged ed. New York: Longman.

Psychomotor Domain

Adapted from Dave, R.H. (1970), "Developing and Writing Behavioral Objectives;" Simpson E. J. (1972). The Classification of Educational Objectives in the Psychomotor Domain. Washington, DC: Gryphon House.

Affective Domain

Adapted from Krathwohl, D.R., Bloom, B.S., and Masia, B.B. (1964). *Taxonomy of Educational Objectives, Book II. Affective domain*. New York: David McKay Company, Inc.

Find taxonomies on following pages

1. Knowledge and Cognitive Processing Domain

		Cognitive processing			
		1. Remember	2. Understand	3. Apply	4. Analyze, Evaluate, or Create
Knowledge	A. Factual				
	B. Conceptual		Articulate how communication is a series of choices with individual and collective impacts Differentiate how a variety of scenarios (both as speakers and as listeners) impact the ability to generate high quality information gathering Identify how communication and investigation skills impact case development	Build an effective communication plan for 3 simulated exercises Use t-funneling and "journalism questions" to focus or broaden conversations. Conduct effective interviews, counseling sessions, and negotiations using the basic processes of interviewing techniques Demonstrate in interview/counseling session/negotiation that effective communication choices can impact the quality of outcomes (practice and final assessment)	Identify choice points from simulated exercises that directed the conversation in a specific direction Evaluate relationship of direction of communication to case development and outcomes
	C. Procedural		Describe in their own words how communication style impacts outcomes/quality of information shared or received		
	D. Meta-cognitive			Discuss through reflective writing what communication choices they made during simulated exercises	Demonstrate critical reflection in what worked/didn't work and how communication choices might be improved or changed in future exercises

Knowledge types	Definition	Examples
Factual	Basic elements to be acquainted with the discipline and solve problems	Terminology, vocabulary, elements, and details
Conceptual	Interrelationship among basic elements	Categories, principles, theories, models, and structures
Procedural	How to do something *(overlaps with psychomotor domain)*	Subject-specific skills, methods of inquiry and criteria for using, and techniques and procedures
Meta-cognitive	Knowing about knowing	Strategic knowledge, reflections, and self-knowledge

Cognitive processing	Definition	Action Verbs
Remember	Retrieve relevant knowledge from long-term memory	Retain, recall, recognize, memorize, recollect, think of, define, identify, list, name, record, repeat, underline, select
Understand	Construct meaning from instructional messages; can be in oral, written or graphic formats	Interpret, exemplify, classify, summarize, infer, compare, explain, give examples of, describe in own words, differentiate between, discriminate, restate, review, translate, respond, practice, discuss, identify, review, simulate
Apply	Carry out procedures	Execute, implement, apply, demonstrate, dramatize, generalize, illustrate, operate, operationalize, practice, use, utilize, initiate
Analyze	Break material into parts and determine relationships	Differentiate, organize, attribute, analyze, appraise, categorize, compare, conclude, contrast, correlate, deduce, diagram, distinguish, estimate, examine, experiment, infer, predict, question, solve, diagnose
Evaluate	Make judgments based upon criteria or standards	Check, critique, assess, judge, appraise, choose, compare, evaluate, measure, rate, revise, score, select, validate, value
Create	Put elements together into coherent or functional whole, reorganize into new patterns	Generate, plan, produce, invent, arrange, assemble, collect, compose, construct, create, design, develop, formulate, manage, modify, organize, prepare, propose, synthesize

2. Psychomotor Domain: (can be used by experiential faculty to set goals for lawyering skill development)

	Definition	Action Verbs	Your Course Goals
Perception	Actively using sensory cues to attend to the behavioral skill. E.g., student observes a seasoned attorney perform the behavior.	Choose, describe, detect, differentiate, distinguish, identify, isolate, relate, select, separate	Speaking: word choice, phrasing, tone, speed, refraining from speaking Listening: body language, parroting/reflective questions, exploring gaps/follow ups
Imitation	Copying the behavior. The student attempts the behavior, with direction and feedback from an experienced person. The student shows desire and motivation to learn the behavior.	Adhere, begin, attempt, carry out, copy, duplicate, follow, mimic, repeat, replicate, start, try	
Practice	Using the behavior repeatedly. The student performs the behavior multiple times, and her actions become more automatic and smooth. The experienced person need not be present.	Codify, discriminate, display, order, organize, systematize, weigh, discuss, theorize, formulate, balance, examine, adhere to	opportunities and feedback loops throughout the units—5 interviews, 3 counseling sessions, 2 negotiations (all formative assessments)
Naturalization	Performing two or more skills in combination or sequence, with consistency and ease. The student can combine the behavior with other behaviors independently and with little mental exertion.	Adapt, automatize, combine, complete, demonstrate, internalize, master, perform, show, succeed	
Origination	Creating new behaviors, combinations, or sequences to respond to a new situation. The student creates new methodologies or techniques to improve on or re-imagine how the needs can be met.	Create, design, compose, refine, arrange	Process feedback and experiences through reflection—what went well, what didn't go well, self-awareness to influence future choices

3. **Affective Domain:** (can be used to set goals related to professional values, affect, or work approach, *e.g.*, with regard to the attorney client relationship, the rule of law, or other professional value)

	Definition	Action Verbs	Your Course Goals
Receive	Be aware of; attend to something; be willing to tolerate it.	Accept, attend, develop, ask, recognize, listen for, describe, differentiate, receive, identify, tolerate	Recognize the import of building speaking/listening skills
Respond	Incorporate a new behavior as a result of the experience.	Complete, comply, cooperate, discuss, examine, obey, assist, respond, follow, volunteer, perform	Examine an awareness of when to adjust pattern, focus, change or redirect course of conversation
Value	Show specific involvement or commitment.	Accept, defend, devote oneself to, pursue, seek, justify, join, debate, value	Defend impact of client-centered focus throughout
Organize	Integrate a new value into one's general set of values, giving due ranking among other priorities.	Codify, discriminate, display, order, organize, systematize, weigh, discuss, theorize, formulate, balance, examine, adhere to	order questions/inquiries in a way that makes most effective use of time and information
Internalize the value set	Act consistently, conscientiously, and pro-actively with the new value.	Internalize, verify, be rated high in the value, require, resolve	

Using the taxonomies on the previous pages, draft your top 1–2 Course Goals:

By the end of the course, my students will:

1. Engage in effective collaborative relationships (across domains) to further the position of their assigned simulation clients.
2. Internalize frameworks for speaking and listening that support a client-centered lawyering approach to their attorney-client relationship with their simulation client.

Checklist

- Do my goals fit within the Animating Theory for the course (Worksheet 1)?
- Do my goals reflect the learning priorities I have set for the course (Worksheet 4)?
- Are my goals clear, observable, and measurable (Worksheets 6 and 8)?
- Do my goals reflect the situational limits of my course and my full responsibilities (Worksheet 3)?

Worksheet 6: Identify Observable Evidence of Student Mastery

Visualize the student who excels in the course you are designing. What does the student's performance or work product look like? That is your evidence of student mastery. The student's work is not at the level of a veteran attorney's; it's A-level work as a student in your course. Look at your picture closely, using the following six categories, or facets, of concrete, observable performance to assist your efforts.[9] A "masterful" student performance may well involve synchronous use of multiple facets. After you identify your evidence of mastery, then you will i) create a final assessment exercise to allow your students to exhibit this evidence (Worksheet 7) and ii) create an assessment rubric that defines levels of student performance (Worksheet 8).

Facet of understanding	Associated verbs & Starter phrases	Evidence of student's mastery in your course
Explanation: Students are able to provide thorough and well-supported accounts of topics, events, or actions, backed by reasoning, facts, or experience. Students are able to develop a theory of how and why, supported by evidence, law, and experience.	Demonstrate, derive, describe, design, exhibit, express, instruct, justify, model, predict, prove, show, synthesize, teach Students will be able to: Explain/teach [x], Give examples of [x]; Make connections with [x]; Offer a theory of [x]; Avoid misconceptions, such as [x].	Students can explain how to use speaking and listening techniques to gather and share high quality information, including explaining how to use journalism questions and t-funneling to broaden or narrow interview and collaborative communication foci appropriately.
Interpretation: Students are able to interpret and analyze the importance, meaning, or significance of their knowledge/skill, with context and awareness of multiple interpretations. Students can create meaning from a set of facts and law, with attention to ambiguity, uncertainty, opacity, emotional content, and diverse perspectives.	Create analogies, critique, document, evaluate, illustrate, judge, make sense of, provide metaphors, read between the lines, represent, tell a story of. Students will be able to: Interpret the [x]; Tell a revealing story of [x]; Provide an apt analogy for [x]; Show the importance or meaning of [x]; Translate [x]; Relate [x] to your experience (or the experiences of others).	Students can evaluate the importance of effective communication techniques across the spectrum of interviews; counseling sessions; and negotiation meetings.

9. Adapted and expanded from Wiggins, G., & McTighe, J., UNDERSTANDING BY DESIGN (2nd ed. 2005) (describing six facets of understanding).

Application-Adaptation: Students use and adapt the knowledge/skill acquired to new situations and contexts, showing flexibility and adaptability. Students can design, develop, test, and refine responses to a new problem or dilemma presented.	Adapt, create, de-bug, design, exhibit, invent, perform, produce, propose, solve, test, use Students will be able to: Apply [x] in a new circumstance; Show or demonstrate [x]; Use in the context of [x]; Design/invent [x]; Overcome a challenge or constraint, such as [x].	Students can translate (transfer) speaking and listening techniques across collaborative domains such as client, witness (non-client), opposing counsel, court/courtroom communications, etc. Students can use speaking and listening techniques across a variety of lawyering situations including litigation, transactional, and administrative cases.
Perspective: Students can take a step back to appreciate a broader view, critically assess the value or importance of a topic. Students can identify, critique, and give credence to multiple valid perspectives regarding a topic.	Analyze, argue, compare, contrast, criticize, infer Students will be able to: Analyze [x]; See from the viewpoint of [x]; Compare and contrast [x]; Critique [x]; Critically examine assumptions such as [x]; Show how [x]; See the limits of [x].	Students can discuss the limitations and benefits of the client-centered lawyering-model across simulated environments. Students can recognize when communication styles require flexibility based on the needs of the communication partner.
Empathy: Students show the ability to embrace the feelings, reasoning, motivations, and perspectives of others with acceptance and non-judgment. Open-minded insight to others.	Assume the role of, believe, be like, be open to, consider, imagine, relate, role-play. Students will be able to: Walk in the shoes of [x]; Experience directly and see [x]; Reach a common understanding with another concerning [x]; Entertain the seemingly odd or alien view that [x]; Anticipate possible concerns of others regarding [x] based on their interests, values, and circumstances.	Students can reach common understanding with their clients/opposing counsel/witnesses/court about what information is being communicated and how—use the client-centered model and reflection to engage with their own judgments and assumptions about motivations, limitations, etc.
Self-Knowledge: Students accept that their style, preferences, and habits are specific to them and affect their views of events, information, and other people. Students can evaluate their professional development with appreciation of what came easily or not and why; can evaluate personal, emotional responses with detachment.	Be aware of, realize, recognize, reflect, self-assess. Students will be able to: Recognize their own prejudice(s) about [x]; Identify the lens through which they view [x]; Explain how they came to understand [x]; Realize that even with all they now know, they still don't really understand [x].	Students can constructively critique in critical written self-reflection their own performances as well as the performances of their teammates in their individual and collective execution of each final assessment. Students can constructively self-critique in open classroom setting.

Checklist

- Does my mastery evidence flow from my course goals and teaching priorities?
- Does my mastery evidence facilitate exploration of the Animating Theory for the course?
- Is my evidence of student mastery observable and measureable in an assessment exercise?

DRC Process Notes:

My first introduction to course design was through Wiggins & McTighe and the Backward Design methodology. Because of this, I became comfortable with using the Facets of Understanding to define my course goals; my goals are supported by Bloom's taxonomies, but they are grounded in the Facets. While the Backward Design methodology was not necessarily created for skills courses at the graduate level, I find them to fit well with bigger picture issues like developing empathy, locating client values on the spectrum with personal values, and a myriad of other law school skills-oriented pedagogical goals.

Worksheet 7: Create a Final Assessment Exercise

Create a final assessment exercise that will allow you to observe and evaluate each piece of mastery evidence listed. Before crafting the assessment exercise, revisit the enduring learning priorities you established (Worksheet 4) and your course goals (Worksheet 5). Use the measurable language in the goals and the mastery evidence (Worksheet 6) to create the content framework for your final assessment exercise. Note: you may use more than one assessment exercise to determine the final grade for your course.

- Choose the vehicle: a piece(s) of writing, a portfolio, an oral presentation or live performance (to professor or before another audience), etc.
- Quantity—Length: Consider how short or long the students' performance or work product should be to showcase their mastery. For instance, if you want to assess the students' level of reflection, can the students meet your expectations in 250 words, 1,000, or 5,000 words? If you want to assess the students' ability to conduct a summation for the jury, should the summation last 5 minutes, 15 minutes, 30 minutes, or more?
- Quantity—Parts: Determine the number of parts or exercises. While it might be ideal to create an assessment exercise that synthesizes the full constellation of knowledge, skills, and values represented in the course goal, often it might be impracticable to create a single assessment exercise that allows the students to produce evidence of full mastery. How would you segment the parts of the assessment?
- Practicalities: Consider the situational factors that impact what is manageable for you to assess.
- Design the subject and the prompts: This is the meat of the assessment. What are you asking your students to do? Make certain that your prompts, length, and parts will summon the work product or performance that elicits your desired mastery evidence.

Vehicle	Live performance of final interview, final counseling session, final negotiation for a semester-long simulated conflict/client scenario.
Quantity (length, parts)	Interview and counseling session: 20 minutes per team over 2 class periods. Negotiation: 50 minutes per pair of teams scheduled during final exam period.
Timing/sequence	1. Initial interview—meet client for first time, conduct introductory interview and begin exploratory questioning. 2. Counseling session—new facts emerge that require counseling session with client about choices/next steps. 3. Negotiation with opposing party in conflict to attempt resolution of the conflict. Everyone comes fresh to the summative assessments—honor code warning not to discuss until all groups have completed the assessment; no peer learning allowed in summative assessments.
Practicalities	Students will necessarily need to engage in subsequent conversations with the simulation client—requires actor to be available for those meetings, particularly in the case of the negotiation. Adequate assessment time for interview and counseling is challenging—evening and/or weekend meetings for assessment are impractical. Split grading—group on the performance, individual on reflection. Developing fact patterns for semester-long simulation—4 currently solidified, can cycle through the patterns.

Subject and prompts	Dispute-oriented fact pattern with both litigation and non-legal resolution options. Case facts—limited information provided at the outset of the interview. Interview and reflective writing instructions and prompts.

DRC Process Notes:

As the attendance in my course has grown over the years, I have had to consider how to assess effectively the skill development while not creating too much of a time strain with my Clinic Director and other responsibilities. It has been an interesting balance to achieve. Each summative assessment consists of 2 parts—the group exercise and the individual reflection. I encourage the students to work consistently together in their teams outside the classroom to build their working relationship and to start identifying where each might provide strength to the graded exercises. Because reflection, feedback, and critique are built into the daily structure and conduct of the course, and because I provide the students with a detailed reflective writing rubric, I am comfortable that self-reflection and critique serve the larger course goals and provide for meaningful assessment on an individual level.

Worksheet 8: Prepare an Analytic Rubric

Whether your course is graded or not, you should assess each student's learning: 1) to inform the students of what they have in fact mastered or not; and 2) to inform you of your teaching effectiveness. An analytic rubric serves both purposes by imparting detailed feedback to each student and by enabling you to analyze where students are having trouble. If you give the rubric to students with the assessment exercise, the rubric also communicates your expectations so that they can self-assess their work before submitting it.

An analytic rubric is easily written as a grid:

- Vertical axis: Identify the assessment (evaluative) criteria to track the course goal and mastery evidence. You may include additional criteria not specifically tied to the course goals (e.g., writing mechanics, class participation), but do not let their grading value dilute the assessment of the course goal. Identify up to 6 criteria.
    - Describe the different elements of performance for each assessment criterion. You may include more than one element of performance in each criterion.
- Horizontal axis: Set and label the different proficiency levels. Levels can be labeled as grades, numeric ranges, or descriptors like exceptional, competent, and developing.
    - Each proficiency level for an assessment criterion should address each performance element in the assessment criterion.

Course Goal (from Worksheet 5): Internalize frameworks for speaking and listening that support a client-centered lawyering approach to their attorney-client relationship with their simulation client. (Note: This rubric is for the final interviewing simulation only.) (Reflection on what are our communication tendencies and how we get stuck in them)

Evaluative criterion; weighting	Highest proficiency	Mid-level proficiency	Low level proficiency
Obtain the basic facts relevant to the case, as well as broader contextual facts and weaknesses.	Active use of funneling and "journalism" questions in question development and fact exploration. Recognizes and follows up on items that generate new lines of inquiry. Identifies and addresses gaps in information and inquires about those gaps. Directly inquires about potential problems areas. Uses verbal and non-verbal indicators of comfort with awkward or difficult information.	Inconsistent use of funneling and "journalism" questions. More questions lead than allow for the client to tell the story. Inconsistently follows up on items that generate new lines of inquiry. Inconsistently identifies and addresses gaps in information and inquires about those gaps. Inconsistently inquires about potential problems areas. Verbal and non-verbal that student is uncomfortable with awkward or difficult information. Inconsistently follows up on awkward or difficult information.	Questions are primarily leading and are not designed to elicit information as much as confirm lawyer assessments, e.g., does not identify that personal judgments and assumptions are impacting the form of questions and responses. Provides no opportunity for the client to tell the story. Fails to follow up on items that are unclear or may open new lines of inquiry. Cannot identify gaps in information. Fails to ask questions or identify weak spots, awkward, or difficult information about the client's case.
Assess the client's needs and goals for the case and the representation.	Prepared to discuss a variety of legal and non-legal approaches to the client's articulated conflict. Able to discuss with comfort and authority relevant law impacting the conflict. Prepared to answer client questions about the legal system. Provides enough detail in answers to satisfy client curiosity or concern.	Prepared to discuss a variety of legal and non-legal approaches to the client's articulated conflict. Able to discuss with comfort and authority relevant law impacting the conflict. Prepared to answer client questions about the legal system. Provides enough detail in answers to satisfy client curiosity or concern.	Prepared to discuss only legal options or not prepared to discuss options at all. Discomfort with explaining relevant law. Student actively indicates the student is not prepared to discuss the client's questions. Active indications that the student is unwilling to discuss the legal system or conduct of the matter. Cannot provide answers to client questions that satisfy curiosity or concern.

Provide information about the legal system, relevant law, available options, etc.	Prepared to discuss a variety of legal and non-legal approaches to the client's articulated conflict. Able to discuss with comfort and authority relevant law impacting the conflict. Prepared to answer client questions about the legal system. Provides enough detail in answers to satisfy client curiosity or concern.	Prepared to discuss a variety of legal and non-legal approaches to the client's articulated conflict. Able to discuss with comfort and authority relevant law impacting the conflict. Prepared to answer client questions about the legal system. Provides enough detail in answers to satisfy client curiosity or concern.	Prepared to discuss only legal options or not prepared to discuss options at all. Discomfort with explaining relevant law. Student actively indicates the student is not prepared to discuss the client's questions. Active indications that the student is unwilling to discuss the legal system or conduct of the matter. Cannot provide answers to client questions that satisfy curiosity or concern.
Establish an effective working relationship with the client.	Always uses active listening, empathic verbal responses. Develops and uses an effective introduction strategy, ice-breaker, and conversational tone. Comfortable with pauses and silence. Accurately reflects back to the client what the client has said. Makes direct inquiries into vocabulary with which the student is unfamiliar. Avoids using legalese or technical language. Eye contact, lean in/lean out (body language conveying interesting and engagement).	Some evidence of active listening and empathic verbal responses. Body language is inconsistently open. Introduction strategy, ice-breaker, and conversational tone are awkward/do not support a comfortable environment. Somewhat comfortable with pauses and silence but will talk through pauses to fill the time and space. Accurately reflects back to the client what the client has said. Inconsistently makes direct inquiries into vocabulary with which the student is unfamiliar. Uses some legalese or technical language.	Fails to listen to client and cannot reflect back what the client has said in any meaningful way. Uses aggressive or hostile body language and verbal cues. Fails to introduce self or others. Conversational tone is absent. Fails to explore vocabulary and/or makes assumptions about client intent or meaning—no follow up. over-uses legal and technical language. Fails to identify where client misunderstanding may be generated by attorney-conduct.

Checklist:

- Does my rubric track my mastery evidence and the prompt for the final assessment exercise?
- Does my rubric align with the course goals?
- If I include criteria not related to the course goal, do they comprise a minimal part of the assessment?
- Are the evaluative criteria specific and clear?
- Are the proficiency descriptions written in neutral, clear terms using consistent terms and components across each level?

Worksheet 9: Draft Course Outcomes

In this Worksheet, you will convert your course goals into multiple learning outcomes and check whether you have achieved the right level of specificity and effectiveness for assessment purposes. Develop a maximum of 6 outcomes per course goal.

- Align each outcome to one or more specific course goal(s).
- Each outcome should be written as a single statement; do not join multiple outcomes within one statement.
- Use verbs that represent observable and measurable performance (live, written, other type of performance). For each outcome, choose the single verb that represents the deepest level of performance that you want for that outcome; avoid compound verbs.
- Because the ABA now requires at least 6 experiential credits for graduation, you might want to align any clinic, field placement, or simulation course to at least some outcomes that relate directly to both your course goals and your school's program outcomes.

Course Goal (from Worksheet 5): Engage in effective collaborative relationships (across domains) to further the position of their assigned simulation client.

Students should be able to . . .

Knowledge, skills and/or values	Verb (performance)	Object (the learning statement)	Condition and/or Criterion
Recognize how their individual communication style(s) impact capacity to engage in effective collaborative relationships.	Identify	Communications style(s) and pattern(s)	To appreciate how one's personal style supports or detracts from the effectiveness of the team in the summative assessment exercises.

Course Goal (from Worksheet 5): Internalize frameworks for speaking and listening that support a client-centered lawyering approach to their attorney-client relationship with their simulation client.

Students should be able to . . .

Knowledge, skills and/or values	Verb (performance)	Object (the learning statement)	Condition and/or Criterion
Ask questions that generate high-quality information	Use	Journalism questions, t-funneling, and active listening	To manage and direct client conversations in furtherance of the simulated case.
Use t-funneling techniques to focus conversation	Be flexible	In generating questions and conducting funnel-like follow up	To explore the factual circumstances, context, and motivations of the communication partner.

Use feedback cues to convey engagement with clients, counsel, partners, etc.	offer	Body language, verbal critique, and positive responses	In a constructive manner that keeps communication channels open.

Checklist:

- Do the course outcomes describe what students should know, do, and/or value in order to complete the final assessment successfully?
- Are the course outcomes described with verbs that represent observable, measurable behaviors?
- Are the course outcomes expressed individually, not jointly?
- Do the course outcomes align with a course goal?
- Do the course outcomes align with the ABA-required program outcomes, in whole or in part? (optional)

DRC Process Notes:

When I began teaching this course, I found *The Clinic Seminar* by Epstein, Aiken, & Mlyniec (2014) to be an important resource. I still use many of the guides from the teaching manual as frameworks for assessment and feedback.

Worksheet 10: Organize Topics and Learning Activities across the Entire Course

Once you have identified the course outcomes, start identifying the learning activities and lawyering tasks that will enable students to develop the knowledge, skills, or values necessary to achieve each outcome. These activities will then help you choose the materials for the course and to plan individual units and lessons. You will want to organize the units into a sequence that promotes effective learning through smooth and clear transitions from unit to unit.

Situational factors

Before laying out the specific learning activities, re-examine the situational factors that will enable or constrain the types of learning activities you can incorporate, when or how they should be sequenced, and the like. Some of your situational factors may include the pre-requisite knowledge, skills, or values expected of students before taking your course or the availability of a boot camp week or clinic orientation.

Models for organizing and sequencing course content

Consider generally your course's organization. The models below will help you to sequence the course topics, outcomes, and learning activities and to decide what foundation needs to be laid and when. You may combine multiple organizational models.

- *Order of importance*: Because students have highest enthusiasm for a course at the beginning, embed the most important (or difficult) concepts earliest.
- *Order of process*: Sequence material along the arc of a process, beginning to end, *e.g.*, litigation sequence (complaint to trial); attorney-client relationship (first meeting through resolution of the matter; first meeting to transition to the next student-lawyer).
- *Simple to complex*: Because students can build confidence in mastering simple topics and skills, start with these before tackling higher level, more complex tasks.
- *Dependent or supportive relationship between units of study*: If the learning is cumulative, start with the concepts or skills that represent pre-requisite knowledge or skill necessary (or helpful) for later units.
- *Cause & Effect:* Introduce a range of problems and then follow with types of solutions to be applied (*e.g.*, claims and remedies).
- *Spiral or cyclical*: Introduce and revisit concepts or skills multiple times throughout the term, adding complexity with each repetition.
- *General to specific vs. Concrete to abstract*: Introduce general principles & then apply to specific situations. Alternatively, start with specific examples of a phenomenon and move toward what they represent at the conceptual or abstract level.
- *Thematic or topical:* Use when individual units represent independent concepts. Plan transitions carefully. (*e.g.*, a survey course.)

ABA experiential course design standards

Standard 304 provides the elements that any course intended to be counted toward the experiential graduation requirement must have. For each mode of skills teaching (simulation, clinic, externship) Standard 304 includes additional requirements.

Std. 304 (a): Experiential courses [include] simulation courses, law clinics, and field placements that must be primarily experiential in nature and must:

1) Integrate doctrine, theory, skills, and legal ethics, and engage students in performance of one or more of the professional skills identified in Standard 302;
2) Develop the concepts underlying the professional skills being taught;
3) Provide multiple opportunities for performance;
4) Provide opportunities for student performance, self-evaluation, and feedback from a faculty member, or, for a field placement, a site supervisor;
5) A classroom instructional component; or, for a field placement, a classroom instructional component, regularly scheduled tutorials, or other means of ongoing, contemporaneous, faculty-guided reflection; and
6) Provide direct supervision of the student's performance by the faculty member; or, for a field placement, provide direct supervision of the student's performance by a faculty member or a site supervisor.

Topic	Course outcomes in measurable terms	Learning activities / Lawyering tasks	Materials to aid student performance
	What will students be able to think, do, or value to complete the final assessment successfully? Use info developed in Worksheet 9. Organize in a coherent sequence. **By the end of the semester, students will be able to:**	What exercises, performances, discussions, or other learning activity will help students to prepare for and succeed in the final assessment? Identify whether an activity is designed as an introduction (I), practice opportunity (P), or mastery vehicle (M).	What readings, media, information, lecture, and other aids will my students need to perform the lawyering and learning activities successfully? Will it be used before, during, or after the class?
Collaborative Problem Solving	Engage in effective collaborative relationships (across domains) to further the position of their assigned simulation client.	Game 1: Farmer Brown's Cows— 3 members in a group; farmer dies, leaves will that bequeaths to 3 children his herd; division of the herd is in fractions not even numbers. Resolve the dispute between the children about the herd's division. Game introduces students on the first day to the team model of assessment throughout the course. Game 2: Broken Squares— 6 members in a group must recreate 5 equal-sized squares from cut up pieces; students cannot talk, gesture or steal pieces from each other; collaborative exercise taking away major forms of communication Game 3: Lego— 3 members in a group, 3 exercises using Lego bricks to build/question/rebuild. Primary goals include surfacing question formation, listening, judgments and assumptions, quality of information discovered/elicited, word choice.	Lecture In-class debriefing of exercises using reflection prompts and directed questions Text reading TED-talk on listening

Topic	Course outcomes in measurable terms	Learning activities / Lawyering tasks	Materials to aid student performance
Client-Centered Lawyering	Internalize frameworks for speaking and listening that support a client-centered lawyering approach to their attorney-client relationship with their simulation client.	Intro. lecture on basic client-centered lawyering model Intro lecture on integrating Wyoming RPC into lawyering relationships Hypothetical: Rich Aunt's Will Dispute (completed as individuals)—wealthy aunt dies leaving a will dispute over cash inheritance; what factors motivate students to choose litigation of the will over settling the will dispute (connect back to this exercise later to change focus from individual to client) Large Group Discussion—what are the most critical motivators for choosing to settle/choosing to hire a lawyer; and why. Connect back to client representation—introduction to principles of working from client-centered focus (keep this self-focused to help students recognize how their value systems influence their choice-making; return later to shift focus outward).	Lecture In-class debriefing of exercises using reflection prompts and directed questions Text reading Wyoming Rules of Professional Conduct reading

Interviewing	Internalize frameworks for speaking and listening that support a client-centered lawyering approach to their attorney-client relationship with their simulation client. Engage in effective collaborative relationships (across domains) to further the position of their assigned simulation client.	Revisit Lego game—break down some of the lessons introduced in the Lego brick games—how did the way questioner asked questions influence the quality of the information revealed by the builder; when the Lego bricks were different between the builder and the re-builder, how did that influence capacity to recreate the original build—how does this connect back to judgments and assumptions, information quality, what it means to be a listener, etc. Formative exercises in identifying basic facts of case, "bad" facts, client motivations, context, etc. Groups of 3 not the assigned law firms—changing groups requires students to be aware of different communication styles with which they are unfamiliar (break them out of the mold of knowing their law firm teammates). In class reflection on how each individual influences the dynamic of the conversation. Introduction to the neuroscience of how fear impacts responses. 3-dimensional model of the brain using the hand and "flipping the lid" vs. having the brain be "online." Formative exercise on interviewing a witness and on interviewing a transactional client—different goals, motivators in different lawyering situations (building relationships across lawyering environments and situations).	Lecture In-class debriefing of exercises using reflection prompts and directed questions Text reading Wyoming Rules of Professional Conduct reading Written feedback on reflective memos and summative assessment exercises

Topic	Course outcomes in measurable terms	Learning activities / Lawyering tasks	Materials to aid student performance
Supportive Lawyering Processes: Case Theory, Fact Investigation, Case Planning	Internalize frameworks for speaking and listening that support a client-centered lawyering approach to their attorney-client relationship with their simulation client.	Develop case theory (limited word count) outside of class for semester-long simulation client; bring to class for large group discussion—use elements of storytelling to tease out for students how well they listened to their client interview, primary motivators for client, relevant opposing facts/pieces. Draw connection in class with classroom exercise that connects the reworked case theory with factual investigation—how to build a factual case using the case theory as a guide/reference point. Work through as a group how case theory and fact investigation can impact case planning; cycle back to the iterative nature of information gathering/case theory/changes in case planning needs or focus.	In class work on case theory development In class work on case planning In-class debriefing of exercises using reflection prompts and directed questions Wyoming Rules of Civil Procedure reading Wyoming Rules of Professional Conduct reading
Client Counseling	Internalize frameworks for assessing and preparing for client counseling sessions that support a client-centered lawyering approach to the attorney-client relationship with their simulation client. Engage in effective collaborative relationships (across domains) to further the position of their assigned simulation client.	Revisit Rich Aunt Hypothetical from outward-focused perspective—we did this once talking about you, how does it change if you're talking about advising someone else? Formative exercise in advising Hilary Clinton during the development of the "email scandal" using newspaper articles and blog posts written during 3 critical periods (revelation of the issue, 2 months later, 1 year later); similar exercise on advising Brett Kavanaugh at specific points in his SCOTUS confirmation conflict—if the lawyer is not litigating but is simply advising on next steps, what are perceived motivators, context, client needs, client goals (long and short term). Formative exercises in advising—practice separate components of client-centered model, listening; Groups of 3 not the assigned law firms—changing groups requires students to be aware of different communication styles with which they are unfamiliar (break them out of the mold of knowing their law firm teammates).	Lecture In-class debriefing of exercises using reflection prompts and directed questions Text reading Guest speaker—communication intelligence Newspaper articles/ blog posts Written feedback on reflective memos and summative assessment exercises

Negotiation	Internalize frameworks for speaking and listening that support a client-centered lawyering approach to their attorney-client relationship with their simulation client and with opposing counsel. Engage in effective collaborative relationships (across domains) to further the position of their assigned simulation client.	Formative exercises in negotiating various disputes—Groups of 3 are the assigned law firms—begin working on reconciling the various negotiation-style tendencies of the law firm members to identify the strengths and weaknesses of each other's' approaches. Formative exercise in writing down various negotiated agreements—are the students hearing what they think they are hearing? Are they communicating it properly in writing—why is writing it down important; how does writing it down surface misunderstandings in communication, differences in articulating salient negotiated points; how do you resolve differences in understanding using communication styles, speaking, and listening Formative exercises on identifying commonalities, Zones of Potential Agreement, Best, Most likely, and Worst Alternatives to a Negotiated Agreement; powers/rights/interests, negotiation styles and strategies.	Lecture In-class debriefing of exercises using reflection prompts and directed questions Text readings Blog posts/articles on writing it down Wyoming Rules of Professional Conduct reading Written feedback on reflective memos and summative assessment exercises (students may choose to pick this up from me at the start of the next semester as this assessment happens at the very end of the semester during exam week).

Checklist:

- Do the course materials, learning activities, and lawyering tasks provide sufficient foundation for student progress toward course mastery?
- Does the order of materials, learning activities, and lawyering tasks allow my students to apply their learning repeatedly, to make progress toward mastery of the course outcomes?
- Do the learning exercises and lawyering activities include ones where I expect course mastery for each Enduring Learning element (Worksheet 4)?
- Do the course materials, learning activities, and lawyering tasks allow my students to consider the Animating Theory and Exploratory Questions for the course on multiple occasions throughout the semester (Worksheets 1 and 2)?
- Do the learning activities and lawyering tasks cover each criterion in ABA Standards 304 (as applied to all experiential courses and to the provisions specific to my type of course)??

Worksheet 11: Plan Units of Student Learning Activities

For each unit (a single topic/learning activity or chunk of topics or activities), create a plan for work that your students will do before, during, and after class. Make sure that you identify how you will "know" that the students learned what you planned. That might be your own reflection and assessment at the end of the class, supervision, or unit, or it might be some other evidence of student learning (whether direct from the student, or indirect from another source).

Course Unit: Collaborative Problem Solving (connected to introduction to critical self-reflection)

Relevant Course Outcomes (from Worksheet 9): Recognize how individual communication style(s) impact capacity to engage in effective collaborative relationships.

Increase student self-awareness about individual communication styles.

How will students prepare for the unit/class?	What will students do in class to prepare them to reach the outcomes?	How will I know they learned what I wanted them to learn?
Read: Text assignment on problem-solving and collaboration Non-text reading on communication styles Listen: TED-talk on listening skills Out-of-Class Exercise: Prepare personal story about listening, storytelling, being misunderstood Short lecture: Active listening as a communication skill; Lawyers as problem-solvers; Collaborative relationships across lawyering domains; Connecting communication to collaboration	Game 1: Farmer Brown's Cows —play game in small groups —analyze answers in large group —discuss problem-solving approaches within group —evaluate the impact of various approaches —connect to client representation Game 2: Broken Squares —play game in small groups—no speaking, grabbing, etc. —discuss reasons behind limitations on communication strategies —discuss impact of forced collaboration —evaluate the impact of various approaches —connect to client representation Game 3: Lego —play game in small groups— 2 variations (all same blocks, one block different) —debrief game in large group —discuss impact of question formation, presumptions, assumptions, etc. on how questions asked and how answers interpreted —evaluate the impact of various approaches —discuss implications for collaborative work between team members —discuss implications for collaborative work with client —discuss implications for collaborative work in other legal environments (court, negotiations, factual investigations, etc.)	Students can identify how they approached solving the problem given whatever limitations are articulated. Students can identify the impact of listening skills on the resolutions in each game. Students can identify what teammates bring to the dynamic. Students can identify what their individual approach added to or detracted from the small group dynamic. Students can begin assessing whether and how they will need to be flexible in the sustained collaborative relationship of their team for the semester. Students can discuss whether and how they would make different communication choices to support stronger collaborative relationships throughout the semester.

Checklist:

- Do the unit activities align with one or more of my course's learning outcomes?
- Do the unit activities have a clear purpose to help students learn?
- Is the unit structured to build on existing learning, give clear direction, and give opportunity to practice what students are expected to do?
- Do the unit activities give students time to develop their own thoughts and positions, and to hear others' ideas, perspectives, or positions?
- Do I hold my students accountable for doing the activity, including by giving them feedback?
- Do I provide opportunity for students to reflect on the activities and connect them to their prior learning?

DRC Process Notes:

I start the course with this unit for a few reasons:

1. They do already know how to ask questions, but they may not be intentional about it or cognizant of the ways in which their individual communication styles impact their connections with other people.

2. The lessons of the games we play in this unit build on each other and provide an anchor for approaching lessons that happen later in the course. For instance, Farmer Brown is seemingly unsolvable unless the students stop thinking about it in legal terms and instead think about it as a math equation (foundation for thinking creatively about legal and non-legal options). Broken Squares keeps the students from speaking to each other and requires them to be observant about body language, task sharing, etc. (foundation for engaging in a meaningful manner with clients in a client-centered fashion). The Lego games provide a window into quality of questions, making judgments and assumptions about meaning, listening skills, what common understanding means, and the like. All 3 sets of games require the students work together with people they do not know (or know well, considering the size of the classes) with the aim of surfacing what it means to work as part of a unit.

3. Start the students on the reflective journey they will take over the semester, including identifying what they as individuals and their teammates bring to the dynamic of the class.

Course: Disability Law Clinic, Carwina Weng

Worksheet 1: Animating Theory

To identify the learning goals for your course, first consider the subject matter generally. Because a subject matter has more content than a course can cover, start by articulating the key reason students should take your course. That reason is your course's Animating Theory. Grant Wiggins and Jay McTighe coined a colloquial term for this, "The Big Idea."[10]

Once you choose your Animating Theory, you will flesh it out with a set of Exploratory Questions (Worksheet 2) that illuminate the challenges you want your students to grapple with. Setting the Animating Theory and Exploratory Questions allows you to build your course from course goal, to mastery evidence, to learning activities. The Animating Theory is not the same as your course goal(s) or learning outcomes; it underlies both. You may have more than one, but restrict yourself to at most two so that student learning is focused. Here, less is more.

The Animating Theory for the Course:

- Refers to core concepts, principles, and theories in a field of study—What unifies the field of study? What makes a skill worthwhile or effective?
- Organizes large bodies of information, skills, or values.
- Is amenable to transfer to new fields of study, new situations, and across disciplines.
- Is abstract and requires investigation to probe its implications.

Considerations for a Skills-focused Course:

- What does the lawyering skill help you do more effectively or efficiently for a client?
- What are the underlying concepts or objectives of the skill?
- When and how do you use the skill (strategy and tactics)?
- Why does the skill work?

Examples: The Animating Theory need not be phrased as a complete sentence. A "motto" works.

- Persuasion: Know your audience.
- Sociology: People in a community depend on each other for the things they need.
- History: History is written by the victors.
- Law: The best lawyer is the best prepared lawyer.

Identify the Animating Theory(ies) for your course.

Lawyer as problem solver.
Human-centered approach—respectful, open, nonjudgmental, collaborative.

Checklist:

- Does my animating theory provide a concise statement, principle, theory, or generalization?
- Does it stand the test of time, allowing students' thoughts about it to develop and evolve over time?

---

10. See Wiggins, G., & McTighe, J., UNDERSTANDING BY DESIGN (2nd ed. 2005).

- Can it promote in-depth understanding and help make sense of the subject matter?
- Can it promote in-depth understanding and help make sense of the subject matter?

CW Process Notes:

I teach a litigation clinic focused on government benefits, but most students will not get an administrative hearing during their one semester in clinic. Nor do most of my students want to become litigators. And almost none is interested in government benefits, other administrative law practices, or poverty law. Most merely want a live-client experience.

Consequently, I want the Operating Principle to be accessible and engaging to all students who are taking the clinic. When I first started teaching clinic, I conceptualized this vision as helping students to find their voices as lawyers—how they interact with clients and others, how they approach problems, how they communicate in writing. I see these issues as involving affect and skills, as I hope students will learn the value of human-centered lawyering and the skills to imbue all their lawyering with that value. When I encountered the world of professional identity formation, I realized I had a ready-made framework in which to operate explicitly and intentionally.

Professional identity formation focuses on how a student becomes a professional, with attention to values, skills, traits, and interests. I came to focus on the skill of problem-solving (and the role of lawyer as problem solvers) as students in law school are focused so much on legal analysis as "what lawyers do" without necessarily understanding why lawyers need to be able to analyze and why clients seek out lawyers. Focusing on problem-solving was one way to add context to what lawyers do for clients. The fact that I knew the ABA standards would include problem-solving as a required program outcome cemented this choice, as I am concerned with a common trait in teaching: to expect students to be able to do something without actually teaching them how to.

I couple problem-solving with human-centeredness as this value is so important in a service profession. Indeed, problem-solving and human-centeredness together well: the way a lawyer approaches problem-solving and the effectiveness of the skill depend on how the lawyer works with/for the client, how they conceptualize the problem and the stakeholders, and how they understand nonlegal aspects of the problem. In addition, being human-centered cuts across all other roles and services lawyers provide.

Thus, I would say my final Animating Theory is a role-based one: "lawyers as human-centered problem solvers."

Worksheet 2: Develop Exploratory Questions

Questions are used to study the Animating Theory for the course and to ground student learning. These questions are open-ended and probing in nature rather than intended to yield specific answers.

An Exploratory Question:

- Opens the Animating Theory for the course to genuine inquiry.
- Provokes lively discussion, sustained inquiry, and new understanding, as well as more questions.
- Requires students to consider alternatives, weigh evidence, support their ideas, and justify their answers.
- Stimulates vital, on-going rethinking of assumptions, prior understanding, and personal experience.
- Naturally recurs, creating opportunities for transfer to other situations and subjects.

Examples of Exploratory Questions that amplify the value of your Animating Theory:

- Persuasion: What's in it for my audience? What are the ethics of persuasion?
- Government and public policy: What makes a good government? How does cultural identity inform one's views of government and its role in society?
- History/Precedent: What patterns recur throughout history and common law? Is all history biased?

Identify 1–2 Exploration Questions for each Animating Theory.

Animating Theory 1: Human-centered Legal Services

How do a lawyer's personal values, identity, and traits affect their ability to serve clients?
What do clients want from their lawyers?

Animating Theory 2: Lawyers as Problem Solvers

What makes a lawyer an effective problem solver?
How does problem-solving interact with other skills and roles of a lawyer?

Checklist:

- Are my Exploratory Questions open-ended, nonjudgmental, meaningful, and purposeful?
- Do the questions have emotional appeal?
- Do the questions have more than one coherent answer?
- Do the questions probe for deeper meaning and explore ideas and beliefs?
- Do the questions encourage peer learning and collaboration?

CW Process Notes:

I started working from the lawyer outward, in progress toward human-centered problem-solving. So, I made human-centeredness the first principle and have students think about who they are and why that matters to the kind of lawyer the will be (core professional identity formation query). Then I want students to think about what their clients want, with the goal of getting students to think about non-law expertise related wants. With the second principle, I want students to bring in their thoughts on human-centeredness into this professional role, to explore how the ability to think about clients as whole human beings and partners affects problem-solving. Then, I want students to think about how improving their skill in problem-solving has ripple effects in other areas of lawyering. I also thought that giving students a specific problem-solving model to work with would help to make explicit practices they have probably used already in solving problems and to give them a clear framework to build on in making their own skills intentional.

Worksheet 3: Identify Situational Factors That Affect Teaching and Learning

The first two Worksheets lay out the scope of the course on a grand scale. Now situate your ambitions for student learning within the realities of your course, the school's curriculum, your students' semesters, and the scope of all your responsibilities. Some of these situational factors are assets to use wisely and fruitfully. Others are limitations. Affirmatively acknowledging that, in your clinic, field placement, or simulation course, you simply cannot cover all that your students need to know, be able to do, or value will help you to make pedagogical choices to maximize student learning.

Possible situational factors

Your school's J.D. program learning outcomes (including the ABA-mandated outcomes)	ABA Standard 3.02 requires problem-solving as an outcome.
Length (e.g., semester, year), number of credits, number of hours in field, casework, or classroom	3-credit, 1-semester course, open to 2Ls and 3Ls. Most students carry a full non-clinic load, co- and extra-curriculars, job search
Grading scheme	Letter grades, not curved
Student preparedness (typical, high/low)	Less training now in teamwork, cultural competence, professional identity formation. Some students have a service learning experience in 1L year
Student motivations	Primary interest is in client interaction, not in working with clients with disabilities or litigations. Some interest in working with veterans
Uniformity, dissimilarity, or variety of student work (in type and complexity)	Litigation focus with two heavily backlogged agencies—students can end up with very different experiences.

Opportunities with community partners (and their needs)	Varies
Personal responsibilities that constrain my availability for class or individual student engagement	My service load and family obligations
Other factors	Administrative pressure to keep enrollment up, conventional wisdom regarding bar courses vs. clinics

Checklist:

- Do I capture factors that are opportunities for me to maximize the learning in my course?
- Do I capture the most salient factors that limit the scope of what students can reasonably learn in my course?
- Do I capture the most salient factors that limit my ability to execute a course plan and engage my students?

Worksheet 4: Prioritize Learning for Transfer (durability)

Allow your Animating Theory to percolate. Break it down into specific priorities for your students' learning. Identify the knowledge and understandings, skills, and/or values that are essential to the Animating Theory of your course. Prioritize those elements based on long-term importance to the students' learning. The highest level (enduring learning) should be learning that is transferable to different contexts in their professional lives.

Even though your course may cover content in all three levels of priority, your course goals (Worksheet 5) and final assessments (Worksheet 7) will focus on the knowledge and understandings, skills, and/or values that you intend to be long-lived (enduring) for your students.

Enduring learning:

Knowledge—who they are; problem-solving model
Skill—perspective taking and problem-solving
Value—human centeredness, collaboration

Important for students to know:

Knowledge—lawyering as story telling
Skill—clear, straightforward communicating
Value—importance of preparation and reflection

Worth being familiar with:

Knowledge—Social Security Administration and Veterans' Affairs Disability Compensation program basic requirements
Skill—analyzing statutes and regulations

Checklist:

- Do the elements listed as *Enduring Learning* help students to synthesize individual lessons and readings into a deeper understanding of the Animating Theory?
- Do the *Enduring Learning* elements lay a foundation for further study of this subject matter?
- Do the *Enduring Learning* elements help students to figure out issues in the subject matter that are more difficult to master?

CW Process Notes:

My focus is definitely on universal skills & values over the specifics needed to practice in disability benefits. Most of my students have no interest in this practice area (or legal services practice). I want skills & values they will recognize as immediately useful & transferable. Disability benefits is just the forum I've chosen for them to practice in.

Worksheet 5: Use Learning Taxonomies to Craft Course Goals[11]

Now that you've identified your learning priorities, you will distill the enduring learning into course goals. Course goals represent the essential i) knowledge and understandings, ii) skills, and/or iii) values that you intend your students to attain by the end of the term. One way to unify the enduring learning into goals is to ask: "How will my students be different by the end of the course?" To answer this question in a way that can be assessed at the end of the course, we have collected taxonomies of learning that capture the complexity and depth of learning you want your students to attain. The taxonomies further assist you to establish observable and measurable course goals (amenable to assessment, Worksheets 6 and 7).

The taxonomies cover the three domains of learning:

1. Cognitive domain: Focuses on knowledge, comprehension, and critical thinking.
2. Psychomotor domain: Encompasses learning geared toward executing specific tasks (*e.g.*, client counseling, negotiating with opposing counsel, witness interviewing).
3. Affective domain: Relates to awareness and growth in values, attitudes, and emotional control (*e.g.*, values embedded in the attorney-client relationship, toward justice, and relating to professional identity formation).

The taxonomy grids on the next three pages organize each domain of learning hierarchically. As you move through the grids (left to right; top to bottom) the categories describe learning at deeper

11. Course Development Institute, Indiana University Center for Innovative Teaching and Learning.

levels of difficulty. Use these grids to choose the deepest point(s) that correspond to a realistic learning goal for your course.

The grids, their terminology, and hierarchy are offered as an aid. Some of your learning priorities might fit within more than one taxonomy, and the Action Verbs that exemplify a category might resonate more than the category of learning does. Choose what works for you. Don't let the taxonomies push your learning goal toward something that doesn't feel right to you. Maybe you will pencil in learning targets for your course in several cells on separate grids; that will allow you to test out different ways to characterize the course goal(s) you want to pursue. In the end you should articulate 1–2 course goals. In drafting these goals, keep your verb singular, not compound, as a verb representing the farthest/deepest taxonomy cell that encapsulates your goal will necessarily include the less complex learning needed to reach that goal.

In the following three pages:

- Review the taxonomy for each domain.
- Reflect on your ambitions for your course. Pencil notes in any of the cells.
- Review your notes and distill them to one to two course goals (last page).

The course goals will form the bedrock for your course. Everything else—the final assessment, rubric, outcomes and learning activities—will be aligned to the course goals.

Sources:

Knowledge and Cognitive Processing Domain

Adapted from Anderson, L.W., Krathwohl, D.R. et. al. (2001). *A Taxonomy for Learning, Teaching, and Assessing: A Revision of Bloom's Taxonomy of Educational Objectives*. Abridged ed. New York: Longman.

Psychomotor Domain

Adapted from Dave, R.H. (1970), "Developing and Writing Behavioral Objectives;" Simpson E. J. (1972). The Classification of Educational Objectives in the Psychomotor Domain. Washington, DC: Gryphon House.

Affective Domain

Adapted from Krathwohl, D.R., Bloom, B.S., and Masia, B.B. (1964). *Taxonomy of Educational Objectives, Book II. Affective domain*. New York: David McKay Company, Inc.

Find taxonomies on following pages

1. Knowledge and Cognitive Processing Domain

		Cognitive processing			
		1. Remember	2. Understand	3. Apply	4. Analyze, Evaluate, or Create
Knowledge	A. Factual	[your course goals]			
	B. Conceptual				
	C. Procedural				
	D. Meta-cognitive				I expect students to be able to analyze their use of the problem-solving model in specific instances and to evaluate their progress overall, including identifying steps to continue growing.

Knowledge types	Definition	Examples
Factual	Basic elements to be acquainted with the discipline and solve problems	Terminology, vocabulary, elements, and details
Conceptual	Interrelationship among basic elements	Categories, principles, theories, models, and structures
Procedural	How to do something *(overlaps with psychomotor domain)*	Subject-specific skills, methods of inquiry and criteria for using, and techniques and procedures
Meta-cognitive	Knowing about knowing	Strategic knowledge, reflections, and self-knowledge

Cognitive processing	Definition	Action Verbs
Remember	Retrieve relevant knowledge from long-term memory	Retain, recall, recognize, memorize, recollect, think of, define, identify, list, name, record, repeat, underline, select
Understand	Construct meaning from instructional messages; can be in oral, written or graphic formats	Interpret, exemplify, classify, summarize, infer, compare, explain, give examples of, describe in own words, differentiate between, discriminate, restate, review, translate, respond, practice, discuss, identify, review, simulate
Apply	Carry out procedures	Execute, implement, apply, demonstrate, dramatize, generalize, illustrate, operate, operationalize, practice, use, utilize, initiate

Analyze	Break material into parts and determine relationships	Differentiate, organize, attribute, analyze, appraise, categorize, compare, conclude, contrast, correlate, deduce, diagram, distinguish, estimate, examine, experiment, infer, predict, question, solve, diagnose
Evaluate	Make judgments based upon criteria or standards	Check, critique, assess, judge, appraise, choose, compare, evaluate, measure, rate, revise, score, select, validate, value
Create	Put elements together into coherent or functional whole, reorganize into new patterns	Generate, plan, produce, invent, arrange, assemble, collect, compose, construct, create, design, develop, formulate, manage, modify, organize, prepare, propose, synthesize

2. Psychomotor Domain: (can be used by experiential faculty to set goals for lawyering skill development)

	Definition	Action Verbs	Your Course Goals
Perception	Actively using sensory cues to attend to the behavioral skill. E.g., student observes a seasoned attorney perform the behavior.	Choose, describe, detect, differentiate, distinguish, identify, isolate, relate, select, separate	
Imitation	Copying the behavior. The student attempts the behavior, with direction and feedback from an experienced person. The student shows desire and motivation to learn the behavior.	Adhere, begin, attempt, carry out, copy, duplicate, follow, mimic, repeat, replicate, start, try	
Practice	Using the behavior repeatedly. The student performs the behavior multiple times, and her actions become more automatic and smooth. The experienced person need not be present.	Codify, discriminate, display, order, organize, systematize, weigh, discuss, theorize, formulate, balance, examine, adhere to	Because I am providing the students with a specific model in problem-solving, the psychomotor taxonomy is useful to gauge their facility with the model. I want most students to be able to practice the model, without having to look it up each time they use it. I anticipate that some students will also achieve the naturalizing stage, especially if they have more life experience.

Naturalization	Performing two or more skills in combination or sequence, with consistency and ease. The student can combine the behavior with other behaviors independently and with little mental exertion.	Adapt, automatize, combine, complete, demonstrate, internalize, master, perform, show, succeed	
Origination	Creating new behaviors, combinations, or sequences to respond to a new situation. The student creates new methodologies or techniques to improve on or re-imagine how the needs can be met.	Create, design, compose, refine, arrange	

3. **Affective Domain:** (can be used to set goals related to professional values, affect, or work approach, *e.g.*, with regard to the attorney client relationship, the rule of law, or other professional value)

	Definition	Action Verbs	Your Course Goals
Receive	Be aware of; attend to something; be willing to tolerate it.	Accept, attend, develop, ask, recognize, listen for, describe, differentiate, receive, identify, tolerate	
Respond	Incorporate a new behavior as a result of the experience.	Complete, comply, cooperate, discuss, examine, obey, assist, respond, follow, volunteer, perform	Human centeredness brings affect into the lawyering equation. The expectation is that students will display behaviors that demonstrate their acceptance of this value. So, I am marking a goal in this dimension as well. As my students are now coming into clinic with less exposure to clients and empathy, I am setting the goal lower to be more realistic about where they might move to.
Value	Show specific involvement or commitment.	Accept, defend, devote oneself to, pursue, seek, justify, join, debate, value	I would still expect some students to get into the valuing stage.
Organize	Integrate a new value into one's general set of values, giving due ranking among other priorities.	Codify, discriminate, display, order, organize, systematize, weigh, discuss, theorize, formulate, balance, examine, adhere to	

Internalize the value set	Act consistently, conscientiously, and pro-actively with the new value.	Internalize, verify, be rated high in the value, require, resolve	

Using the taxonomies on the previous pages, draft your top 1–2 Course Goals:

By the end of the course, my students will:

> Be able to address real-life lawyering problems and client matters effectively by applying the provided problem-solving model and by following a human-centered approach.

Checklist

- Do my goals fit within the Animating Theory for the course (Worksheet 1)?
- Do my goals reflect the learning priorities I have set for the course (Worksheet 4)?
- Are my goals clear, observable, and measurable (Worksheets 6 and 8)?
- Do my goals reflect the situational limits of my course and my full responsibilities (Worksheet 3)?

Worksheet 6: Identify Observable Evidence of Student Mastery

Visualize the student who excels in the course you are designing. What does the student's performance or work product look like? That is your evidence of student mastery. The student's work is not at the level of a veteran attorney's; it's A-level work as a student in your course. Look at your picture closely, using the following six categories, or facets, of concrete, observable performance to assist your efforts.[12] A "masterful" student performance may well involve synchronous use of multiple facets. After you identify your evidence of mastery, then you will i) create a final assessment exercise to allow your students to exhibit this evidence (Worksheet 7) and ii) create an assessment rubric that defines levels of student performance (Worksheet 8).

Facet of understanding	Associated verbs & Starter phrases	Evidence of student's mastery in your course
Explanation: Students are able to provide thorough and well-supported accounts of topics, events, or actions, backed by reasoning, facts, or experience. Students are able to develop a theory of how and why, supported by evidence, law, and experience.	Demonstrate, derive, describe, design, exhibit, express, instruct, justify, model, predict, prove, show, synthesize, teach Students will be able to: Explain/teach [x], Give examples of [x]; Make connections with [x]; Offer a theory of [x]; Avoid misconceptions, such as [x].	

12. Adapted and expanded from Wiggins, G., & McTighe, J., UNDERSTANDING BY DESIGN (2nd ed. 2005) (describing six facets of understanding).

Interpretation: Students are able to interpret and analyze the importance, meaning, or significance of their knowledge/skill, with context and awareness of multiple interpretations. Students can create meaning from a set of facts and law, with attention to ambiguity, uncertainty, opacity, emotional content, and diverse perspectives.	Create analogies, critique, document, evaluate, illustrate, judge, make sense of, provide metaphors, read between the lines, represent, tell a story of. Students will be able to: Interpret the [x]; Tell a revealing story of [x]; Provide an apt analogy for [x]; Show the importance or meaning of [x]; Translate [x]; Relate [x] to your experience (or the experiences of others).	Make sense of how they used the model in their clinic work.
Application-Adaptation: Students use and adapt the knowledge/skill acquired to new situations and contexts, showing flexibility and adaptability. Students can design, develop, test, and refine responses to a new problem or dilemma presented.	Adapt, create, de-bug, design, exhibit, invent, perform, produce, propose, solve, test, use Students will be able to: Apply [x] in a new circumstance; Show or demonstrate [x]; Use in the context of [x]; Design/invent [x]; Overcome a challenge or constraint, such as [x].	Use independently the model in two contexts: a client-related problem and a personal professional development problem.
Perspective: Students can take a step back to appreciate a broader view, critically assess the value or importance of a topic. Students can identify, critique, and give credence to multiple valid perspectives regarding a topic.	Analyze, argue, compare, contrast, criticize, infer Students will be able to: Analyze [x]; See from the viewpoint of [x]; Compare and contrast [x]; Critique [x]; Critically examine assumptions such as [x]; Show how [x]; See the limits of [x].	Use the elements of the model that require specific attention to learning about and adapting to the perspectives of others (clients and others involved in the problem).
Empathy: Students show the ability to embrace the feelings, reasoning, motivations, and perspectives of others with acceptance and non-judgment. Open-minded insight to others.	Assume the role of, believe, be like, be open to, consider, imagine, relate, role-play. Students will be able to: Walk in the shoes of [x]; Experience directly and see [x]; Reach a common understanding with another concerning [x]; Entertain the seemingly odd or alien view that [x]; Anticipate possible concerns of others regarding [x] based on their interests, values, and circumstances.	

Self-Knowledge:		
Students accept that their style, preferences, and habits are specific to them and affect their views of events, information, and other people. Students can evaluate their professional development with appreciation of what came easily or not and why; can evaluate personal, emotional responses with detachment.	Be aware of, realize, recognize, reflect, self-assess. Students will be able to: Recognize their own prejudice(s) about [x]; Identify the lens through which they view [x]; Explain how they came to understand [x]; Realize that even with all they now know, they still don't really understand [x].	Examine how their prior knowledge, personal preferences and dislikes, impacted how they engaged problem-solving and how they changed through the process.

Checklist

- Does my mastery evidence flow from my course goals and teaching priorities?
- Does my mastery evidence facilitate exploration of the Animating Theory for the course?
- Is my evidence of student mastery observable and measureable in an assessment exercise?

Worksheet 7: Create a Final Assessment Exercise

Create a final assessment exercise that will allow you to observe and evaluate each piece of mastery evidence listed. Before crafting the assessment exercise, revisit the enduring learning priorities you established (Worksheet 4) and your course goals (Worksheet 5). Use the measurable language in the goals and the mastery evidence (Worksheet 6) to create the content framework for your final assessment exercise. Note: you may use more than one assessment exercise to determine the final grade for your course.

- Choose the vehicle: a piece(s) of writing, a portfolio, an oral presentation or live performance (to professor or before another audience), etc.
- Quantity—Length: Consider how short or long the students' performance or work product should be to showcase their mastery. For instance, if you want to assess the students' level of reflection, can the students meet your expectations in 250 words, 1,000, or 5,000 words? If you want to assess the students' ability to conduct a summation for the jury, should the summation last 5 minutes, 15 minutes, 30 minutes, or more?
- Quantity—Parts: Determine the number of parts or exercises. While it might be ideal to create an assessment exercise that synthesizes the full constellation of knowledge, skills, and values represented in the course goal, often it might be impracticable to create a single assessment exercise that allows the students to produce evidence of full mastery. How would you segment the parts of the assessment?
- Practicalities: Consider the situational factors that impact what is manageable for you to assess.
- Design the subject and the prompts: This is the meat of the assessment. What are you asking your students to do? Make certain that your prompts, length, and parts will summon the work product or performance that elicits your desired mastery evidence.

Vehicle	Capstone portfolio comprised of three separate essays (2 analytical of individual problems; 1 assessing progress), due at the end of the semester.
Quantity (length, parts)	Each essay is limited to 1,250 words.
Timing/sequence	
Practicalities	8 students; three weeks to give a letter grade to the registrar, and I have a personal deadline to give student feedback within 2 weeks as well. Grading portfolios while reviewing client files and continuing any necessary legal work.
Subject and prompts	(for 2 analytical essays) Write two essays each describing, reflecting upon, and critiquing your involvement with a challenging problem encountered during the clinic. Choose one problem where your problem-solving worked well and a second where your problem-solving steps did not work as well. Choose problems that helped you grow. The growth you describe might be more the pure skill of problem-solving or it might be contextualized to specific lawyering situations, e.g., client interaction, development of the theory of the case. Describe the problem and context; explain how you tackled each problem (strategies, solutions, and implementation). Evaluate your problem-solving (early planning based on readings, hunches, prior experience; patterns in approach; tactics that worked or didn't; solution effectiveness from the perspective of others impacted).
Materials to develop	None in particular, but work with students throughout semester to identify experiences that might be included in the portfolio.

Worksheet 8: Prepare an Analytic Rubric

Whether your course is graded or not, you should assess each student's learning: 1) to inform the students of what they have in fact mastered or not; and 2) to inform you of your teaching effectiveness. An analytic rubric serves both purposes by imparting detailed feedback to each student and by enabling you to analyze where students are having trouble. If you give the rubric to students with the assessment exercise, the rubric also communicates your expectations so that they can self-assess their work before submitting it.

An analytic rubric is easily written as a grid:

- Vertical axis: Identify the assessment (evaluative) criteria to track the course goal and mastery evidence. You may include additional criteria not specifically tied to the course goals (e.g., writing mechanics, class participation), but do not let their grading value dilute the assessment of the course goal. Identify up to 6 criteria.
  - Describe the different elements of performance for each assessment criterion. You may include more than one element of performance in each criterion.

- Horizontal axis: Set and label the different proficiency levels. Levels can be labeled as grades, numeric ranges, or descriptors like exceptional, competent, and developing.
    - Each proficiency level for an assessment criterion should address each performance element in the assessment criterion.

Course Goal (from Worksheet 5): Students will be able to address real-life lawyering and client problems effectively and collaboratively by following the problem-solving model.

Individual Problem Assessment (2, each worth 20 points)

Evaluative criterion; weighting	Highest proficiency	Mid-level proficiency	Low level proficiency
Choice of Problem (10%)	Identifies a problem that was challenging to you personally and complicated substantively without being insurmountable.	Identifies a problem that was not reasonably challenging or complicated.	Identifies a problem for which you did not implement/ evaluate a solution or which you did not process sufficiently to learn from.
Description of the Problem and your Problem- Solving (30%)	Provides vivid, specific details that allow me to understand the problem, its context, the stakeholders, and your thought processes, emotions, and actions in solving the problem using the model we learned.	Provides sufficient detail to allow me to understand what was going on but missing the details that tell me what you did and why.	Provides perfunctory detail that doesn't allow me to understand what was going on.
Evaluation (50%)	Assesses the effectiveness of your problem-solving, in terms of both the outcome and process. Explains your conclusions with support from your description of the problem and your problem-solving efforts, the readings, or other life experiences.	Assesses effectiveness without sufficient support to allow me to understand the assessment.	Assessment is incomplete (only outcome or process but not both) OR lacks support.
Writing Mechanics (10%)	0-3 grammar, spelling, or usage errors. 0 run-ons or fragments. Logical organization with appropriate roadmap, signposts, and transitions. Clear, supported conclusion.	4-8 grammar, spelling, or usage errors. 1-2 run-ons or fragments. Logical organization but missing roadmap, signpost, or transitions. Vague OR unsupported conclusion.	>8 grammar, spelling, or usage errors. >2 run-ons or fragments. Confusing organization. Missing conclusion.

Semester Assessment & Plan (1, worth 60 points)

Evaluative criteria	Excellent: A, A-	Competent: B+, B, B-	Developing: C+ & below
Analysis: Look back: Where did your skill level start and end? How did you develop your problem-solving skills? How collaborative & human-centered were you? What internal or external factors, including the Model we used, helped/hindered? (45%)	Assesses the proficiency of your problem-solving over the course of the semester, using the proficiency spectrum provided on p. 5. Provides detailed support from your teamwork, class work, and client work, including the two assessments included in the portfolio; the Model and course readings; or other life experiences to allow me to understand the assessment.	Assesses proficiency without sufficient support from your work, the Model, readings, or life experiences to allow me to understand the assessment.	Lacks an assessment from the proficiency spectrum OR support (e.g., states conclusions or opinions without explanation based in fact).
Synthesis: Look ahead: What will you do next to build on the learning of this semester? How will you transfer your learning to new contexts? What priorities will help you to grow over the next year? (45%)	Identifies 1-2 challenges, steps, or explorations that you're taking on as a result of the analysis, which will allow you to build on this learning (e.g., new context, connection to new learning). Explains these challenges, etc. with sufficient detail for me to understand what you will do and why.	Identifies 1-2 next challenges, steps, or explorations but these are more backwards looking (what I've already learned) rather than forward looking (how I will I improve or use this learning in a different context); OR Lacks sufficient detail for me to understand either what you will do or why.	Identifies too many challenges, steps or explorations (>2); OR lacks detail.
Writing Mechanics (10%)	0-3 grammar, spelling, or usage errors. 0 run-ons or fragments. Logical organization with appropriate roadmap, signposts, and transitions. Clear, supported conclusion.	4-8 grammar, spelling, or usage errors. 1-2 run-ons or fragments. Logical organization but missing roadmap, signpost, or transitions. Vague OR unsupported conclusion.	>8 grammar, spelling, or usage errors. >2 run-ons or fragments. Confusing organization. Missing conclusion.

Checklist:

- Does my rubric track my mastery evidence and the prompt for the final assessment exercise?
- Does my rubric align with the course goals?
- If I include criteria not related to the course goal, do they comprise a minimal part of the assessment?
- Are the evaluative criteria specific and clear?
- Are the proficiency descriptions written in neutral, clear terms using consistent terms and components across each level?

Worksheet 9: Draft Course Outcomes

In this Worksheet, you will convert your course goals into multiple learning outcomes and check whether you have achieved the right level of specificity and effectiveness for assessment purposes. Develop a maximum of 6 outcomes per course goal.

- Align each outcome to one or more specific course goal(s).
- Each outcome should be written as a single statement; do not join multiple outcomes within one statement.
- Use verbs that represent observable and measurable performance (live, written, other type of performance). For each outcome, choose the single verb that represents the deepest level of performance that you want for that outcome; avoid compound verbs.
- Because the ABA now requires at least 6 experiential credits for graduation, you might want to align any clinic, field placement, or simulation course to at least some outcomes that relate directly to both your course goals and your school's program outcomes.

Course Goal (from Worksheet 5): Students will be able to address real-life lawyering and client problems effectively and collaboratively following the problem-solving model

Course Goal:	Students will be able to: Verb (performance)	Object (the learning statement)	Condition and/or Criterion
Know the Brest-Krieger model; value collaboration	Apply	Brest-Krieger model	Humanistically with client.
Skill—asking questions to be able to diagnose the problem, to identify its causes, to brainstorm options that will advance the client's position	Ask	Questions	To elicit factual detail, emotions, interests, values, motivations, and priorities relevant to the problem.
Skill—take perspective	Explain	The perspectives of different stakeholders	In a client or lawyering problem.
Skill—interaction Value—identities of others (cultural competence, empathy)	Interact	With clients, co-counsel, and others	With respect for their cultural and personal identities.
Skill—self evaluation	Evaluate	Their growth	In problem-solving.

Checklist:

- Do the course outcomes describe what students should know, do, and/or value in order to complete the final assessment successfully?
- Are the course outcomes described with verbs that represent observable, measurable behaviors?
- Are the course outcomes expressed individually, not jointly?
- Do the course outcomes align with a course goal?
- Do the course outcomes align with the ABA-required program outcomes, in whole or in part? (optional)

Worksheet 10: Organize Topics and Learning Activities across the Entire Course

Once you have identified the course outcomes, start identifying the learning activities and lawyering tasks that will enable students to develop the knowledge, skills, or values necessary to achieve each outcome. These activities will then help you choose the materials for the course and to plan individual units and lessons. You will want to organize the units into a sequence that promotes effective learning through smooth and clear transitions from unit to unit.

Situational factors

Before laying out the specific learning activities, re-examine the situational factors that will enable or constrain the types of learning activities you can incorporate, when or how they should be sequenced, and the like. Some of your situational factors may include the pre-requisite knowledge, skills, or values expected of students before taking your course or the availability of a boot camp week or clinic orientation.

Models for organizing and sequencing course content

Consider generally your course's organization. The models below will help you to sequence the course topics, outcomes, and learning activities and to decide what foundation needs to be laid and when. You may combine multiple organizational models.

- *Order of importance*: Because students have highest enthusiasm for a course at the beginning, embed the most important (or difficult) concepts earliest.
- *Order of process*: Sequence material along the arc of a process, beginning to end, *e.g.*, litigation sequence (complaint to trial); attorney-client relationship (first meeting through resolution of the matter; first meeting to transition to the next student-lawyer).
- *Simple to complex*: Because students can build confidence in mastering simple topics and skills, start with these before tackling higher level, more complex tasks.
- *Dependent or supportive relationship between units of study*: If the learning is cumulative, start with the concepts or skills that represent pre-requisite knowledge or skill necessary (or helpful) for later units.
- *Cause & Effect:* Introduce a range of problems and then follow with types of solutions to be applied (*e.g.*, claims and remedies).
- *Spiral or cyclical*: Introduce and revisit concepts or skills multiple times throughout the term, adding complexity with each repetition.
- *General to specific vs. Concrete to abstract*: Introduce general principles & then apply to specific situations. Alternatively, start with specific examples of a phenomenon and move toward what they represent at the conceptual or abstract level.
- *Thematic or topical:* Use when individual units represent independent concepts. Plan transitions carefully. (*e.g.*, a survey course.)

ABA experiential course design standards

Standard 304 provides the elements that any course intended to be counted toward the experiential graduation requirement must have. For each mode of skills teaching (simulation, clinic, externship) Standard 304 includes additional requirements.

Std. 304 (a): Experiential courses [include] simulation courses, law clinics, and field placements that must be primarily experiential in nature and must:

1) Integrate doctrine, theory, skills, and legal ethics, and engage students in performance of one or more of the professional skills identified in Standard 302;
2) Develop the concepts underlying the professional skills being taught;
3) Provide multiple opportunities for performance;
4) Provide opportunities for student performance, self-evaluation, and feedback from a faculty member, or, for a field placement, a site supervisor;
5) A classroom instructional component; or, for a field placement, a classroom instructional component, regularly scheduled tutorials, or other means of ongoing, contemporaneous, faculty-guided reflection; and
6) Provide direct supervision of the student's performance by the faculty member; or, for a field placement, provide direct supervision of the student's performance by a faculty member or a site supervisor.

Topic	Course outcomes in measurable terms	Learning activities / Lawyering tasks	Materials to aid student performance
	What will students be able to think, do, or value to complete the final assessment successfully? Use info developed in Worksheet 9. Organize in a coherent sequence. **By the end of the semester, students will be able to:**	What exercises, performances, discussions, or other learning activity will help students to prepare for and succeed in the final assessment? Identify whether an activity is designed as an introduction (I), practice opportunity (P), or mastery vehicle (M).	What readings, media, information, lecture, and other aids will my students need to perform the lawyering and learning activities successfully? Will it be used before, during, or after the class?
Orientation	—Interact with clients & classmates (develop knowledge about selves and classmates; clients; agencies) —Take into account perspective —Evaluate growth	—Introduce self; finding 5-10 things that everyone in the class has in common (I) —Quick write: describe the clinic's clients and something you are looking forward to/ concerned about in working with them (I) —Share 1-2 learning goals (I)	—Multimedia on people with disabilities (e.g., ethnographies, "working with" guides) —Articles about Social Security Admin, Veterans Affairs, regarding problems that claimants face
Law	(Substantive law is not an express learning outcome. But it is necessary to support students in doing fieldwork and to lay groundwork for practicing problem-solving methodologies)	—Accountability exercise to ensure students prepared for class (I) —Chart: identify the differences in how Social Security Disability (SSD), Supplemental Security Income, and Veteran's Affairs work (I) —Research & integrate as needed (P)	—Practice manual excerpts —Online resources —Agency organization, process, and determination charts

Problem-Solving	—Apply problem-solving model (PS) in a human-centered, collaborative manner —Perspective taking —Evaluate growth	—Puzzle—put in order the steps of the model. (I) —As a class, work through scenarios employing problem-solving model as way to address lawyering issues (P) —Refection: What part of the PS model helped me the most in the scenario, client matters, and/or teamwork matters? Why? (I, P, CM)	—Textbook readings: introduction to problem-solving and our model
Oral Communication Skills	—Interact with client (using skills of empathy, listening, and being present) —Perspective taking	—Improvisational Comedy listening exercises—focus on being present and listening carefully and accurately (I, P) —Active listening exercise (I, P)	—Readings explaining communicating —Readings on empathy vs. sympathy
Interviewing (longer unit; revisit through-supervision & case rounds)[13]	Interact with client - Sharing - Grounding - Closing Ask questions - Content: evidence; characterization - Form of question - Organization Perspective taking Apply PS model	—I model an intake interview; all students critique. Why do I make certain choices? How do I know? (I) —Team planning for simulation, using PS framework and readings for guidance (I, P) —Teams conduct simulation with client. Critique, with client (P) —Field work: Client intakes & on-going interviews (P, CM)) —Case Rounds after 1st real client interviews—common issues? (P)	—Reading on interviewing —Intake primer —Simulation scenario —SSD decision after hearing (what is legally relevant) —Working with military service members and veterans —Working with clients with mental health diagnoses —5 Habits —Metaphor: making a pizza; difference between evidence and fact finding
Case Planning	—Perspective taking —Apply PS Model	—Simulation 1: Closing arguments—theory of case and client; working with canned evidence; adding in additional evidence (I, P) —Simulation 2: In teams, plan development of client's claim; conduct research, discovery (P) —Field work: client matters; supervision—what needs to be requested? How? What must be submitted? (P, CM)	—Readings on models of organization, case development —Reading on Storytelling (characters, setting, plot) —Readings on medical records & dummy file —Ethics: all-evidence rule

13. For the unit on Oral communication skills and Interviewing, see Worksheet 11 below, for details on planning the student learning activities (prep and in-class) and assessing whether the students learned what was hoped.

Topic	Course outcomes in measurable terms	Learning activities / Lawyering tasks	Materials to aid student performance
Written Communication	—Interact with client and others —Perspective taking —Apply PS model	—Fieldwork: letters to clients and others; email; drafting wills, statements; drafting letter briefs (P, CM) —Fieldwork: peer review (P, CM) —Case Rounds (P, CM)	—PowerPoint on Design Process —Text on Plain English
Advocacy (longer unit; field work dependent)	—Interact with client and others —Ask questions —Perspective taking —Apply PS model	—Critique transcript of ALJ hearing (I) Plan and simulate direct- and cross-examinations (P) —Ethics: discussions as to candor to the tribunal (I) —Field work: conduct hearings (P, CM) —Case Rounds (P, CM)	—Readings on advocacy models —Practice manuals for Social Security Disability and VA practice —Simulation file —Agency rules on ethics
Systems & Reflection	—Perspective taking —Apply PS model —Evaluate growth	—Quick write: who are our clients? What have we learned from them? How do they want to be viewed? (P, CM) —Systems analysis (P, CM)—how do Social Security and Veterans Affairs view our clients? Why? How do we change parts of the system? (P, CM) —Student presentations: sharing and teaching about an issue that has resonated with them from the semester (P, CM)	—Readings about cultural aspects of disability, from an individual perspective —Readings about models of disability law (systems view) —Readings about lawyering and social work

Checklist:

- Do the course materials, learning activities, and lawyering tasks provide sufficient foundation for student progress toward course mastery?
- Does the order of materials, learning activities, and lawyering tasks allow my students to apply their learning repeatedly, to make progress toward mastery of the course outcomes?
- Do the learning exercises and lawyering activities include ones where I expect course mastery for each Enduring Learning element (Worksheet 4)?
- Do the course materials, learning activities, and lawyering tasks allow my students to consider the Animating Theory and Exploratory Questions for the course on multiple occasions throughout the semester (Worksheets 1 and 2)?
- Do the learning activities and lawyering tasks cover each criterion in ABA Standards 304 (as applied to all experiential courses and to the provisions specific to my type of course)??

Worksheet 11: Plan Units of Student Learning Activities

For each unit (a single topic/learning activity or chunk of topics or activities), create a plan for work that your students will do before, during, and after class. Make sure that you identify how you will "know" that the students learned what you planned. That might be your own reflection and assessment at the end of the class, supervision, or unit, or it might be some other evidence of student learning (whether direct from the student, or indirect from another source).

Course Unit: Working with your Clients: Oral Communications and Interviewing

Relevant Course Outcomes (from Worksheet 9): Interact with clients and others with respect for cultural, personal, and professional identities.

Ask questions to probe for factual detail, emotion, perspectives, interests, values, motivations, and priorities relevant to the problem.

Consider the perspectives of different stakeholders in a client or lawyering problem.

How will students prepare for the unit/class?	What will students do in class to prepare them to reach the outcomes?	How will I know they learned what I wanted them to learn?
Watch video about interacting with people with disabilities Read the Spoon Theory (understanding chronic pain) Read text chapters on interviewing and my primer on interviewing Read Working with Clients with Behavioral Health Problems; Working with Military Families and Veterans; 5 Habits Read sample ALJ decision	Class 1: Orientation—quick write: what do I think our clients will be like? What am I looking forward to or worried about in working with them? Class 2: Communicating—Being present and listening. Improvisational comedy exercises: "Yes, and," Last Word, and Repeater. Discuss how to use these in interviewing Discuss client's perspective Class 3: Intro to interviewing: Mini-decoding lecture: pizza metaphor; evidence vs. conclusions; lawyer's role. Sample Interview Review difference between conclusions and evidence; between what an ALJ finds as facts and what an ALJ heard in evidence Teacher models an intake interview with client actor. Active listening exercise: acknowledge, motivate, redirect Class 4: Question Forms Practice chronology and probing questions, active listening techniques Class 5: Students do mock interview of client who is a veteran with PTSD and bipolar disorder Class 6–7: Case rounds to revisit issues in communicating and interviewing, including cultural competence. Start with personal identity exercise & Habits 1, 3–4.	What are our clients like—ask again at end of semester Communicating: feedback during the exercises and later, in planning and in supervision, can repeat the exercises, see whether students are doing them independently Question forms: feedback during class; review of interview plans; debrief from interviews Mock interview: feedback from client, me and peers. Set goals for targeted practice through interview plans and interviews Case Rounds: discussion, use of 5 Habits

Checklist:

- Do the unit activities align with one or more of my course's learning outcomes?
- Do the unit activities have a clear purpose to help students learn?
- Is the unit structured to build on existing learning, give clear direction, and give opportunity to practice what students are expected to do?
- Do the unit activities give students time to develop their own thoughts and positions, and to hear others' ideas, perspectives, or positions?
- Do I hold my students accountable for doing the activity, including by giving them feedback?
- Do I provide opportunity for students to reflect on the activities and connect them to their prior learning?

CW Process Notes

This unit is spaced out over a lot of the course. I introduce our clients in the first class of the clinic, through class preparation, and ask the students in class to tell me what they think our clients will be like. I compare their thoughts then to their thoughts at the end of the semester to see if there is growth in how they view and interact with our clients. Primarily, I want them to move beyond thinking of our clients as "disabled" and "victimized" to thinking of them as people with disabilities who are the protagonists in the stories they bring us (and that we retell to the agencies). That perspective shift can take longer so it gets started first.

The more tangible skills of communicating and interviewing are added in quickly. I then break down interacting with clients into very basic communication/interaction skills (being present and listening) and technical interviewing skills (asking questions, other forms of active listening). We spend a class on communication using improv exercises that help students to listen closely and to build on what clients tell them, instead of jumping into skeptic mode and thinking about their next question. We then move into "see one, do one," with the student watching me interview a mock client and then the students interviewing their own mock clients. That brings us into question forms and types. We plan questions for the mock interview together in class, using our problem-solving model, to identify categories of questions, concerns and questions the client might have, etc. Then the students do the own interviews and we debrief. This set of classroom activities gives us lots of reference points throughout the semester to work from, and exercises that we can pull out in supervision to refresh our skills.

Course: Learning from Practice—Professional Judgment Seminar (companion seminar to externship), Meg Reuter

Worksheet 1: Animating Theory

To identify the learning goals for your course, first consider the subject matter generally. Because a subject matter has more content than a course can cover, start by articulating the key reason students should take your course. That reason is your course's Animating Theory. Grant Wiggins and Jay McTighe coined a colloquial term for this, "The Big Idea."[13]

Once you choose your Animating Theory, you will flesh it out with a set of Exploratory Questions (Worksheet 2) that illuminate the challenges you want your students to grapple with. Setting the Animating Theory and Exploratory Questions allows you to build your course from course goal, to mastery evidence, to learning activities. The Animating Theory is not the same as your course goal(s) or learning outcomes; it underlies both. You may have more than one, but restrict yourself to at most two so that student learning is focused. Here, less is more.

The Animating Theory for the Course:

- Refers to core concepts, principles, and theories in a field of study—What unifies the field of study? What makes a skill worthwhile or effective?
- Organizes large bodies of information, skills, or values.
- Is amenable to transfer to new fields of study, new situations, and across disciplines.
- Is abstract and requires investigation to probe its implications.

Considerations for a Skills-focused Course:

- What does the lawyering skill help you do more effectively or efficiently for a client?
- What are the underlying concepts or objectives of the skill?
- When and how do you use the skill (strategy and tactics)?
- Why does the skill work?

Examples: The Animating Theory need not be phrased as a complete sentence. A "motto" works.

- Persuasion: Know your audience.
- Sociology: People in a community depend on each other for the things they need.
- History: History is written by the victors.
- Law: The best lawyer is the best prepared lawyer.

Identify the Animating Theory(ies) for your course.

Society expects lawyers to have the skills for professional judgment and practical wisdom.
Deliberate and reflective practice are critical to achieving the capacity for professional judgment and practical wisdom.

Checklist:

- Does my animating theory provide a concise statement, principle, theory, or generalization?

---

13. See Wiggins, G., & McTighe, J., UNDERSTANDING BY DESIGN (2nd ed. 2005).

- Does it stand the test of time, allowing students' thoughts about it to develop and evolve over time?
- Can it promote in-depth understanding and help make sense of the subject matter?
- Can it promote in-depth understanding and help make sense of the subject matter?

MER Process Notes:

I have taught many versions of a companion seminar to student field placements, generating numerous lists of learning outcomes or teaching goals. Distilled to the core, these outcomes have always included versions of close observation, reflection, self-evaluation, and self-development.

I wanted re-orient the course to focus on biases that we should be aware of, mitigate, and overcome as much as possible. Developing debiasing and reflective skills are the purpose of my course. I started to realize that although cultural and racial biases are my ultimate focus, many other biases present risks to good lawyering. Biases like advocate/partisan bias, confirmation bias, impulses toward obedience, and others start in the same place as cultural biases. I surmised that if I could create a theme about professional judgment, detachment, and objectivity, then I could bring students along from non-threatening biases (e.g.,, advocate bias) to one's that are far more emotionally fraught, like racial biases.

I have paired the professional judgment thread with a thread focused on deliberate and reflective practice. These comprise the underlying methods of the whole course and this is what the students will hear from me frequently.

I believe my theses for the course achieve the basic purposes laid out in the Experiential Learning Design process. In any course where professional identity formation goals predominate, examining various aspects of the lawyerly identity like judgment, wisdom, and reflection are animating concepts. These concepts help to translate sociology, psychology, and behavioral economics research on judgment and decision making to apply to the pragmatics of being an effective high integrity lawyer.

My linking—

- Important emblems of professional judgment and its exercise include expertise, detachment, ability to listen and communicate, and the ability to adapt to a wide variety of audiences and circumstances, among other components.
- Discernment and audience-appropriate communication and relationships require awareness of one's blind spots and cognitive biases as well as the ability to take the perspective of others.
- Law students can begin actively to develop professional judgment now, in their apprentice state.
- The most useful way to overcome or mitigate cognitive biases is to pause, become carefully observant, self-aware, question, and reflect on the what is transpiring around you in your fieldwork, what it means to you personally, and what it means to others.
- I use practical wisdom, drawn from Aristotle's phrónêsis and Donald Schön's theory of reflection as the means to self-development, continuous learning, and professional mastery.

Worksheet 2: Develop Exploratory Questions

Questions are used to study the Animating Theory for the course and to ground student learning. These questions are open-ended and probing in nature rather than intended to yield specific answers.

An Exploratory Question:

- Opens the Animating Theory for the course to genuine inquiry.
- Provokes lively discussion, sustained inquiry, and new understanding, as well as more questions.
- Requires students to consider alternatives, weigh evidence, support their ideas, and justify their answers.
- Stimulates vital, on-going rethinking of assumptions, prior understanding, and personal experience.
- Naturally recurs, creating opportunities for transfer to other situations and subjects.

Examples of Exploratory Questions that amplify the value of your Animating Theory:

- Persuasion: What's in it for my audience? What are the ethics of persuasion?
- Government and public policy: What makes a good government? How does cultural identity inform one's views of government and its role in society?
- History/Precedent: What patterns recur throughout history and common law? Is all history biased?

Identify 1–2 Exploration Questions for each Animating Theory.

Animating Theory 1: Highly regarded, effective lawyers have the skills for and exhibit professional judgment and practical wisdom.

What are the component parts of professional judgment and practical wisdom?
What is the role of empathy in professional judgment?
What is the relationship between professional judgment and leadership?
What are the impediments to developing professional judgment and practical wisdom?

Animating Theory 2: Deliberate and reflective practice are critical to achieving the capacity for professional judgment and practical wisdom.

How does the exercise of deliberate and reflective practice lead to professional judgment and mastery of legal skills?
How is deliberate or reflective practice any different than trying one's best to do good work on any assignment?

Checklist:

- Are my Exploratory Questions open-ended, nonjudgmental, meaningful, and purposeful?
- Do the questions have emotional appeal?
- Do the questions have more than one coherent answer?
- Do the questions probe for deeper meaning and explore ideas and beliefs?
- Do the questions encourage peer learning and collaboration?

MER Process Notes:

My intention is that the students will find it emotionally appealing to begin to think deliberately about their path to become worthy of being a civic leader and to be entrusted with their clients' legal welfare. I am quite aware that there is an irreducible core of students of students who consider this reflective process to be navel-gazing and time wasting. My hope is that they want to engage the question of professional judgment as an analytical challenge of cognitive biases. In subsequent semesters, I have likened the pursuit of professional judgement to development of leadership skill.

Worksheet 3: Identify Situational Factors That Affect Teaching and Learning

The first two Worksheets lay out the scope of the course on a grand scale. Now situate your ambitions for student learning within the realities of your course, the school's curriculum, your students' semesters, and the scope of all your responsibilities. Some of these situational factors are assets to use wisely and fruitfully. Others are limitations. Affirmatively acknowledging that, in your clinic, field placement, or simulation course, you simply cannot cover all that your students need to know, be able to do, or value will help you to make pedagogical choices to maximize student learning.

Possible situational factors

ABA mandated institutional learning outcomes	UMKC is re-examining its institutional learning outcomes currently. The renewed version will have some configuration of reflective practice as part of student professional identity formation.
Length (e.g., semester, year), number of credits, number of hours in field, casework, or classroom	The course is a seminar is separately credited from the field placement course. It's one-credit, graded, non-mandatory, and meets once a week for 75 minutes roughly. The field placement credits are pass/fail.
Uniformity/variety of student work (in type and complexity)	Students in the seminar are doing fieldwork in multiple kinds of law offices (e.g., government, judicial, or non-profit entities, but not private practice). Some students will have individual clients, others organizational clients, and others with no clients (judicial). Students can be in any practice area. I do not have a well-formed frame for exploring any particular type of law practice, practice setting, or clientele.

Checklist:

- Do I capture factors that are opportunities for me to maximize the learning in my course?
- Do I capture the most salient factors that limit the scope of what students can reasonably learn in my course?
- Do I capture the most salient factors that limit my ability to execute a course plan and engage my students?

MER Process Notes:

Usually one would think such an open-ended framework provides beneficial flexibility. In my experience, it is actually a difficult challenge. Students like the seminar when it is tangibly related to their fieldwork; they are often impatient with the course when the topics veer off to things they see as extraneous to their fieldwork and /or career objectives. If the seminar is a survey of lawyering issues relevant to each of the practice areas/settings represented by the externs, it necessarily means that in any given week, we will have content that is of low or no interest to a number of the externs. The more diverse the extern placements the more difficult it is to find the overlapping interests. I identified professional judgment as something to which each student aspires, at some level.

Worksheet 4: Prioritize Learning for Transfer (durability)

Allow your Animating Theory to percolate. Break it down into specific priorities for your students' learning. Identify the knowledge and understandings, skills, and/or values that are essential to the Animating Theory of your course. Prioritize those elements based on long-term importance to the students' learning. The highest level (enduring learning) should be learning that is transferable to different contexts in their professional lives.

Even though your course may cover content in all three levels of priority, your course goals (Worksheet 5) and final assessments (Worksheet 7) will focus on the knowledge and understandings, skills, and/or values that you intend to be long-lived (enduring) for your students.

Enduring learning:

Without deliberate attention to one's cognitive biases, one will be crippled in her abilities to develop professional level judgment.
Overcoming cognitive bias requires both self-awareness and empathy (ability to see through the eyes of others).

Important for students to know:

Methods of self-assessment
Studies of lawyering skills necessary as an effective practitioner; special focus that each study identifies "listening" as one of the top skills needed.

Worth being familiar with:

Attributes and functioning of Daniel Kahneman's System 1 and System 2 Thinking
Attributes and functioning of Donald Schon's cycle of reflective practice
Attributes and functioning of Carol Dweck's growth mindset

Checklist:

- Do the elements listed as *Enduring Learning* help students to synthesize individual lessons and readings into a deeper understanding of the Animating Theory?
- Do the *Enduring Learning* elements lay a foundation for further study of this subject matter?
- Do the *Enduring Learning* elements help students to figure out issues in the subject matter that are more difficult to master?

Worksheet 5: Use Learning Taxonomies to Craft Course Goals[14]

Now that you've identified your learning priorities, you will distill the enduring learning into course goals. Course goals represent the essential i) knowledge and understandings, ii) skills, and/or iii) values that you intend your students to attain by the end of the term. One way to unify the enduring learning into goals is to ask: "How will my students be different by the end of the course?" To answer this question in a way that can be assessed at the end of the course, we have collected taxonomies of learning that capture the complexity and depth of learning you want your students to attain. The taxonomies further assist you to establish observable and measurable course goals (amenable to assessment, Worksheets 6 and 7).

The taxonomies cover the three domains of learning:

1. Cognitive domain: Focuses on knowledge, comprehension, and critical thinking.
2. Psychomotor domain: Encompasses learning geared toward executing specific tasks (*e.g.*, client counseling, negotiating with opposing counsel, witness interviewing).
3. Affective domain: Relates to awareness and growth in values, attitudes, and emotional control (*e.g.*, values embedded in the attorney-client relationship, toward justice, and relating to professional identity formation).

The taxonomy grids on the next three pages organize each domain of learning hierarchically. As you move through the grids (left to right; top to bottom) the categories describe learning at deeper levels of difficulty. Use these grids to choose the deepest point(s) that correspond to a realistic learning goal for your course.

The grids, their terminology, and hierarchy are offered as an aid. Some of your learning priorities might fit within more than one taxonomy, and the Action Verbs that exemplify a category might resonate more than the category of learning does. Choose what works for you. Don't let the taxonomies push your learning goal toward something that doesn't feel right to you. Maybe you will pencil in learning targets for your course in several cells on separate grids; that will allow you to test out different ways to characterize the course goal(s) you want to pursue. In the end you should articulate

14. Course Development Institute, Indiana University Center for Innovative Teaching and Learning.

1–2 course goals. In drafting these goals, keep your verb singular, not compound, as a verb representing the farthest/deepest taxonomy cell that encapsulates your goal will necessarily include the less complex learning needed to reach that goal.

In the following three pages:

- Review the taxonomy for each domain.
- Reflect on your ambitions for your course. Pencil notes in any of the cells.
- Review your notes and distill them to one to two course goals (last page).

The course goals will form the bedrock for your course. Everything else—the final assessment, rubric, outcomes and learning activities—will be aligned to the course goals.

Sources:

Knowledge and Cognitive Processing Domain

Adapted from Anderson, L.W., Krathwohl, D.R. et. al. (2001). *A Taxonomy for Learning, Teaching, and Assessing: A Revision of Bloom's Taxonomy of Educational Objectives.* Abridged ed. New York: Longman.

Psychomotor Domain

Adapted from Dave, R.H. (1970), "Developing and Writing Behavioral Objectives;" Simpson E. J. (1972). The Classification of Educational Objectives in the Psychomotor Domain. Washington, DC: Gryphon House.

Affective Domain

Adapted from Krathwohl, D.R., Bloom, B.S., and Masia, B.B. (1964). *Taxonomy of Educational Objectives, Book II. Affective domain.* New York: David McKay Company, Inc.

Find taxonomies on following pages

1. Knowledge and Cognitive Processing Domain

		Cognitive processing			
		1. Remember	2. Understand	3. Apply	4. Analyze, Evaluate, or Create
Knowledge	A. Factual	[your course goals]			
	B. Conceptual				
	C. Procedural				
	D. Meta-cognitive		Explain and give examples of unconscious biases and how they impact our behaviors. Differentiate between explicit bias, implicit bias, and microaggressions.	Be able to identify instances where, upon reflection, one's behavior was limited by cognitive biases.	

Knowledge types	Definition	Examples
Factual	Basic elements to be acquainted with the discipline and solve problems	Terminology, vocabulary, elements, and details
Conceptual	Interrelationship among basic elements	Categories, principles, theories, models, and structures
Procedural	How to do something *(overlaps with psychomotor domain)*	Subject-specific skills, methods of inquiry and criteria for using, and techniques and procedures
Meta-cognitive	Knowing about knowing	Strategic knowledge, reflections, and self-knowledge

Cognitive processing	Definition	Action Verbs
Remember	Retrieve relevant knowledge from long-term memory	Retain, recall, recognize, memorize, recollect, think of, define, identify, list, name, record, repeat, underline, select
Understand	Construct meaning from instructional messages; can be in oral, written or graphic formats	Interpret, exemplify, classify, summarize, infer, compare, explain, give examples of, describe in own words, differentiate between, discriminate, restate, review, translate, respond, practice, discuss, identify, review, simulate

Apply	Carry out procedures	Execute, implement, apply, demonstrate, dramatize, generalize, illustrate, operate, operationalize, practice, use, utilize, initiate
Analyze	Break material into parts and determine relationships	Differentiate, organize, attribute, analyze, appraise, categorize, compare, conclude, contrast, correlate, deduce, diagram, distinguish, estimate, examine, experiment, infer, predict, question, solve, diagnose
Evaluate	Make judgments based upon criteria or standards	Check, critique, assess, judge, appraise, choose, compare, evaluate, measure, rate, revise, score, select, validate, value
Create	Put elements together into coherent or functional whole, reorganize into new patterns	Generate, plan, produce, invent, arrange, assemble, collect, compose, construct, create, design, develop, formulate, manage, modify, organize, prepare, propose, synthesize

2. Psychomotor Domain: (can be used by experiential faculty to set goals for lawyering skill development)

	Definition	Action Verbs	Your Course Goals
Perception	Actively using sensory cues to attend to the behavioral skill. E.g., student observes a seasoned attorney perform the behavior.	Choose, describe, detect, differentiate, distinguish, identify, isolate, relate, select, separate	
Imitation	Copying the behavior. The student attempts the behavior, with direction and feedback from an experienced person. The student shows desire and motivation to learn the behavior.	Adhere, begin, attempt, carry out, copy, duplicate, follow, mimic, repeat, replicate, start, try	
Practice	Using the behavior repeatedly. The student performs the behavior multiple times, and her actions become more automatic and smooth. The experienced person need not be present.	Codify, discriminate, display, order, organize, systematize, weigh, discuss, theorize, formulate, balance, examine, adhere to	

Naturalization	Performing two or more skills in combination or sequence, with consistency and ease. The student can combine the behavior with other behaviors independently and with little mental exertion.	Adapt, automatize, combine, complete, demonstrate, internalize, master, perform, show, succeed	
Origination	Creating new behaviors, combinations, or sequences to respond to a new situation. The student creates new methodologies or techniques to improve on or re-imagine how the needs can be met.	Create, design, compose, refine, arrange	

3. **Affective Domain:** (can be used to set goals related to professional values, affect, or work approach, *e.g.*, with regard to the attorney client relationship, the rule of law, or other professional value)

	Definition	Action Verbs	Your Course Goals
Receive	Be aware of; attend to something; be willing to tolerate it.	Accept, attend, develop, ask, recognize, listen for, describe, differentiate, receive, identify, tolerate	
Respond	Incorporate a new behavior as a result of the experience.	Complete, comply, cooperate, discuss, examine, obey, assist, respond, follow, volunteer, perform	
Value	Show specific involvement or commitment.	Accept, defend, devote oneself to, pursue, seek, justify, join, debate, value	Develop personal definition of professional judgment
Organize	Integrate a new value into one's general set of values, giving due ranking among other priorities.	Codify, discriminate, display, order, organize, systematize, weigh, discuss, theorize, formulate, balance, examine, adhere to	
Internalize the value set	Act consistently, conscientiously, and pro-actively with the new value.	Internalize, verify, be rated high in the value, require, resolve	Consider and apply the elements of professional judgment with ease and deliberateness.

Using the taxonomies on the previous pages, draft your top 1–2 Course Goals:

By the end of the course, my students will:

1. Develop personal definition of professional judgment that, among other things, takes into account the need to appreciate and interpret a set of circumstances through the eyes of others.
2. Demonstrate the ability to put deliberate and reflective practice into use to amplify his/her learning from experience.

Checklist

- Do my goals fit within the Animating Theory for the course (Worksheet 1)?
- Do my goals reflect the learning priorities I have set for the course (Worksheet 4)?
- Are my goals clear, observable, and measurable (Worksheets 6 and 8)?
- Do my goals reflect the situational limits of my course and my full responsibilities (Worksheet 3)?

Worksheet 6: Identify Observable Evidence of Student Mastery

Visualize the student who excels in the course you are designing. What does the student's performance or work product look like? That is your evidence of student mastery. The student's work is not at the level of a veteran attorney's; it's A-level work as a student in your course. Look at your picture closely, using the following six categories, or facets, of concrete, observable performance to assist your efforts.[15] A "masterful" student performance may well involve synchronous use of multiple facets. After you identify your evidence of mastery, then you will i) create a final assessment exercise to allow your students to exhibit this evidence (Worksheet 7) and ii) create an assessment rubric that defines levels of student performance (Worksheet 8).

Facet of understanding	Associated verbs & Starter phrases	Evidence of student's mastery in your course
Explanation: Students are able to provide thorough and well-supported accounts of topics, events, or actions, backed by reasoning, facts, or experience. Students are able to develop a theory of how and why, supported by evidence, law, and experience.	Demonstrate, derive, describe, design, exhibit, express, instruct, justify, model, predict, prove, show, synthesize, teach Students will be able to: Explain/ teach [x], Give examples of [x]; Make connections with [x]; Offer a theory of [x]; Avoid misconceptions, such as [x].	
Interpretation: Students are able to interpret and analyze the importance, meaning, or significance of their knowledge/skill, with context and awareness of multiple interpretations. Students can create meaning from a set of facts and law, with attention to ambiguity, uncertainty, opacity, emotional content, and diverse perspectives.	Create analogies, critique, document, evaluate, illustrate, judge, make sense of, provide metaphors, read between the lines, represent, tell a story of. Students will be able to: Interpret the [x]; Tell a revealing story of [x]; Provide an apt analogy for [x]; Show the importance or meaning of [x]; Translate [x]; Relate [x] to your experience (or the experiences of others).	
Application-Adaptation: Students use and adapt the knowledge/skill acquired to new situations and contexts, showing flexibility and adaptability. Students can design, develop, test, and refine responses to a new problem or dilemma presented.	Adapt, create, de-bug, design, exhibit, invent, perform, produce, propose, solve, test, use Students will be able to: Apply [x] in a new circumstance; Show or demonstrate [x]; Use in the context of [x]; Design/invent [x]; Overcome a challenge or constraint, such as [x].	Apply readings and class discussions to create a personal definition of professional judgment. Students will present their personal definition in writing or orally, depending on the semester.

15. Adapted and expanded from Wiggins, G., & McTighe, J., Understanding by Design (2nd ed. 2005) (describing six facets of understanding).

Perspective: Students can take a step back to appreciate a broader view, critically assess the value or importance of a topic. Students can identify, critique, and give credence to multiple valid perspectives regarding a topic.	Analyze, argue, compare, contrast, criticize, infer Students will be able to: Analyze [x]; See from the viewpoint of [x]; Compare and contrast [x]; Critique [x]; Critically examine assumptions such as [x]; Show how [x]; See the limits of [x].	Write reflective essays throughout the semester (usually 3 or 4).
Empathy: Students show the ability to embrace the feelings, reasoning, motivations, and perspectives of others with acceptance and non-judgment. Open-minded insight to others.	Assume the role of, believe, be like, be open to, consider, imagine, relate, role-play. Students will be able to: Walk in the shoes of [x]; Experience directly and see [x]; Reach a common understanding with another concerning [x]; Entertain the seemingly odd or alien view that [x]; Anticipate possible concerns of others regarding [x] based on their interests, values, and circumstances.	
Self-Knowledge: Students accept that their style, preferences, and habits are specific to them and affect their views of events, information, and other people. Students can evaluate their professional development with appreciation of what came easily or not and why; can evaluate personal, emotional responses with detachment.	Be aware of, realize, recognize, reflect, self-assess. Students will be able to: Recognize their own prejudice(s) about [x]; Identify the lens through which they view [x]; Explain how they came to understand [x]; Realize that even with all they now know, they still don't really understand [x].	Consider and reflect upon one's field experience to identify where one has grown in skills and awareness. Students will demonstrate in a final retrospective essay on what were there major learning takeaways, what was the most effective method for their learning, how their work affected others and the other's perspective of the student's work.

Checklist

- Does my mastery evidence flow from my course goals and teaching priorities?
- Does my mastery evidence facilitate exploration of the Animating Theory for the course?
- Is my evidence of student mastery observable and measureable in an assessment exercise?

Worksheet 7: Create a Final Assessment Exercise

Create a final assessment exercise that will allow you to observe and evaluate each piece of mastery evidence listed. Before crafting the assessment exercise, revisit the enduring learning priorities you established (Worksheet 4) and your course goals (Worksheet 5). Use the measurable language in the goals and the mastery evidence (Worksheet 6) to create the content framework for your final assessment exercise. Note: you may use more than one assessment exercise to determine the final grade for your course.

- Choose the vehicle: a piece(s) of writing, a portfolio, an oral presentation or live performance (to professor or before another audience), etc.
- Quantity—Length: Consider how short or long the students' performance or work product should be to showcase their mastery. For instance, if you want to assess the students' level of reflection, can the students meet your expectations in 250 words, 1,000, or 5,000 words? If you want to assess the students' ability to conduct a summation for the jury, should the summation last 5 minutes, 15 minutes, 30 minutes, or more?
- Quantity—Parts: Determine the number of parts or exercises. While it might be ideal to create an assessment exercise that synthesizes the full constellation of knowledge, skills, and values represented in the course goal, often it might be impracticable to create a single assessment exercise that allows the students to produce evidence of full mastery. How would you segment the parts of the assessment?
- Practicalities: Consider the situational factors that impact what is manageable for you to assess.
- Design the subject and the prompts: This is the meat of the assessment. What are you asking your students to do? Make certain that your prompts, length, and parts will summon the work product or performance that elicits your desired mastery evidence.

Final Assessment 1: Personal Definition of Professional Judgment

Vehicle	Oral presentation or reflective essay (depending on the semester) of student's personal definition of professional judgment.
Quantity (length, parts)	Oral presentation: 10-minute presentation to professor. Essay: 1,250–1,500 words.
Timing/sequence	End of semester.
Practicalities	Scheduling issues for oral presentations. Additionally, I'd like to be able to figure out a way to do these as class presentations, embedded with peer learning. But it would preclude me from including this in the students' final grade.
Subject and prompts	Professional judgment presentation In a nutshell, students are directed to: • Define professional judgment in your own terms (one to three elements that comprise professional judgment in a meaningful, coherent, and concise manner). • Tie your definition to the readings, class discussions, and/or exercises. • Explain how your understanding of professional judgment has influenced your work in your field placement, in school, or in another leadership context. • Project how you expect to bring your current professional judgment capabilities to a higher level of performance in the near term, whether in work, school or other activity. • Address in a clear-eyed fashion what it will take to overcome barriers to development of such skill levels, whether such barriers are patently obvious or subtle.

Final Assessment 2: Reflection

Vehicle	4 essays, reviewed as a body of reflection and personal growth.
Quantity (length, parts)	First three essays are 750–1,000 words about 1 ½ pages, single spaced. Last retrospective essay is 1,250–1,500 words. Cumulative total 3,500–4,500 words.
Timing/sequence	The essay due dates are evenly distributed over the semester.
Practicalities	Concern that students who are new to reflection (or temperamentally resistant to reflection) would find the essays too onerous and just give me insincere filler. I have settled on 750 to 1,500 words. I have found that these word counts are long enough to make the student pause, but short enough so that it doesn't lead to student resistance and idle filler.

<table>
<tr><td>Subject and prompts</td><td>As part of the Field Placement courses, each student will take time to pause to reflect on his/her experience and prepare reflective essays. Use your essays to examine the broader implications of your placement experiences regarding the practice of law, the lawyer's role, professional effectiveness, and your own learning progress.

A crucial component to the transition from student novice to expert practitioner—and harbinger of lifelong learning—is the art and habit of reflective practice. As explained by Donald A. Schön, philosopher and seminal thinker in this field—reflective practice is a cycle that includes
• observing one's own actions in situ;
• Analyzing those observations, often with the input of others;
• Identifying what one has learned as the basis for new knowledge; and
• Using the new knowledge to inform future actions.

Topics: You are free to choose your own topics for your essays to allow you to write about the issues that are most significant or interesting to you.

Develop skills of close observation. What is going on in the workplace? What are the finer details that allow you to understand something or to surface a question you had not considered before? Importantly take the time to identify where and how you might have jumped to conclusions or assumed something about the people and conduct involved. Take the time to consider the subject of your reflection from the perspective of others.

With those close observations developed, next analyze what they mean for you personally and directly: your skill development, your current ability level or future development needs, your relationships, your learning style, how you might challenge yourself or test alternate approaches to work, or how you find methods for self-assessment and critique. Your reflective essays can give critical examination to larger questions about the nature of justice; the role of law in the wellbeing of a community, and the lawyer's role in the legal system.</td></tr>
</table>

Worksheet 8: Prepare an Analytic Rubric

Whether your course is graded or not, you should assess each student's learning: 1) to inform the students of what they have in fact mastered or not; and 2) to inform you of your teaching effectiveness. An analytic rubric serves both purposes by imparting detailed feedback to each student and by enabling you to analyze where students are having trouble. If you give the rubric to students with the assessment exercise, the rubric also communicates your expectations so that they can self-assess their work before submitting it.

An analytic rubric is easily written as a grid:

- Vertical axis: Identify the assessment (evaluative) criteria to track the course goal and mastery evidence. You may include additional criteria not specifically tied to the course goals (e.g., writing mechanics, class participation), but do not let their grading value dilute the assessment of the course goal. Identify up to 6 criteria.
    - Describe the different elements of performance for each assessment criterion. You may include more than one element of performance in each criterion.
- Horizontal axis: Set and label the different proficiency levels. Levels can be labeled as grades, numeric ranges, or descriptors like exceptional, competent, and developing.
    - Each proficiency level for an assessment criterion should address each performance element in the assessment criterion.

Rubric 1: for Professional Judgment presentation

	Well-developed skill	Emerging, effective work	Under-developed
Personal definition-clarity	Student thesis or definition of professional judgment has 1-3 elements. The thesis is meaningful, coherent, and concise.	Student thesis is overburdened with an extended list of elements that fail to show meaningful distillation or consideration.	Student thesis is disjointed and/or simplistic.
Theoretical context	Student's thesis is supported by multiple and specific references to readings, class discussions, and/or exercises.	Student's thesis has some support, but the contextual references are thin or have weak connection to the thesis.	Student makes little or no reference to the work undertaken in the seminar.
Integrates field learning	Student's thesis is grounded in multiple examples drawn from his/her field experience, whether demonstrating the exercise of professional judgment or a missed opportunity to exhibit professional judgment.	Student's thesis makes some reference(s) to field experience, but in a superficial manner.	Student suggests that he/she had little to no opportunity to observe professional judgment or perspective taking in the course of the field placement.
Personal integration and future orientation	Student offers clear and pragmatic ideas how he/she will incorporate one or more elements of professional judgment in future endeavors (work, school, other leadership activities). Student acknowledges barriers to implementing the characteristics of professional judgment, but has thoughtful ideas how to overcome the impediments.	Student suggests some ways in which to adapt behaviors going forward, but the suggestions are simplistic without acknowledgment that new habits take deliberate attention to incorporate effectively.	Student suggests that he/she currently practices and exhibits all elements that comprise his/her definition of professional judgment.
Blind spots; Self-awareness; Perspective-taking	Student presentation shows self-awareness how his/her experience and preferences can impede professional judgment, whether through the thesis, theoretical context, or personal integration. Presentation shows ability to anticipate, recognize, and readiness to adapt to the viewpoints and cultural values of others.	Presentation refers to one or more of these related concepts, but does not show how they are related and/or have live significance in law practice.	Student glosses over or rejects the imperative that one cannot exhibit professional judgment without having empathy and the ability to understand circumstances through the eyes of another.

Mechanics— Presentation or Writing	Student presented with professional demeanor and enthusiasm in the topic. Student uses appropriate eye contact and gestures. Student's voice is clear, with varied volume, pitch, and pace. Student did not read from notes.	Student's presentation was uncertain and flat. Student failed to have consistent eye contact and direct engagement with the audience (professor), perhaps because of use of note cards.	Student was unprepared, developed a definition of professional judgment that failed to reference class or fieldwork.
	Writing is personal, flows well, and paints a vivid picture. Uses clear and concise sentences, appropriate word choice, effective paragraph structure using topic and transition statements. Negligible errors in grammar, usage, punctuation, or style. Reflects careful and thorough proofreading and line editing.	Writing is strong, but shows weaknesses in flow or structure (e.g., rambling, mechanical, cliché). Sentence structure is competent, but needs editing for transition, concision, and/or word choice. Mostly free of grammatical, spelling, punctuation, and other style errors.	Writing is poorly organized. Writing uses has multiple errors in grammar or usage. Requires extensive editing for concision, word choice; most paragraphs poorly structured. Multiple distracting errors in grammar, punctuation, style, and/or spelling.

Rubric 2: Reflective Writing

	Well-developed skill	Emerging, effective work	Under-developed
Close observation	—Writing shows close observation and purpose. —Writing articulates clearly the topic chosen (e.g., dilemma, questions, or puzzle) and reason for choosing it. —Topic setup provides clear and appropriately detailed background information.	—Topic is well chosen, but the body of the writing does not clearly support or flow from the topic. —Topic setup is sufficient but missing specifics grounding topic to context.	—Writer's focus is not apparent and topic is ill defined. —Topic setup is cursory, with inadequate detail to provide context or explain its importance to the reader.
Perspective-taking	—Writing addresses multiple perspectives, including writer's personal perspective. —Each perspective is supported by appropriate, valid evidence (e.g., direct observation, information learned from others, factual background, and/or additional research, as appropriate).	—Writing addresses multiple perspectives, but fails to identify and examine the perspective of one or more important actors. —The perspectives are supported by some evidence, but may be superficial or rely on unexamined clichés.	—Writing is descriptive and considers the experience largely from the writer's point of view. —Where additional perspectives are addressed, the supporting evidence is cursory or cliché.
Personal engagement	—Writing shows the writer engaged in deep, analytical self-reflection. —Writing shows meaningful personal reaction or struggle on the intellectual-cognitive level and the emotional level. —Writing shows self-awareness and writer's assessment of his/her strengths and weaknesses and contemplates what he/she still needs to learn.	—Writing shows genuine examination of writer's experience and reaction but shows minimal evaluation of (or ability to evaluate) writer's own strengths and weaknesses on both intellectual/cognitive and emotional levels.	—Writing shows minimal introspection in relation to topic or to the perspective of others. —Evaluation of writer's struggle or reaction is minimal or missing.

Lessons learned	—Writing explores insights gained and developments in writer's knowledge, values, or beliefs. —Writing anticipates and projects future actions the writer will take toward personal change, or other relevant development.	—Writing explores one or more lessons learned, but fails to address the writer's status before the experience/reflection, after the experience/reflection; and/or projection into the future.	—Writing is largely descriptive without identifying take-aways or learning that is personal to writer.
Overall quality and depth	—Writing shows full and substantial treatment of the topic, with related analysis, reflection and student growth evident in the piece.	—Writing shows significant treatment of the topic, but the analysis, reflection and/or evidence of student growth is missing or superficial.	—Writing shows cursory treatment of the topic, with limited analysis, reflection, and/or demonstration of personal growth.
Writing mechanics	—Writing is personal, flows well, and paints a vivid picture. —Uses clear and concise sentences, appropriate word choice, effective paragraph structure using topic and transition statements. —Negligible errors in grammar, usage, punctuation, or style. —Reflects careful and thorough proofreading and line editing.	—Writing is strong, but shows weaknesses in flow or structure (e.g., rambling, mechanical, cliché). —Sentence structure is competent, but needs editing for transition, concision, and/or word choice. —Mostly free of grammatical, spelling, punctuation, and other style errors.	—Writing is poorly organized. —Writing uses has multiple errors in grammar or usage. —Requires extensive editing for concision, word choice; most paragraphs poorly structured. —Multiple distracting errors in grammar, punctuation, style, and/or spelling.

Checklist:

- Does my rubric track my mastery evidence and the prompt for the final assessment exercise?
- Does my rubric align with the course goals?
- If I include criteria not related to the course goal, do they comprise a minimal part of the assessment?
- Are the evaluative criteria specific and clear?
- Are the proficiency descriptions written in neutral, clear terms using consistent terms and components across each level?

Worksheet 9: Draft Course Outcomes

In this Worksheet, you will convert your course goals into multiple learning outcomes and check whether you have achieved the right level of specificity and effectiveness for assessment purposes. Develop a maximum of 6 outcomes per course goal.

- Align each outcome to one or more specific course goal(s).
- Each outcome should be written as a single statement; do not join multiple outcomes within one statement.
- Use verbs that represent observable and measurable performance (live, written, other type of performance). For each outcome, choose the single verb that represents the deepest level of performance that you want for that outcome; avoid compound verbs.
- Because the ABA now requires at least 6 experiential credits for graduation, you might want to align any clinic, field placement, or simulation course to at least some outcomes that relate directly to both your course goals and your school's program outcomes.

Course Goal (from Worksheet 5): Develop personal definition of professional judgment that, among other things, considers need to appreciate and interpret a set of circumstances through the eyes of others.

Course Goal (from Worksheet 5): Demonstrate the ability to put deliberate and reflective practice into use to amplify his/her learning from experience.

Students should be able to . . .

Knowledge, skills and/or values	Verb (performance)	Object (the learning statement)	Condition and/or Criterion
Deliberate practice.	Devise	A learning plan	Based on self-assessment and professional development needs.
Deliberate practice.	Effectuate	The learning plan	Through fieldwork experience, careful observation, and continuous self-assessment.
Reflective practice.	Articulate	The benefits of reflective practice.	
Reflective practice.	Apply	Reflective practice in multiple contexts	To amplify learning and professional judgment.
Reflective practice.	Deploy	Active and careful observation skills	To facilitate perspective taking and self-assessment.
Perspective taking and its barriers (cognitive biases) Reflective practice.	Describe	Multiple examples how perception and interpretation	Of the circumstances of others is necessary for professional judgment and effective lawyering.

Perspective taking and its barriers (cognitive biases)	Illustrate	How cognitive biases and patterned behaviors can impede	One's ability to see through the eyes of another.
Perspective taking and its barriers (cognitive biases)	Identify and Evaluate	His/her own cognitive biases, patterned behaviors, and gut reactions	In multiple instances.

Checklist:

- Do the course outcomes describe what students should know, do, and/or value in order to complete the final assessment successfully?
- Are the course outcomes described with verbs that represent observable, measurable behaviors?
- Are the course outcomes expressed individually, not jointly?
- Do the course outcomes align with a course goal?
- Do the course outcomes align with the ABA-required program outcomes, in whole or in part? (optional)

Worksheet 10: Organize Topics and Learning Activities across the Entire Course

Once you have identified the course outcomes, start identifying the learning activities and lawyering tasks that will enable students to develop the knowledge, skills, or values necessary to achieve each outcome. These activities will then help you choose the materials for the course and to plan individual units and lessons. You will want to organize the units into a sequence that promotes effective learning through smooth and clear transitions from unit to unit.

Situational factors

Before laying out the specific learning activities, re-examine the situational factors that will enable or constrain the types of learning activities you can incorporate, when or how they should be sequenced, and the like. Some of your situational factors may include the pre-requisite knowledge, skills, or values expected of students before taking your course or the availability of a boot camp week or clinic orientation.

Models for organizing and sequencing course content

Consider generally your course's organization. The models below will help you to sequence the course topics, outcomes, and learning activities and to decide what foundation needs to be laid and when. You may combine multiple organizational models.

- *Order of importance*: Because students have highest enthusiasm for a course at the beginning, embed the most important (or difficult) concepts earliest.
- *Order of process*: Sequence material along the arc of a process, beginning to end, *e.g.*, litigation sequence (complaint to trial); attorney-client relationship (first meeting through resolution of the matter; first meeting to transition to the next student-lawyer).
- *Simple to complex*: Because students can build confidence in mastering simple topics and skills, start with these before tackling higher level, more complex tasks.

- ***Dependent or supportive relationship between units of study***: If the learning is cumulative, start with the concepts or skills that represent pre-requisite knowledge or skill necessary (or helpful) for later units.
- ***Cause & Effect:*** Introduce a range of problems and then follow with types of solutions to be applied (*e.g.*, claims and remedies).
- ***Spiral or cyclical***: Introduce and revisit concepts or skills multiple times throughout the term, adding complexity with each repetition.
- ***General to specific vs. Concrete to abstract***: Introduce general principles & then apply to specific situations. Alternatively, start with specific examples of a phenomenon and move toward what they represent at the conceptual or abstract level.
- ***Thematic or topical:*** Use when individual units represent independent concepts. Plan transitions carefully. (*e.g.*, a survey course.)

ABA experiential course design standards

Standard 304 provides the elements that any course intended to be counted toward the experiential graduation requirement must have. For each mode of skills teaching (simulation, clinic, externship) Standard 304 includes additional requirements.

Std. 304 (a): Experiential courses [include] simulation courses, law clinics, and field placements that must be primarily experiential in nature and must:

1) Integrate doctrine, theory, skills, and legal ethics, and engage students in performance of one or more of the professional skills identified in Standard 302;
2) Develop the concepts underlying the professional skills being taught;
3) Provide multiple opportunities for performance;
4) Provide opportunities for student performance, self-evaluation, and feedback from a faculty member, or, for a field placement, a site supervisor;
5) A classroom instructional component; or, for a field placement, a classroom instructional component, regularly scheduled tutorials, or other means of ongoing, contemporaneous, faculty-guided reflection; and
6) Provide direct supervision of the student's performance by the faculty member; or, for a field placement, provide direct supervision of the student's performance by a faculty member or a site supervisor.

Topic	Course outcomes in measurable terms	Learning activities / Lawyering tasks	Materials to aid student performance
	What will students be able to think, do, or value to complete the final assessment successfully? Use info developed in Worksheet 9. Organize in a coherent sequence. **By the end of the semester, students will be able to:**	What exercises, performances, discussions, or other learning activity will help students to prepare for and succeed in the final assessment? Identify whether an activity is designed as an introduction (I), practice opportunity (P), or mastery vehicle (M).	What readings, media, information, lecture, and other aids will my students need to perform the lawyering and learning activities successfully? Will it be used before, during, or after the class?
Deliberate practice	Devise a learning plan based on self-assessment and professional development needs. Effectuate the learning plan through fieldwork experience, careful observation, and continuous self-assessment.	Discuss attorney competencies in class. (I) Deconstruct why all studies have some form of "listening" as one of the top critical skills for lawyers (pre-req to perspective taking). (P) Undertake UMKC self-assessment. (I) Write a personal learning plan for the externships, 3-4 lawyering and professional goals. (P) Discuss goals and relevant assignments with mentor attorney. (P) Mid-semester assessment of learning goal progress, discuss with mentor attorney and take mid-course corrections as appropriate. (P) Final essay-retrospective on progress on learning goals, what were more effective and least effective activities in one's learning/growth. (P)	Reports/studies to review /consider: Educating Tomorrow's Lawyers study of skills, work traits, and character values necessary for starting practice; UMKC lawyering skills and aptitudes self-assessment Lecture on other lawyering skills studies such as Shultz-Zedeck, National Conference of Bar Examiners
Reflective practice	Articulate the benefits of reflective practice. Apply reflective practice in multiple contexts to amplify learning and professional judgment. Deploy active and careful observation skills to facilitate perspective taking and self-assessment. Practice self-evaluation.	Small group discussions to dissect the useful elements of selected essay(s); rate the essay along the criteria of the rubric. (I) Class discussion of the same. (I) Write several reflective essays along the semester. (P) Digest faculty comments on essays regarding. (P)	Lecture to introduce Donald Schon and reflective practice; discuss how to look for and use disorienting moments Read 4-6 exemplars of student reflective writing (exemplifying close observation, self-evaluation, and perspective taking) Examine reflective writing rubric

Perspective taking and its barriers (cognitive biases)	Provide multiple examples how perception and interpretation of the circumstances of others is necessary for professional judgment and effective lawyering Illustrate how cognitive biases, patterned behaviors, and gut instincts can obfuscate one's ability to see through the eyes of another. Identify and evaluate his/her own cognitive biases, patterned behaviors, and gut reactions, in multiple instances. Develop techniques to discern perspective of others Adjust his/her approach to others, cognizant of their circumstances, values, and preferences. Practice perspective taking in terms of cultural identity and difference.	Case file assessment exercise; simulated negotiation; need for closure exercise (shows partisan or advocate's bias). (I) IAT (implicit cultural biases). (I) Exercise in anticipating the needs of a new client (unmasking assumptions; inability to generate multiple hypotheses). (P) Miscommunication and diagnosis. (P) Feedback—supervisor and extern perspective; self-awareness exercise in how one reacts to different forms of feedback. (P) A Few Good Men movie montage to reveal cultural difference, how it animates behavior and assumptions, fitting or not fitting one's nominal culture; impact on lawyering. (M)	Lecture on Kahneman's System 1 and 2 thinking (from Thinking, Fast and Slow) List of cognitive biases Navigating Cultural Difference, Learning from Practice Case assessment file (negotiation exercise)
Professional judgment	Synthesize a personal definition of professional judgment that i) is strategic (e.g., anticipates steps necessary to develop his/her capacity for professional judgment); ii) shows meta-cognition regarding one's current developmental limitations and strengths; and iii) incorporates the need to consider the perspective and values of others.	Discussion of personal and interpersonal skills needed; difference and similarity between professional judgment and leadership ability. (I) Mistake and recovery exercise. (P) Essay articulating personal definition of professional judgment (final assessment). (M)	Read Rhode, Lawyers as Leaders, and two pieces from engineering and medicine about professional judgment and the gaps.

Checklist:

- Do the course materials, learning activities, and lawyering tasks provide sufficient foundation for student progress toward course mastery?
- Does the order of materials, learning activities, and lawyering tasks allow my students to apply their learning repeatedly, to make progress toward mastery of the course outcomes?
- Do the learning exercises and lawyering activities include ones where I expect course mastery for each Enduring Learning element (Worksheet 4)?
- Do the course materials, learning activities, and lawyering tasks allow my students to consider the Animating Theory and Exploratory Questions for the course on multiple occasions throughout the semester (Worksheets 1 and 2)?
- Do the learning activities and lawyering tasks cover each criterion in ABA Standards 304 (as applied to all experiential courses and to the provisions specific to my type of course)??

Worksheet 11: Plan Units of Student Learning Activities

For each unit (a single topic/learning activity or chunk of topics or activities), create a plan for work that your students will do before, during, and after class. Make sure that you identify how you will "know" that the students learned what you planned. That might be your own reflection and assessment at the end of the class, supervision, or unit, or it might be some other evidence of student learning (whether direct from the student, or indirect from another source).

Course Unit: Learning and understanding the unconscious bias of advocate or partisan role

Course competencies (from Worksheet 9):

Seeing and experiencing the reality of unconscious cognitive biases.

How will students prepare for the unit/class?	What will students do in class to prepare them to reach the outcomes?	How will I know they learned what I wanted them to learn?
Students are assigned the role of defense or plaintiff's counsel; given identical case files regarding an injury suffered by an accident between a motorcyclist and a car driver. They are told they will conduct a negotiation with opposing counsel next class. They are also told the case has already been decided by a retired judge sitting as a mediator. Students are required to send me the night before the class two assessments of the case—subjective (what is fair) and objective (what the judge decided).	In class, students are paired with opposing counsel and have 15 minutes to negotiate a settlement, keeping track of how many rounds of offers it took to reach a settlement or impasse at the end of the expired time. After the negotiation, final settlements and student reactions to the experience are shared. You might think this is a negotiating exercise. Rather the negotiation is a ruse. The class is designed to demonstrate the unconscious cognitive bias of the partisan or advocate's role. I then tell the class about several social science experiments that tracked lawyers and law students regarding their assessment of a case, even their so-called "objective assessment." On average the plaintiff and defendant's estimates vary by 20%, and straddle the mediator's award. The class assessments always show the same advocate's bias.	We have class discussion to surface the ways in which the advocate's disposition is a tempering disposition that is not always useful. We tease apart the value of "zealous" advocacy for a client (in which case a partisan bias is useful), from the value of objective advising (in which case the lawyer is handicapped in offering professional judgment for the client). In part, I know whether the students i) have learned and integrated the concept that their unconscious biases impact their behaviors unwittingly and ii) that they need methods (practices, habits) to mitigate those impacts, when we switch to the next classes on navigating cultural difference. Are the students ready to talk about the impacts of implicit bias in a meaningful, cursory, reluctant, or hostile manner.

Checklist:

- Do the unit activities align with one or more of my course's learning outcomes?
- Do the unit activities have a clear purpose to help students learn?
- Is the unit structured to build on existing learning, give clear direction, and give opportunity to practice what students are expected to do?

- Do the unit activities give students time to develop their own thoughts and positions, and to hear others' ideas, perspectives, or positions?
- Do I hold my students accountable for doing the activity, including by giving them feedback?
- Do I provide opportunity for students to reflect on the activities and connect them to their prior learning?

Chapter 9

Worksheet Packet

Worksheet 1: Animating Theory

To identify the learning goals for your course, first consider the subject matter generally. Because a subject matter has more content than a course can cover, start by articulating the key reason students should take your course. That reason is your course's Animating Theory. Grant Wiggins and Jay McTighe coined a colloquial term for this, "The Big Idea."[1]

Once you choose your Animating Theory, you will flesh it out with a set of Exploratory Questions (Worksheet 2) that illuminate the challenges you want your students to grapple with. Setting the Animating Theory and Exploratory Questions allows you to build your course from course goal, to mastery evidence, to learning activities. The Animating Theory is not the same as your course goal(s) or learning outcomes; it underlies both. You may have more than one, but restrict yourself to at most two so that student learning is focused. Here, less is more.

The Animating Theory for the Course:

- Refers to core concepts, principles, and theories in a field of study—What unifies the field of study? What makes a skill worthwhile or effective?
- Organizes large bodies of information, skills, or values.
- Is amenable to transfer to new fields of study, new situations, and across disciplines.
- Is abstract and requires investigation to probe its implications.

Considerations for a Skills-focused Course:

- What does the lawyering skill help you do more effectively or efficiently for a client?
- What are the underlying concepts or objectives of the skill?
- When and how do you use the skill (strategy and tactics)?
- Why does the skill work?

Examples: The Animating Theory need not be phrased as a complete sentence. A "motto" works.

- Persuasion: Know your audience.
- Sociology: People in a community depend on each other for the things they need.
- History: History is written by the victors.
- Law: The best lawyer is the best prepared lawyer.

Identify the Animating Theory(ies) for your course.

Checklist:

- Does my animating theory provide a concise statement, principle, theory, or generalization?
- Does it stand the test of time, allowing students' thoughts about it to develop and evolve over time?
- Can it promote in-depth understanding and help make sense of the subject matter?

1. See Wiggins, G., & McTighe, J., UNDERSTANDING BY DESIGN (2nd ed. 2005).

Worksheet 2: Develop Exploratory Questions

Questions are used to study the Animating Theory for the course and to ground student learning. These questions are open-ended and probing in nature rather than intended to yield specific answers.

An Exploratory Question:

- Opens the Animating Theory for the course to genuine inquiry.
- Provokes lively discussion, sustained inquiry, and new understanding, as well as more questions.
- Requires students to consider alternatives, weigh evidence, support their ideas, and justify their answers.
- Stimulates vital, on-going rethinking of assumptions, prior understanding, and personal experience.
- Naturally recurs, creating opportunities for transfer to other situations and subjects.

Examples of Exploratory Questions that amplify the value of your Animating Theory:

- Persuasion: What's in it for my audience? What are the ethics of persuasion?
- Government and public policy: What makes a good government? How does cultural identity inform one's views of government and its role in society?
- History/Precedent: What patterns recur throughout history and common law? Is all history biased?

Identify 1–2 Exploration Questions for each Animating Theory.

Animating Theory 1: ______________________________

Animating Theory 2: ______________________________

Checklist:

- Are my Exploratory Questions open-ended, nonjudgmental, meaningful, and purposeful?
- Do the questions have emotional appeal?
- Do the questions have more than one coherent answer?
- Do the questions probe for deeper meaning and explore ideas and beliefs?
- Do the questions encourage peer learning and collaboration?

Worksheet 3: Identify Situational Factors That Affect Teaching and Learning

The first two Worksheets lay out the scope of the course on a grand scale. Now situate your ambitions for student learning within the realities of your course, the school's curriculum, your students' semesters, and the scope of all your responsibilities. Some of these situational factors are assets to use wisely and fruitfully. Others are limitations. Affirmatively acknowledging that, in your clinic, field placement, or simulation course, you simply cannot cover all that your students need to know, be able to do, or value will help you to make pedagogical choices to maximize student learning.

Add your own situational factors to the chart below.

Possible situational factors

Your school's J.D. program learning outcomes (including the ABA-mandated outcomes)	
Length (e.g., semester, year), number of credits, number of hours in field, casework, or classroom	
Grading scheme	
Student preparedness (typical, high/low)	
Student motivations	
Uniformity, dissimilarity, or variety of student work (in type and complexity)	
Opportunities with community partners (and their needs)	
Personal responsibilities that constrain my availability for class or individual student engagement	
Other factors	
Other factors	

Checklist:

- Do I capture factors that are opportunities for me to maximize the learning in my course?
- Do I capture the most salient factors that limit the scope of what students can reasonably learn in my course?
- Do I capture the most salient factors that limit my ability to execute a course plan and engage my students?

Worksheet 4: Prioritize Learning for Transfer (durability)

Allow your Animating Theory to percolate. Break it down into specific priorities for your students' learning. Identify the knowledge and understandings, skills, and/or values that are essential to the Animating Theory of your course. Prioritize those elements based on long-term importance to the students' learning. The highest level (enduring learning) should be learning that is transferable to different contexts in their professional lives.

Even though your course may cover content in all three levels of priority, your course goals (Worksheet 5) and final assessments (Worksheet 7) will focus on the knowledge and understandings, skills, and/or values that you intend to be long-lived (enduring) for your students.

Identify key learning at each level of priority.

Enduring learning:

Important for students to know:

Worth being familiar with:

Checklist:

- Do the elements listed as *Enduring Learning* help students to synthesize individual lessons and readings into a deeper understanding of the Animating Theory?
- Do the *Enduring Learning* elements lay a foundation for further study of this subject matter?
- Do the *Enduring Learning* elements help students to figure out issues in the subject matter that are more difficult to master?

Worksheet 5: Use Learning Taxonomies to Craft Course Goals[2]

Now that you've identified your learning priorities, you will distill the enduring learning into course goals. Course goals represent the essential i) knowledge and understandings, ii) skills, and/or iii) values that you intend your students to attain by the end of the term. One way to unify the enduring learning into goals is to ask: "How will my students be different by the end of the course?" To answer this question in a way that can be assessed at the end of the course, we have collected taxonomies of learning that capture the complexity and depth of learning you want your students to attain. The taxonomies further assist you to establish observable and measurable course goals (amenable to assessment, Worksheets 6 and 7).

The taxonomies cover the three domains of learning:

1. Cognitive domain: Focuses on knowledge, comprehension, and critical thinking.
2. Psychomotor domain: Encompasses learning geared toward executing specific tasks (*e.g.*, client counseling, negotiating with opposing counsel, witness interviewing).
3. Affective domain: Relates to awareness and growth in values, attitudes, and emotional control (*e.g.*, values embedded in the attorney-client relationship, toward justice, and relating to professional identity formation).

The taxonomy grids on the next three pages organize each domain of learning hierarchically. As you move through the grids (left to right; top to bottom) the categories describe learning at deeper levels of difficulty. Use these grids to choose the deepest point(s) that correspond to a realistic learning goal for your course.

The grids, their terminology, and hierarchy are offered as an aid. Some of your learning priorities might fit within more than one taxonomy, and the Action Verbs that exemplify a category might resonate more than the category of learning does. Choose what works for you. Don't let the taxonomies push your learning goal toward something that doesn't feel right to you. Maybe you will pencil in learning targets for your course in several cells on separate grids; that will allow you to test out different ways to characterize the course goal(s) you want to pursue. In the end you should articulate 1–2 course goals. In drafting these goals, keep your verb singular, not compound, as a verb representing the farthest/deepest taxonomy cell that encapsulates your goal will necessarily include the less complex learning needed to reach that goal.

In the following three pages:

- Review the taxonomy for each domain.
- Reflect on your ambitions for your course. Pencil notes in any of the cells.
- Review your notes and distill them to one to two course goals (last page).

The course goals will form the bedrock for your course. Everything else—the final assessment, rubric, outcomes and learning activities—will be aligned to the course goals.

Sources:

Knowledge and Cognitive Processing Domain

Adapted from Anderson, L.W., Krathwohl, D.R. et. al. (2001). *A Taxonomy for Learning, Teaching, and Assessing: A Revision of Bloom's Taxonomy of Educational Objectives.* Abridged ed. New York: Longman.

2. Course Development Institute, Indiana University Center for Innovative Teaching and Learning.

Psychomotor Domain

Adapted from Dave, R.H. (1970), "Developing and Writing Behavioral Objectives;" Simpson E. J. (1972). The Classification of Educational Objectives in the Psychomotor Domain. Washington, DC: Gryphon House.

Affective Domain

Adapted from Krathwohl, D.R., Bloom, B.S., and Masia, B.B. (1964). *Taxonomy of Educational Objectives, Book II. Affective domain*. New York: David McKay Company, Inc.

On the taxonomies below, mark the highest-order learning and deepest mastery levels that you want students to achieve.

1. Knowledge and Cognitive Processing Domain

		Cognitive processing			
		1. Remember	2. Understand	3. Apply	4. Analyze, Evaluate, or Create
Knowledge	A. Factual	[your course goals]			
	B. Conceptual				
	C. Procedural				
	D. Meta-cognitive				

Knowledge types	Definition	Examples
Factual	Basic elements to be acquainted with the discipline and solve problems	Terminology, vocabulary, elements, and details
Conceptual	Interrelationship among basic elements	Categories, principles, theories, models, and structures
Procedural	How to do something *(overlaps with psychomotor domain)*	Subject-specific skills, methods of inquiry and criteria for using, and techniques and procedures
Meta-cognitive	Knowing about knowing	Strategic knowledge, reflections, and self-knowledge

Cognitive processing	Definition	Action Verbs
Remember	Retrieve relevant knowledge from long-term memory	Retain, recall, recognize, memorize, recollect, think of, define, identify, list, name, record, repeat, underline, select
Understand	Construct meaning from instructional messages; can be in oral, written or graphic formats	Interpret, exemplify, classify, summarize, infer, compare, explain, give examples of, describe in own words, differentiate between, discriminate, restate, review, translate, respond, practice, discuss, identify, review, simulate

Apply	Carry out procedures	Execute, implement, apply, demonstrate, dramatize, generalize, illustrate, operate, operationalize, practice, use, utilize, initiate
Analyze	Break material into parts and determine relationships	Differentiate, organize, attribute, analyze, appraise, categorize, compare, conclude, contrast, correlate, deduce, diagram, distinguish, estimate, examine, experiment, infer, predict, question, solve, diagnose
Evaluate	Make judgments based upon criteria or standards	Check, critique, assess, judge, appraise, choose, compare, evaluate, measure, rate, revise, score, select, validate, value
Create	Put elements together into coherent or functional whole, reorganize into new patterns	Generate, plan, produce, invent, arrange, assemble, collect, compose, construct, create, design, develop, formulate, manage, modify, organize, prepare, propose, synthesize

2. Psychomotor Domain: (can be used by experiential faculty to set goals for lawyering skill development)

	Definition	Action Verbs	Your Course Goals
Perception	Actively using sensory cues to attend to the behavioral skill. E.g., student observes a seasoned attorney perform the behavior.	Choose, describe, detect, differentiate, distinguish, identify, isolate, relate, select, separate	
Imitation	Copying the behavior. The student attempts the behavior, with direction and feedback from an experienced person. The student shows desire and motivation to learn the behavior.	Adhere, begin, attempt, carry out, copy, duplicate, follow, mimic, repeat, replicate, start, try	
Practice	Using the behavior repeatedly. The student performs the behavior multiple times, and her actions become more automatic and smooth. The experienced person need not be present.	Codify, discriminate, display, order, organize, systematize, weigh, discuss, theorize, formulate, balance, examine, adhere to	
Naturalization	Performing two or more skills in combination or sequence, with consistency and ease. The student can combine the behavior with other behaviors independently and with little mental exertion.	Adapt, automatize, combine, complete, demonstrate, internalize, master, perform, show, succeed	
Origination	Creating new behaviors, combinations, or sequences to respond to a new situation. The student creates new methodologies or techniques to improve on or re-imagine how the needs can be met.	Create, design, compose, refine, arrange	

3. **Affective Domain:** (can be used to set goals related to professional values, affect, or work approach, *e.g.*, with regard to the attorney client relationship, the rule of law, or other professional value)

	Definition	Action Verbs	Your Course Goals
Receive	Be aware of; attend to something; be willing to tolerate it.	Accept, attend, develop, ask, recognize, listen for, describe, differentiate, receive, identify, tolerate	
Respond	Incorporate a new behavior as a result of the experience.	Complete, comply, cooperate, discuss, examine, obey, assist, respond, follow, volunteer, perform	
Value	Show specific involvement or commitment.	Accept, defend, devote oneself to, pursue, seek, justify, join, debate, value	
Organize	Integrate a new value into one's general set of values, giving due ranking among other priorities.	Codify, discriminate, display, order, organize, systematize, weigh, discuss, theorize, formulate, balance, examine, adhere to	
Internalize the value set	Act consistently, conscientiously, and pro-actively with the new value.	Internalize, verify, be rated high in the value, require, resolve	

Using the taxonomies on the previous pages, draft your top 1–2 Course Goals:

By the end of the course, my students will:

Checklist

- Do my goals fit within the Animating Theory for the course (Worksheet 1)?
- Do my goals reflect the learning priorities I have set for the course (Worksheet 4)?
- Are my goals clear, observable, and measurable (Worksheets 6 and 8)?
- Do my goals reflect the situational limits of my course and my full responsibilities (Worksheet 3)?

Worksheet 6: Identify Observable Evidence of Student Mastery

Visualize the student who excels in the course you are designing. What does the student's performance or work product look like? That is your evidence of student mastery. The student's work is not at the level of a veteran attorney's; it's A-level work as a student in your course. Look at your picture closely, using the following six categories, or facets, of concrete, observable performance to assist your efforts.[3] A "masterful" student performance may well involve synchronous use of multiple facets. After you identify your evidence of mastery, then you will i) create a final assessment exercise to allow your students to exhibit this evidence (Worksheet 7) and ii) create an assessment rubric that defines levels of student performance (Worksheet 8).

Fill in the chart below with your desired mastery evidence.

Facet of understanding	Associated verbs & Starter phrases	Evidence of student's mastery in your course
Explanation: Students are able to provide thorough and well-supported accounts of topics, events, or actions, backed by reasoning, facts, or experience. Students are able to develop a theory of how and why, supported by evidence, law, and experience.	Demonstrate, derive, describe, design, exhibit, express, instruct, justify, model, predict, prove, show, synthesize, teach Students will be able to: Explain/ teach [x], Give examples of [x]; Make connections with [x]; Offer a theory of [x]; Avoid misconceptions, such as [x].	
Interpretation: Students are able to interpret and analyze the importance, meaning, or significance of their knowledge/ skill, with context and awareness of multiple interpretations. Students can create meaning from a set of facts and law, with attention to ambiguity, uncertainty, opacity, emotional content, and diverse perspectives.	Create analogies, critique, document, evaluate, illustrate, judge, make sense of, provide metaphors, read between the lines, represent, tell a story of. Students will be able to: Interpret the [x]; Tell a revealing story of [x]; Provide an apt analogy for [x]; Show the importance or meaning of [x]; Translate [x]; Relate [x] to your experience (or the experiences of others).	
Application-Adaptation: Students use and adapt the knowledge/skill acquired to new situations and contexts, showing flexibility and adaptability. Students can design, develop, test, and refine responses to a new problem or dilemma presented.	Adapt, create, de-bug, design, exhibit, invent, perform, produce, propose, solve, test, use Students will be able to: Apply [x] in a new circumstance; Show or demonstrate [x]; Use in the context of [x]; Design/invent [x]; Overcome a challenge or constraint, such as [x].	

3. Adapted and expanded from Wiggins, G., & McTighe, J., UNDERSTANDING BY DESIGN (2nd ed. 2005) (describing six facets of understanding).

Perspective: Students can take a step back to appreciate a broader view, critically assess the value or importance of a topic. Students can identify, critique, and give credence to multiple valid perspectives regarding a topic.	Analyze, argue, compare, contrast, criticize, infer Students will be able to: Analyze [x]; See from the viewpoint of [x]; Compare and contrast [x]; Critique [x]; Critically examine assumptions such as [x]; Show how [x]; See the limits of [x].	
Empathy: Students show the ability to embrace the feelings, reasoning, motivations, and perspectives of others with acceptance and non-judgment. Open-minded insight to others.	Assume the role of, believe, be like, be open to, consider, imagine, relate, role-play. Students will be able to: Walk in the shoes of [x]; Experience directly and see [x]; Reach a common understanding with another concerning [x]; Entertain the seemingly odd or alien view that [x]; Anticipate possible concerns of others regarding [x] based on their interests, values, and circumstances.	
Self-Knowledge: Students accept that their style, preferences, and habits are specific to them and affect their views of events, information, and other people. Students can evaluate their professional development with appreciation of what came easily or not and why; can evaluate personal, emotional responses with detachment.	Be aware of, realize, recognize, reflect, self-assess. Students will be able to: Recognize their own prejudice(s) about [x]; Identify the lens through which they view [x]; Explain how they came to understand [x]; Realize that even with all they now know, they still don't really understand [x].	

Checklist

- Does my mastery evidence flow from my course goals and teaching priorities?
- Does my mastery evidence facilitate exploration of the Animating Theory for the course?
- Is my evidence of student mastery observable and measureable in an assessment exercise?

Worksheet 7: Create a Final Assessment Exercise

Create a final assessment exercise that will allow you to observe and evaluate each piece of mastery evidence listed. Before crafting the assessment exercise, revisit the enduring learning priorities you established (Worksheet 4) and your course goals (Worksheet 5). Use the measurable language in the goals and the mastery evidence (Worksheet 6) to create the content framework for your final assessment exercise. Note: you may use more than one assessment exercise to determine the final grade for your course.

- Choose the vehicle: a piece(s) of writing, a portfolio, an oral presentation or live performance (to professor or before another audience), etc.
- Quantity—Length: Consider how short or long the students' performance or work product should be to showcase their mastery. For instance, if you want to assess the students' level of reflection, can the students meet your expectations in 250 words, 1,000, or 5,000 words? If you want to assess the students' ability to conduct a summation for the jury, should the summation last 5 minutes, 15 minutes, 30 minutes, or more?
- Quantity—Parts: Determine the number of parts or exercises. While it might be ideal to create an assessment exercise that synthesizes the full constellation of knowledge, skills, and values represented in the course goal, often it might be impracticable to create a single assessment exercise that allows the students to produce evidence of full mastery. How would you segment the parts of the assessment?
- Practicalities: Consider the situational factors that impact what is manageable for you to assess.
- Design the subject and the prompts: This is the meat of the assessment. What are you asking your students to do? Make certain that your prompts, length, and parts will summon the work product or performance that elicits your desired mastery evidence.

Plan and draft a final assessment exercise.

Vehicle	
Quantity (length and parts)	
Timing/sequence	
Practicalities	
Subject and prompts	

Worksheet 8: Prepare an Analytic Rubric

Whether your course is graded or not, you should assess each student's learning: 1) to inform the students of what they have in fact mastered or not; and 2) to inform you of your teaching effectiveness. An analytic rubric serves both purposes by imparting detailed feedback to each student and by enabling you to analyze where students are having trouble. If you give the rubric to students with the assessment exercise, the rubric also communicates your expectations so that they can self-assess their work before submitting it.

An analytic rubric is easily written as a grid:

- Vertical axis: Identify the assessment (evaluative) criteria to track the course goal and mastery evidence. You may include additional criteria not specifically tied to the course goals (e.g., writing mechanics, class participation), but do not let their grading value dilute the assessment of the course goal. Identify up to 6 criteria.
    - Describe the different elements of performance for each assessment criterion. You may include more than one element of performance in each criterion.
- Horizontal axis: Set and label the different proficiency levels. Levels can be labeled as grades, numeric ranges, or descriptors like exceptional, competent, and developing.
    - Each proficiency level for an assessment criterion should address each performance element in the assessment criterion.

Draft a rubric for your final assessment. Restate your course goal for reference.

Course Goal (from Worksheet 5): ______________________________

Evaluative criterion; weighting	Highest proficiency	Mid-level proficiency	Low level proficiency
Criterion 1 (weight or % of grade)			

Checklist:

- Does my rubric track my mastery evidence and the prompt for the final assessment exercise?
- Does my rubric align with the course goals?
- If I include criteria not related to the course goal, do they comprise a minimal part of the assessment?
- Are the evaluative criteria specific and clear?
- Are the proficiency descriptions written in neutral, clear terms using consistent terms and components across each level?

Worksheet 9: Draft Course Outcomes

In this Worksheet, you will convert your course goals into multiple learning outcomes and check whether you have achieved the right level of specificity and effectiveness for assessment purposes. Develop a maximum of 6 outcomes per course goal.

- Align each outcome to one or more specific course goal(s).
- Each outcome should be written as a single statement; do not join multiple outcomes within one statement.
- Use verbs that represent observable and measurable performance (live, written, other type of performance). For each outcome, choose the single verb that represents the deepest level of performance that you want for that outcome; avoid compound verbs.
- Because the ABA now requires at least 6 experiential credits for graduation, you might want to align any clinic, field placement, or simulation course to at least some outcomes that relate directly to both your course goals and your school's program outcomes.

Draft 1–6 course outcomes for each course goal.

Course Goal (from Worksheet 5): ____________________

Knowledge, skills and/or values	Students will be able to: Verb (performance)	Object (the learning statement)	Condition and/or Criterion

Checklist:

- Do the course outcomes describe what students should know, do, and/or value in order to complete the final assessment successfully?
- Are the course outcomes described with verbs that represent observable, measurable behaviors?
- Are the course outcomes expressed individually, not jointly?
- Do the course outcomes align with a course goal?
- Do the course outcomes align with the ABA-required program outcomes, in whole or in part? (optional)

Worksheet 10: Organize Topics and Learning Activities across the Entire Course

Once you have identified the course outcomes, start identifying the learning activities and lawyering tasks that will enable students to develop the knowledge, skills, or values necessary to achieve each outcome. These activities will then help you choose the materials for the course and to plan individual units and lessons. You will want to organize the units into a sequence that promotes effective learning through smooth and clear transitions from unit to unit.

Situational factors

Before laying out the specific learning activities, re-examine the situational factors that will enable or constrain the types of learning activities you can incorporate, when or how they should be sequenced, and the like. Some of your situational factors may include the pre-requisite knowledge, skills, or values expected of students before taking your course or the availability of a boot camp week or clinic orientation.

Models for organizing and sequencing course content

Consider generally your course's organization. The models below will help you to sequence the course topics, outcomes, and learning activities and to decide what foundation needs to be laid and when. You may combine multiple organizational models.

- *Order of importance*: Because students have highest enthusiasm for a course at the beginning, embed the most important (or difficult) concepts earliest.
- *Order of process*: Sequence material along the arc of a process, beginning to end, *e.g.*, litigation sequence (complaint to trial); attorney-client relationship (first meeting through resolution of the matter; first meeting to transition to the next student-lawyer).
- *Simple to complex*: Because students can build confidence in mastering simple topics and skills, start with these before tackling higher level, more complex tasks.
- *Dependent or supportive relationship between units of study*: If the learning is cumulative, start with the concepts or skills that represent pre-requisite knowledge or skill necessary (or helpful) for later units.
- *Cause & Effect:* Introduce a range of problems and then follow with types of solutions to be applied (*e.g.*, claims and remedies).
- *Spiral or cyclical*: Introduce and revisit concepts or skills multiple times throughout the term, adding complexity with each repetition.
- *General to specific vs. Concrete to abstract*: Introduce general principles & then apply to specific situations. Alternatively, start with specific examples of a phenomenon and move toward what they represent at the conceptual or abstract level.
- *Thematic or topical:* Use when individual units represent independent concepts. Plan transitions carefully. (*e.g.*, a survey course.)

ABA experiential course design standards

Standard 304 provides the elements that any course intended to be counted toward the experiential graduation requirement must have. For each mode of skills teaching (simulation, clinic, externship) Standard 304 includes additional requirements.

Std. 304 (a): Experiential courses [include] simulation courses, law clinics, and field placements that must be primarily experiential in nature and must:

1) Integrate doctrine, theory, skills, and legal ethics, and engage students in performance of one or more of the professional skills identified in Standard 302;
2) Develop the concepts underlying the professional skills being taught;
3) Provide multiple opportunities for performance;
4) Provide opportunities for student performance, self-evaluation, and feedback from a faculty member, or, for a field placement, a site supervisor;
5) A classroom instructional component; or, for a field placement, a classroom instructional component, regularly scheduled tutorials, or other means of ongoing, contemporaneous, faculty-guided reflection; and
6) Provide direct supervision of the student's performance by the faculty member; or, for a field placement, provide direct supervision of the student's performance by a faculty member or a site supervisor.

Complete the chart below, starting with the area that makes the most sense to you.

Topic	Course outcomes in measurable terms	Learning activities / Lawyering tasks	Materials to aid student performance
	What will students be able to think, do, or value to complete the final assessment successfully? Use info developed in Worksheet 9. Organize in a coherent sequence. **By the end of the semester, students will be able to:**	What exercises, performances, discussions, or other learning activity will help students to prepare for and succeed in the final assessment? Identify whether an activity is designed as an introduction (I), practice opportunity (P), or mastery vehicle (M).	What readings, media, information, lecture, and other aids will my students need to perform the lawyering and learning activities successfully? Will it be used before, during, or after the class?

Checklist:

- Do the course materials, learning activities, and lawyering tasks provide sufficient foundation for student progress toward course mastery?
- Does the order of materials, learning activities, and lawyering tasks allow my students to apply their learning repeatedly, to make progress toward mastery of the course outcomes?
- Do the learning exercises and lawyering activities include ones where I expect course mastery for each Enduring Learning element (Worksheet 4)?
- Do the course materials, learning activities, and lawyering tasks allow my students to consider the Animating Theory and Exploratory Questions for the course on multiple occasions throughout the semester (Worksheets 1 and 2)?
- Do the learning activities and lawyering tasks cover each criterion in ABA Standards 304 (as applied to all experiential courses and to the provisions specific to my type of course)??

Worksheet 11: Plan Units of Student Learning Activities

For each unit (a single topic/learning activity or chunk of topics or activities), create a plan for work that your students will do before, during, and after class. Make sure that you identify how you will "know" that the students learned what you planned. That might be your own reflection and assessment at the end of the class, supervision, or unit, or it might be some other evidence of student learning (whether direct from the student, or indirect from another source).

Create a plan for each unit of content. Remember that the activities can span more than one class and need not be contiguous.

Course Unit: ______________________________

Relevant Course Outcomes (from Worksheet 9): ______________________________

How will students prepare for the unit/class?	What will students do in class to prepare them to reach the outcomes?	How will I know they learned what I wanted them to learn?

Checklist:

- Do the unit activities align with one or more of my course's learning outcomes?
- Do the unit activities have a clear purpose to help students learn?
- Is the unit structured to build on existing learning, give clear direction, and give opportunity to practice what students are expected to do?
- Do the unit activities give students time to develop their own thoughts and positions, and to hear others' ideas, perspectives, or positions?
- Do I hold my students accountable for doing the activity, including by giving them feedback?
- Do I provide opportunity for students to reflect on the activities and connect them to their prior learning?

Glossary

Alignment: When a course's learning objectives, activities, and assessments match up so students learn what the educator intends and the educator can accurately assess what students are learning, considering the desired course goals and outcomes, then course alignment exists. *See Ch 2, Sec E.*

Animating Theory: The principles and desires an educator holds for a course that ground the course both methodologically and theoretically; the intellectual home of the course that defines its place in the larger subject matter. *See Ch 3, Sec A.*

Assessment: The act of making judgments about how a student is performing in a course. Giving value and ranking to student performance. *See Ch 5.*

Assessment Tool or Exercise: Used to measure a student's strengths and weaknesses in a course. Effective assessment tools contain the following components: planning; intentional design and development that includes a description of the context and conditions of the assessment, the tasks to be performed by the student, and detailed evidence criteria the educator will use to measure success in performance; and quality checks. See also **Formative Assessment** and **Summative Assessment.** *See Ch 5.*

Capstone: A final multifaceted assessment exercise or activity designed to encourage students to think critically, solve challenging problems, and integrate learning from across the course. *See example at Ch 5, Sec E, Disability Law Clinic.*

Client-Centered Lawyering: A multidimensional approach to developing a lawyer-client relationship characterized in part by locating the client as the primary priority-setter and choice-maker. *See examples at Ch 8, worksheets for Criminal Defense Clinic; Interviewing, Counseling and Negotiation; and Disability Law Clinic.*

Course Goal: The overarching purpose of the course characterized by an identification of what knowledge, skills, or values an educator wishes her students to acquire. *See Ch 4.*

Course (Learning) Outcomes: The component parts of the **Course Goals.** Course outcomes are articulated as student achievements or work product. Course outcomes prescribe what students are expected to demonstrate they have learned, *e.g.*, student can conduct a high quality, client-centered interview. *Ch 7, Secs A and B.*

Design Process: A methodology for organizing instructional goals and desired outcomes within an identified pedagogical framework and based on an identified learning theory. In the experiential learning design model, a variety of learning theories and/or instructional goals can inform the specific aspects of the course design process. *See Ch 2, Secs C and D.*

Domains of Learning: A hierarchical framework for categorizing types of learning with the intent of moving a student from memorization to higher forms of thinking and, consequently, transfer. Benjamin Bloom developed the original learning domains in the 1950s; over time the domains have been expanded. *See Ch 4, Secs A, B, and C.*

- **Cognitive (Knowing):** The ability to process and reproduce information. The Cognitive Domain entails the following levels of thinking: remember, understand, apply, analyze, evaluate, and create.
- **Psychomotor (Doing):** In its original conception, the Psychomotor Domain referred to the use of coordinated motor skills to physically control objects. In the experiential learning context, this book reframes the domain to emphasize the ability of the student to complete the tasks (develop the skills) she is learning in the course. Levels at this domain are: perception, imitation, practice, naturalization, and origination.
- **Affective (Valuing):** Relates to our attitudes, feelings, and ethics in response to things and situations. It includes five learning levels: receiving, responding, valuing, organization, and characterization.

Evaluative Criteria: The key learning areas educators seek to strengthen in a course. **Evaluative Criteria** are different from **Rubrics** in that the evaluative criteria, comprise the components of the final assessment exercise that the educator will evaluate using the performance levels included in a rubric. *See Ch 6, Sec B.*

Exploratory Questions: The questions upon which an educator builds the essential understandings of the course. Exploratory questions support students in getting to the important ideas of the course because they do not bear one correct answer; they are open to discussion, investigation, and disagreement. As a course design tool, the exploratory questions should be defined at the beginning of the process. As with all steps in the design process, exploratory questions should and can be revisited as the goals of the course evolve. *See Ch 3, Sec B.*

Facets of Understanding: A non-hierarchical articulation of different aspects of "understanding" in the learning context, as conceived by Grant Wiggins and Jay McTighe. Different learning tasks or activities may focus on one or multiple facets depending on the desired course goals and course outcomes. *See Ch 5, Sec A.*

Formative Assessment: A range of formal and informal exercises or activities that monitor student learning to provide ongoing feedback and help students identify their strengths and weaknesses and target areas that need work. Formative assessments share the dual purpose of improving student learning and improving educator teaching and may be graded or ungraded. *See Ch 5.*

Learning Activities: The cumulative choices of readings, discussions, simulations, and other activities that provide the foundation of learning for the course. In the EL model, learning activities are chosen last and are designed to ensure that course outcomes and mastery can be met, thereby aligning the learning with the course goal or goals. *See Ch 7, Secs C and D.*

Mastery: Related to Bloom's theory of learning, mastery learning requires that a student become more than proficient in basic skills before moving upward in the learning hierarchy from basic skills to higher, more complex ways of thinking. Educators define mastery for their courses using explicit, objective benchmarks in performance criteria that signal the requisite learning has occurred for the student. *See also* **Mastery Evidence**. *See Ch 5, Secs A and B.*

Mastery Evidence: The tangible evidence that demonstrates a student developed the understanding or capability articulated in a specific course goal or goals. An educator assesses mastery evidence by applying assessment tools that connect the definition of subject mastery to articulated learning goals for the course. *See Ch 5, Secs A and B.*

Objectives: Statements that define the learning expectations of a curriculum, course, lesson or activity relative to demonstrable skills or knowledge that will be acquired by a student while in the course. Learning objectives tend to describe specific, discrete units of knowledge and skills that can be accomplished over the course timeframe.

Observable and Measurable Goals & Outcomes: Related to **Mastery Evidence**. Refers to behaviors or applications that enable an educator to determine students' understanding of what they have learned, including valid ways of distinguishing between understanding and mere recall. Observable and measurable outcomes and goals are based on objective standards and clearly articulable benchmarks, not subjective interpretations or straight scoring on assessment tools such as exams. *See Ch 5.*

Performance Levels: Determine the degree of performance which has been met and will provide for consistent and objective assessment and better feedback to students. The same descriptors can be used for different criteria within one rubric. *See also* **Rubric**. *See Ch 6, Sec B.*

Rubric: An identification of the criteria an educator will use in evaluating student performance. An effective rubric identifies key performance indicators at multiple levels of proficiency. *See Ch 6, Sec A.*

- **Checklists:** Often described as "in the family of a rubric but not quite a rubric." Can offer a yes/no format for deciding if a student can demonstrate skills, knowledge, or behaviors that support accomplishing specific criteria.
- **Holistic:** The most general kind of rubric structure. A holistic rubric lists three to five levels of performance, along with a broad description of the characteristics that define each level. Desired characteristics are placed together in each level of performance and a single score is given for the entire activity. Does not usually require an educator to provide individualized targeted feedback.
- **Analytic:** The most specific rubric structure. An analytic rubric breaks down the characteristics of an assignment into parts, allowing the scorer to itemize and define exactly what aspects are strong, and which ones need improvement. In contrast to holistic rubrics, analytic rubrics give students a clearer picture of why they got the score they got.

Sequencing Instruction: Choosing an order in which to teach the course. Sequencing includes both the ordering of units within the broader topics and the individual activities, readings, and other learning tools an educator uses within each topic. An effective instructional sequence provides the student with an understandable pattern of progression such that the student can make meaning from the learning. *See Ch 7, Secs C and D.*

Situational Factors & Realities: The context and conditions in which a course operates. Effective course design is dependent on a realistic evaluation of not only how many credit hours a course commands but also institutional constraints, student constraints, available resources, etc. *See Ch 3, Sec C.*

Summative Assessment: An assessment tool used to measure student learning at the end of an instructional unit. Summative assessments can be discrete to the learning unit or can build on and integrate information taught over the life of the course. *See also* **Capstone.** *See Ch 5.*

Taxonomies: *See also* **Learning Domains.**

Transfer of Learning: Generally relates to the application of knowledge from one situation to another, *i.e.*, the ability of a student to use previously acquired knowledge and skills in new situations. Teaching for transfer is related to developing mastery in a subject or skill such that when a student is faced with a different situation or application of the knowledge they can draw from their mastery to apply the learning in unfamiliar settings. *See Ch 5.*

Thanks to Alicia Alvarez, Susan Bennett, Christine Cimini, and Jayesh Rathod for teaching the design process workshops with us, to all the faculty who have participated in the workshops, and to Wendy Myers for her design and administrative assistance.

Special thanks to Grant Wiggins, Jay McTighe, and the Indiana University Center for Innovative Teaching and Learning for their inspiration. Any flaws in building on their work are, of course, our responsibility.